D1546398

"This extraordinary book is a Rosetta Stone for financial leaders and anyone who wishes to transform his or her relationship with money. Kim Ann Curtin brilliantly bridges the world of investment with the journey of awakening. She demonstrates that it is possible to claim inner reward amidst our quest to succeed in the marketplace. If every financier read this book and applied its principles, the world would be a far happier and more prosperous place."
—ALAN COHEN, author of *The Dragon Doesn't Live Here Anymore*

"Kim Ann Curtin elevates and deepens the debate over necessary reform of Wall Street and today's unstable global casino finance. Deeply researching Adam Smith's overlooked *The Theory of Moral Sentiments* provides context for this research into the deeper motivations and worldviews of the 'Wall Street 50' in finance whom Curtin interviews. Beyond blaming and shaming, she identifies positive trends, thus showcasing possibilities for reforming markets, metrics, and models for more sustainable financing of our common human future."
—HAZEL HENDERSON, author of *Mapping the Global Transition to the Solar Age* and *Ethical Markets: Growing the Green Economy*, and President, Ethical Markets Media (USA and Brazil) Certified B Corporation

"Wall Street's backbone is trust. And there is no osteoporosis of trust; it crumbles all at once. *Transforming Wall Street: A Conscious Path for a New Future* provides us with financiers who honor and understand this trust, proving that capitalists can indeed live consciously."
—HIS HOLINESS SRI SRI RAVI SHANKAR

"Kim Ann Curtin's experience coaching 'conscious capitalism' comes through as she captures the practices of 50 leading Wall Street financiers, academics, and futurists who allow Wall Street to serve not greed but the greater good."
—KEITH FERRAZZI, author of the #1 *New York Times* bestseller *Never Eat Alone* and *Who's Got Your Back*

"There is no conflict between making money and morality. As Barry Ritholtz, who is quoted here, succinctly states, 'It comes back to integrity. If you have integrity, it doesn't matter what you do for a living.' The evils often attributed to capitalism almost invariably come from other sources, such as crony capitalism, which is the exact opposite. Self-interest is not the same as selfishness. Such narrow thinking would fail to delineate between the motivated entrepreneur and the armed robber; the former enhances society's wealth through self-interest, while the latter destroys it through selfishness. The idea that the corporation's job is to maximize shareholder value is a myth that neither serves the interests of society, the corporation, or ironically, even shareholders (beyond the short-term). These are just a sampling of the ideas explored in *Transforming Wall Street*, a book that probes fifty leading Wall Street figures for their insights on more important questions than how to make money in the markets."

—JACK SCHWAGER, author of *Market Wizards*

"This book is a superbly textured insight into the world of Wall Street. By skillfully mixing the perspectives of fifty 'participants' Kim Ann Curtin addresses one of the critical questions of today—can one harmonize a spiritual sensitivity with the realities of working in the financial community? The book is useful on many levels—from entry level to the board room. There is no jargon; there is no rote. Reading this book is an enlightening and thrilling experience. Buy it and read it."

—ROBERT MONKS, shareholder activist and author
of *The New Global Investors: How Shareowners Can
Unlock Sustainable Prosperity Worldwide*

"There are a lot of good people on Wall Street, but the most notorious ones are known to the public for the wrong reasons. Every day, conscious capitalism faces resistance on Wall Street. We need more good people on Wall Street. This book sheds light on the good actors and provides readers with a toolkit to follow in their footsteps."

—BRAD KATSUYAMA, President and CEO, IEX Group, Inc.

"Kim Ann Curtin does a real service by showing people that there is more to Adam Smith than greed and reminding us of what he really believed." —DR. CRAIG SMITH, School of Social and Political Sciences, The University of Glasgow

"In *Transforming Wall Street*, Kim Ann Curtin strips away layers of justifications and misconceptions to provide us with the true essence of capitalism and how it can be consciously used to maximize human potential. She deftly weaves together historic turning points and contemporary thought leaders to create a compelling argument that by using our economic systems more deliberately, we will be far more satisfied with the outcomes."

—AMY DOMINI, founder of Domini Social Investments and author of *Socially Responsible Investing: Making a Difference and Making Money*

"Through her interviews, Curtin defines what true capitalism can be and should be. She exposes the situations that have hindered capitalism, such as government interference in free markets, from fulfilling its potential for long-term prosperity for everyone. Well worth reading."

—JOHN A. ALLISON, President and CEO of the Cato Institute, Retired Chairman and CEO, BB&T

"*Forcibly inspiring!* Kim Ann Curtin brilliantly restores our faith in the fact that there is heroism in capitalism. She showcases a select group of practitioners who embrace the philosophy that best business practices are achieved when lives are bettered and communities are strengthened ahead of profits. In *Transforming Wall Street: A Conscious Path for a New Future*, Curtin introduces us to some leaders who define this new paradigm—those conscious visionaries who have changed the world not just by making money and driving shareholder returns BUT by leaving people better than they found them."

—CYNTHIA D. DIBARTOLO, ESQ., Chief Executive Officer, Tigress Financial Partners LLC

"In *Transforming Wall Street*, Kim Ann Curtin's rigorous research into modern day capitalism has managed to unearth some of its finest stalwarts, and in so doing, gets to the essence of what makes this economic system work and wherein lies its strengths and vulnerabilities. This is masterful writing, laced with honest and compelling arguments. A recommended read for all who would seek to learn more about capitalism's past, present, and future."
—DON SEYMOUR, founder, DMS Offshore Investment Services Ltd.

"Kim Ann Curtin's book *Transforming Wall Street* is full of interesting and innovative ideas about human nature, our interests in and motivations regarding money, and how we can apply capitalism in ways that will make our economy, society, and personal lives more satisfying. It is well worth reading."
—JOHN C. WHITEHEAD, former Co-Chairman and Partner of Goldman Sachs, a former US Deputy Secretary of State and former director of the NYSE

"Kim Ann Curtin has bravely faced facts in the much-maligned recent history of Wall Street and woven together interviews from some of today's most accomplished thinkers and players to create a brocade of strategies for conscious leadership that will, if implemented, make our financial power centers both successful and responsible again."
—MARSHALL GOLDSMITH, author of the *New York Times* and global bestseller *What Got You Here Won't Get You There*

"It's only through practicing mindfulness with the intention of everyone's financial benefit that you can call yourself a true fiduciary. Kim's book reflects her inner wisdom in applying this process to our collective benefit." —MICHAEL MARTIN, MartinKronicle.com author, *The Inner Voice of Trading*

"Room to Read's early development thrived thanks in large part to the conscious capitalism of Wall Street that Kim Ann Curtin eloquently discusses. Curtin's analysis of the Wall Street 50 is a fantastic account of how the banking and hedge fund communities can—and are—making a tremendous impact on social causes. Room to Read's global literacy and girls' education efforts have impacted over 8 million children in Asia and Africa due in large part to philanthropic leadership and support from the finance community. *Transforming Wall Street* is a rousing take on the future of Wall Street's contribution not only to Main Street but also to communities in Asia and Africa."

—JOHN WOOD, founder, Room to Read and author
of *Leaving Microsoft to Change the World*

"When it comes to spreading Conscious Capitalism, Wall Street and the financial sector are the final frontier, and to many, the greatest obstacle. Kim Ann Curtin's book is a wonderfully positive and inclusive contribution to the dialogue of how the financial sector can reconnect with its invaluable and inherent higher purpose, which is to enable the spread of human and planetary flourishing by shepherding societal resources and directing them towards the most impactful areas. The breadth of thinking and depth of wisdom in this book are quite breathtaking. Let us all hope that it falls on receptive ears in the canyons of Wall Street and in financial capitals around the world."

—RAJ SISODIA, FW Olin Distinguished Professor of Global
Business and Whole Foods Market Research Scholar in
Conscious Capitalism, Babson College, and Co-founder
and Co-Chairman, Conscious Capitalism Inc.

TRANSFORMING WALL STREET

A Conscious Path for a New Future

KIM ANN CURTIN

The Wall Street Coach

AVIVA
PUBLISHING
New York

Published by
Aviva Publishing
Lake Placid, NY
518-523-1320
www.avivapubs.com

First edition

Ordering information for print editions:

Quantity sales. Special discounts are available on quantity purchases by corporations, associations, and others. For details, contact the "Special Sales Department" at The Wall Street Coach, PO Box 1401, New York, NY 10163. 646-420-2099.

Orders for college textbook/course adoption use. Please contact The Wall Street Coach, 646-420-2099.

Orders for US trade bookstores and wholesalers. Please contact The Wall Street Coach, 646-420-2099. Email: info@thewallstreetcoach.com

Hardcover print edition ISBN 978-1-94098-459-9
Library of Congress Control Number: 2014949516

Disclaimer: All interviews in this book have been edited for grammar and punctuation and to remove the repetitions and idiosyncrasies of human speech. They have also been edited for space to fit this book, but all the content is true to the spirit of what the interviewees originally said.

Editor: Tyler Tichelaar
Copyeditor and proofreader: Larry Alexander
Cover design: Alina Wilczynski, moonkissed media
Interior design: Karen Giangreco

I dedicate this book to Monsignor Thomas J. Hartman.

Without your love, support, and encouragement,
I simply would not be here.

Is the system going to flatten you out and deny you your humanity, or are you going to be able to make use of the system to the attainment of human purposes?
—JOSEPH CAMPBELL

Yesterday I was clever, so I wanted to change the world. Today I am wise, so I am changing myself.
—RUMI

That which you call your soul or spirit is your consciousness, and that which you call "free will" is your mind's freedom to think or not, the only will you have, your only freedom, the choice that controls all the choices you make and determines your life and character.
—AYN RAND, *Atlas Shrugged*

Awareness is the greatest agent for change.
—ECKHART TOLLE, *A New Earth*

You never change things by fighting the existing reality. To change something, build a new model that makes the existing model obsolete.
—R. BUCKMINSTER FULLER

Contents

TRANSFORMING WALL STREET

A Conscious Path for a New Future

Preface

A few years back, Michael Lewis, in a Bloomberg interview, said he felt that those at the top of the Wall Street structure needed to display more "social obligation." And the way to restore that was through *shame*.

While I agree with Mr. Lewis that we are absolutely in need of a Wall Street that honors its "social obligation" more successfully, I disagree it is through shame that we will or can accomplish this goal.

This book offers an alternative path to that restoration by focusing on what we *do want* for and from Wall Street and its leaders instead of what we *don't want*. We have spent a lot of time, energy, and focus on those who have shown no integrity in the world of finance. We are well aware of the breaches of integrity that have occurred. We are clear on the lack of ethics displayed. We are painfully aware of the global impact this behavior has had and continues to have. We have been disgusted and repelled by much reprehensible behavior. It has discouraged and saddened many, but none more so than those who view themselves as capitalists. As any true capitalist knows, what we have witnessed is not capitalism but the very antithesis of it.

I propose the time has come to shift our attention toward what we want. To speak to the qualities we desire. If we want a Wall Street that capitalists can be proud of, then let us focus on those whom we can already be proud of and look at the qualities they share and encourage the same from the rest of our leaders, especially those in the making.

As an executive coach, one of my more powerful influences is Appreciative Inquiry (AI). Wikipedia describes it as:

> That which takes an asset-based approach, believing that every organization, and every person in an organization, has positive aspects that can be built upon. And that to focus on only the dysfunction can actually cause organizations to become worse

or fail to become better. AI argues, *when all members of an organization are motivated to understand and value the most favorable features of its culture, it can make rapid improvements.* [Emphasis mine]

I believe rapid improvements are needed and that the stories shared by the men and women I interviewed for this book will assist in creating these improvements.

These interviews took place between 2011–2014. I sought out the men and women of Wall Street who were working in integrity, the ones who were conscious. What do I mean by conscious? Those awake and aware—of their action and inaction. Those who are striving to work and live consciously. Those who follow their own moral code.

Doing my own research and welcoming friends, colleagues, and industry leaders' suggestions (including the public's via social media), I began a search for Wall Streeters who fit this definition of being conscious; then I decided on the number fifty for two reasons: 1) I felt fifty was a number high enough to have some gravitas, and 2) it reminded me of *Hawaii Five-O*, the elite forces unit that I loved on TV as a young girl. Since the slang expression "Five-O" is still used to indicate the presence of police in the area, I thought how apt that my Five-O are the "presence" of consciousness on Wall Street. Since then, a friend pointed out that fifty also represents the states in our union. So now I think of it as there being a Wall Streeter to inspire every state! Much to my delight, I discovered there are actually way more than fifty, but I had to stop somewhere.

As an executive coach, I'm about encouraging more consciousness for my individual clients and the organizations I advise. As a citizen of this country, not to mention the world, I definitely want to see more consciousness on Wall Street (and Main Street). I also want to encourage our younger generation to pursue capitalism consciously—to believe they can achieve great success without selling out one's soul. I believe conscious capitalism is not only possible but the way out and the way forward. Who better to assist in proving this theory true than those who are the conscious capitalists of Wall Street? From the

Wall Street Five-O we can learn how these capitalists not only live and work consciously but attribute their success to this quality. Their stories, I hope, will inspire Wall Street and Main Street to strive for this balance and emulate their qualities. They speak about the challenges they've faced (and face) and how they rose (and rise) to meet them. They discuss temptations resisted and how they managed to overcome them.

What does living consciously mean to them? How do they balance living consciously while capitalistically? Who influenced them? What are their values? How are they able to stay true to their integrity when large sums of money are at stake? If given magic wands, what would they do regarding Wall Street? What is their advice to those entering or working on Wall Street now? How does one become more awake and aware? These are the questions they answer in the pages that follow.

Additionally, I sought out what I describe as *Teachers of Consciousness*. These teachers and their wisdom have assisted me in my own awakening, expanding my consciousness along the way. I've asked them for the best advice to give someone interested in becoming more awake—how one might begin.

The Wall Street 50 are neither angels nor saints (nor are the *Teachers of Consciousness*). In fact, they would be the first ones to say they are far from perfect, yet they are worthy of emulation and our admiration. Their stories of conscious leadership are encouraging, and I hope they will inspire and move you into action. They are living examples of how capitalism can indeed live in harmony with consciousness.

> *Our fate is shaped from within ourselves*
> *outward, never from without inward.*
> **—JACQUES LUSSEYRAN**

Introduction

Why I Wrote This Book

"You want to write a book about the conscious men and women of Wall Street? People will think it's some sort of *Saturday Night Live* comedy skit!" That was the response from a friend when I told him of my idea over three years ago. "People are too angry at Wall Street right now for this book to ever work." My friend might very well have been correct, but it's too late now, because in spite of the truth of his statements, I had to do it anyway. In the beginning, I had only considered writing a book about my own journey and what I had learned along the way. Yet the anti-capitalistic energy out there really gnawed at me and I just couldn't shake it, and after witnessing a sign at an Occupy Wall Street protest that showed a man in a suit lynched from a tree, my decision was made.

I want to say right from the start that I'm not in denial about the problems on Wall Street. I did not support the bailouts. I don't believe that is what capitalism is about. Actual fraud, and a willful cheating of honest people out of billions of dollars occurred. It was on many levels institutional, not just a few bad apples. And yet not a single person of stature has gone to jail or even trial. The media remains mostly a mouthpiece of the government and Wall Street, and it has not spoken truth to power; not only did it not offer up any serious solutions nor encourage any, but it also positioned what did occur as capitalistic when what happened and is still happening is the antithesis of it. "Crony capitalism," is what Adam Smith, the "Father of Capitalism," decried and what motivated him to write *The Wealth of Nations*. Most people don't really understand Smith's teachings, but I assure you he would be horrified over the behavior we've seen. When he spoke about *The Wealth of Nations*, he was talking about *what all the people of a nation* experience—not just those in business.

Regulations and laws exist to protect the people, and when they are flouted willfully and systemically, government needs to respond vigorously and with meaningful justice.

While reading Adam Smith's *Theory of Moral Sentiments*, the umbrella under which *The Wealth of Nations* actually sits, I realized that in addition to Smith accepting (more than advocating) man's natural tendency to be concerned with his own self-interest, he also spoke of how we have a moral responsibility to our neighbor and community. He also said it is a given that mankind experiences empathy for others. I believe if we were to follow Smith's philosophy, then we would practice and experience true "conscious" capitalism, the way it was meant to be.

One day walking past the Strand bookstore in Union Square, New York, I saw a sign in the window with this Toni Morrison quote, "If there's a book that you want to read, but it hasn't been written yet, then you must write it." So after watching three years of complaints, anger, and protests, and not seeing the changes that we had hoped to see, I thought I'd write this book.

How I Tackled This Project

In spite of what I acknowledge regarding the massive fraud that has occurred, this book comes out of my personal belief that there still are actually more men and women in finance that have integrity than those who do not. As one colleague said to me, "It wouldn't work otherwise!" Yet this book is not a scientific study. It is one woman's quest to discover whether what she believes in her heart is true: that capitalism is a good thing, that one can be successful while retaining one's integrity, and that the more financially successful one is, the more good one can do in the world.

Having worked in finance now for more than fifteen years, I have had the privilege and honor to know countless men and women who have integrity in this industry. I have known many who lead moral lives personally and professionally. I think it's important to acknowledge them. Are there jerks? Sure. They exist and I'm not denying them, but they are simply not the majority, and while I'm not ignoring the issues that exist in this industry and how serious they are, I believe the best way to tackle them is to focus on what we want more of and to learn from those who have been successful at navigating the financial world with their integrity intact. I hope their stories will inspire and encourage others to follow their lead. It's time we have conscious leaders to look up to in this industry and perhaps those who are less aware or half asleep will awake and begin to see that one can indeed be a successful capitalist while retaining one's soul or, at the very least, the conscious leaders will be emboldened to begin to crowd out those who are not.

My search for those who are conscious or act with integrity on Wall Street first began by word of mouth. I'd ask friends and colleagues whom they thought qualified. Then I began to post on social media, asking the public to recommend those they thought were the good guys of Wall Street. The names started to pour in. In the end, I researched and interviewed over ninety people—many of whom currently work on The Street or in finance in some capacity, a handful

I see as the titans of finance, and some who previously worked on Wall Street. Once the men and women from Wall Street whom I consider "conscious financiers" shared their personal journeys with me, I became even more inspired to bring their stories forward. I believe these *Wall Street 50* who share their experiences will breed hope and, ultimately, inspire others in the industry and beyond to emulate them. I then sought out the four professors whose work had enlightened me in understanding capitalism more clearly and understanding who Adam Smith really was and what he advocated. Then last, but certainly not least, I interviewed those whom I call the "*Teachers of Consciousness*," teachers who have had an impact on my own personal growth and have done what I call, "the work on themselves." Each of them has studied, developed, and increased his or her own consciousness through a variety of methods, and they share in common the experience of having been face to face with their own dragons in the basement of their souls. I have always sought out teachers who have been "through it." And each of these teachers has. They share how you, yes you, can expand your own vision. They have influenced my own awakening, and I hope they will influence yours.

A lot of these Wall Street 50 are world renowned, yet amazingly not one of them asked me for a non-disclosure agreement. They gave me amazing access to meet with them one-on-one without seeing my questions first, nor having a PR person present. They answered my questions while allowing me to record our conversations. Keep in mind they knew I had not yet secured a publisher, nor did I have the professional credentials as a reporter or a writer. What made them agree? I believe it was their desire to be heard. I believe each of these men and women strive to live and work consciously. They are as upset and frustrated with the unconsciousness on Wall Street as anyone. Perhaps they were simply glad that someone noticed they were operating under a set of values.

It's important to note that only one self-selected himself. Frank Casey emailed me, having seen my post on Albourne Village seeking conscious financiers. He wrote me and spoke about how he and his colleagues spent nearly nine years trying to stop Bernie Madoff. After speaking to Frank multiple times and hearing his astonishing story of unstoppableness, I chose to include him. I remember being thrilled that he had reached out since I knew he was one of the threesome who brought down Madoff. I had watched in horror and disbelief, along with the rest of the world, when that scandal broke, and I was pretty excited to speak with one of the men who helped bring him down. I was especially curious to find out what it was that motivated him to be so dogged about it—they worked on it for ten years! Frank, along with Harry Markopolos and Neil Chelo, spent years imploring the authorities to shut Madoff down, and in spite of being ignored by every government agency for an entire decade, they didn't stop.

I wish I had been able to interview more women, but I struggled to find women who would agree to be interviewed. Women in general seemed to be less comfortable being in the spotlight in this industry since it is still quite the man's world. I think that is too bad because I believe more women in this industry would help. I want to encourage more women to join this industry. One of my Teachers of Consciousness described this situation as needing more *hina* (feminine) energy. Kauila Clark, who is respectfully regarded as a Hawaiian Kahu, a Keeper and a Guardian of Hawai'i's ancient wisdom, said the industry is currently filled with only *ku* energy (male energy) and when anything or anyone has too much of either energy—it will be out of balance.

Some people will scoff at this book. That's okay. I believe that what you seek, you find. Energy flows where attention goes. I believe there is consciousness on Wall Street, but not as much as there needs to be. Being the proponent that I am of Appreciative Inquiry, I know the way to get more of something in an organization is to focus on what you want, not what you don't. One of the books I read early in my research was Michael Martin's *The Inner Voice of Trading*. In it, he quotes Ed Seykota, a well-known commodities trader who pioneered Systems trading, as saying, "each person gets what they want from their trading." Meaning that we are the co-creators (albeit unknowingly) of our experiences. I believe not only is that true, but that to some extent every person co-creates what he or she gets from life as well, and that has to do with a person's consciousness and how he views and engages with the world around him.

It is also because I believe in co-creation that I wrote this book. I believe that if people believe capitalism is wrong, or that wealth can only be achieved in an illicit way, that will unconsciously prevent people from attaining or even seeking wealth, for fear of being tarnished in some way.

Many soulful people think that money is dirty or bad or wrong. The word *rich* has become a derogatory adjective. I believe money is energy. And that we can re-design our relationship to money into one that is fueled with love and abundance instead of fear and scarcity. Together, we can perform a "blood transfusion" on the money we earn, create, spend, and donate. Barbara Wilder speaks about this in her book *Money is Love*. Barbara teaches that as we begin to remove our negative thoughts and feelings surrounding money and we redefine money as love, we bring the power of love into all of our monetary transactions. Barbara states, "This in turn opens our hearts to allow money to flow abundantly into our lives and from this place of harmony we can then send money back out into the world on a flow of love and gratitude. Money healed can begin to heal all that it touches. And because money flows like blood through the planet, diseased it causes disease, but infused with love, money can become rejuvenating. . . . Money is the blood of the planet. Heal the money and we can heal the world."

I believe we all have a relationship with money whether we are connected to it or not. How we choose, consciously or unconsciously, to co-create with it drives us into either having more or less of it in our lives.

Susan Davis, one of my Wall Street 50 and the founder and president of Capital Missions talked about this point with me in one of the interviews I conducted. Here is what she said:

> The reason I chose to operate in a for-profit world, as opposed to a not-for-profit world, is that in the for-profit world, you make your own money, so you control your own destiny, whereas in a not-for-profit world, you have to be kind of hat-in-hand to donors

who are really difficult to find and to keep in touch with. So, that's why I wanted to be self-funding. But my intention behind money has always been love, and your intention behind anything is what actually manifests, and so when your intention is love, you manifest love. Money is really just a medium; you could be manifesting help, or you could be manifesting a garden to feed your family; there are so many things that can be manifested, but when corporations only focus on making money, even if it means destroying the Earth that supports us, well then "this" manifested money won't build but destroy, so first it has to be healed. . . . It has been very well proven that altruistic people are happier, healthier, and live longer, and people are more likely to act generously than not. But since we've set up our global economy based on an incorrect assumption that humans are selfish and greedy, we are suffering the consequences now of that belief. When we destroy the Earth that supports each of us with its air, water, and soil, then we need to change the intention. That's why I went into finance—because we have to fix this thing. We made a major mistake; we have got a ladder up against the wrong wall, and we have to get our ladder up against the right wall and get everybody on Earth up that ladder because we have to restore the Earth that supports us instead of destroying it. That's why I focused on finance.

Imagine the power of co-creation when we use money as if it were love to build, not to destroy, to serve others too rather than to hoard it only for ourselves. Ultimately, I'd like to see these fifty conscious Wall Streeters be brought together in a consortium to co-create solutions globally. They could become a Special Forces Unit that informs all leaders of the world on economic issues. A think tank of sorts. They could create the new model of finance. My friend, Andrew Hewitt—creator of Game Changers 500, which takes the Fortune 500 idea and instead lists the 500 most purpose-driven organizations—recently suggested we put before them these questions: "What does the new model of finance look like? What kind of ecosystem will support it?"

Perhaps the new model of finance begins with crafting principle-based practices as well as principle-based regulation. I can remember during Occupy Wall Street seeing some finance people try to begin a dialogue with some of those in the Occupy movement to educate them on what issues really needed to be focused on. I'll never forget Peter Schiff, author of *How an Economy Grows and Why It Crashes*, patiently trying to educate the crowd, despite being yelled at, that it wasn't capitalism, but crony capitalism, that was the enemy, and how their movement and platform could be more successful if they understood that.

Now more than ever, it's time to hear from the conscious leaders in the finance industry. That is why I sought these fifty out. They have much to say and all of Wall Street needs to hear from them as well as the other conscious leaders in this industry. I want those who slumber in this industry to be roused awake, and those on the fence to come forward and begin the transformation of finance. My hope is that this book and these fifty will encourage a movement that will begin the creation of a new Wall Street. How? By encouraging more people to become aware of how they work and live. The philosopher, futurist, inventor, and global thinker, R. Buckminster Fuller, said, "If humanity does not opt for integrity, we are through completely. It is absolutely touch and go. Each one of us could make the difference." I hope this book will inspire more individuals to *make that difference.*

In David Whyte's book *The Heart Aroused: Poetry & the Preservation of Soul in Corporate America*, he opens with this quote from Irene Claremont de Castillejo:

> Only a few achieve the colossal task of holding together, without being split asunder, the clarity of their vision alongside an ability to take their place in a materialistic world. They are the modern heroes . . . artists at least have a form within which they can hold their own conflicting opposites together. But there are some who have no recognized artistic form to serve this purpose, they are the artists of the living. To my mind these last are the supreme heroes in our soulless society.

You, reader, are that hero. The time has come for you to come forth and create the change you and the rest of the world seek for and from Wall Street. Together we can co-create this change by waking up, standing up, speaking up—first to our souls, then to our families and friends, then to our colleagues, our staff, our CEOs, and board members—about the way we run our firms. We can do this with our wallets in addition to our words and our choices.

How? It starts as everything does . . . with ourselves. We begin by waking up, by increasing our own self-awareness, and by developing our emotional and spiritual intelligence, and as our own consciousness and awareness expands we increase the level of it in our world. It is time for the conscious capitalists to take back Wall Street and the entire financial world. This is the time and we are the people.

It is better to light a candle than to curse the darkness.
—CHINESE PROVERB

The Wall Street 50, the Professors, and the Teachers of Consciousness

THE WALL STREET 50

In writing this book I interviewed over seventy people who either work or have worked on Wall Street, and I've slimmed those down to what I call *The Wall Street 50*. These fifty people are quoted on the following pages:

BILL ACKMAN, founder, Pershing Square Capital Management

DARA ALBRIGHT, founder, NowStreet

JOHN ALLISON, former CEO, BB&T Bank

JOHN BOGLE, founder, The Vanguard Group

JOSHUA BROWN, CEO, Ritholtz Wealth Management

ERIC CARANGELO, VP, State Street

FRANK R. CASEY, member of The Fox Hounds

GLEN DAILEY, Glen Capital Management

ROB DAVIS, founder, Hedge Funds Care, Help For Children

SUSAN DAVIS, founder, Capital Missions

CYNTHIA DIBARTOLO, founder, Tigress Financial Partners

AMY DOMINI, founder, Domini Social Investments

JONAH FORD, co-founder, Ceres Hedge

JOSEPH GRANO, founder, Centurion Holdings

ALEX GREEN, founder, The Oxford Club

ERIC GRESCHNER, founder, Regatta Research

OSWALD GRUBEL, former Group CEO, UBS AG

MORIHIKO GOTO, founder, Goto Capital Markets Inc.

JANET HANSON, founder, 85 Broads

CARLA HARRIS, managing director, Morgan Stanley

HAZEL HENDERSON, founder, Ethical Markets Media

MAYRA HERNÁNDEZ, Grupo Financiero Banorte

R. PAUL HERMAN, founder, HIP Investor

MARLEE-JO JACOBSON, founder, SafeMoneyMetrics

ERIKA KARP, founder, Cornerstone Capital

BRAD KATSUYAMA, co-founder and CEO, IEX Group Inc

HENRY KAUFMAN, former managing director, Salomon Bros Inc.

DR. ANDREW KUPER, founder, LeapFrog Investments

SCHUYLER "SKY" LANCE, co-founder, SustainVC LLC

PETER LEEDS, founder and CEO, PeterLeeds.com

MISHA RUBIN (LYUVE), partner, Ernst & Young

MICHAEL MARTIN, trader and author

ROBERT MONKS, shareholder activist and author

MAKOTO OZAWA, trader, Fountainhead Capital

DEEPAK PAREKH, Chairman of HDFC

JOSEPH PERELLA, partner, Perella Weinberg Partners

ARNAUD POISSONNIER, founder, Babyloan

ANDREW H. PRITCHARD, Independent IB and Sales

BARRY RITHOLTZ, founder, Ritholtz Wealth Management

JAMES B. ROGERS, founder, Beeland Interests

ANDREW SCHEFFER, finance advisor, Buddhist monk

JACK SCHWAGER, author, *Market Wizards*

GEORGE SCHWARTZ, COO, Boston Private Bank & Trust

DON SEYMOUR, founder, DMS Offshore Investment Services Ltd.

AARON SMYLE, founder, Smyle & Associates

MICHAEL STUART, co-founder, Clark & Stuart

JASON APOLLO VOSS, content director, CFA Institute

SOL WAKSMAN, founder and president, BarclayHedge Ltd.

JOHN WHITEHEAD, former Co-Chair, Goldman Sachs

FRED WILSON, co-founder, Union Square Ventures

THE PROFESSORS

I interviewed these professors for Part I: Capitalism: A Defense. They articulate in a simple and compelling way how misinformed our corporations and educational systems are regarding capitalism. These professors speak to what capitalism was meant to be and what it originally hoped to achieve:

PROFESSOR MICHAEL PORTER, Bishop William Lawrence University Professor at Harvard Business School

PROFESSOR LYNN STOUT, Distinguished Professor of Corporate and Business Law, Cornell University

PROFESSOR CHRISTOPHER J. BERRY, FRSE Emeritus Professor (Political Theory), Honorary Professorial Research Fellow, School of Social and Political Sciences, University of Glasgow

PROFESSOR CRAIG SMITH, Adam Smith Lecturer in the Scottish Enlightenment (School of Social and Political Sciences) University of Glasgow

THE TEACHERS OF CONSCIOUSNESS

These teachers are featured throughout the book to assist the reader in understanding how to live and work more consciously while capitalistically:

PATRICIA ABURDENE, social forecaster and author of *Conscious Money*

PETER BLOCK, consultant and author of *The Answer to How is Yes: Acting on What Matters*

KAUILA CLARK, Hawaiian Kahu

ALAN H. COHEN, M.A., author of *The Dragon Doesn't Live Here Anymore*

CHIP CONLEY, author of *Peak: How Great Companies Get Their Mojo from Maslow*

RAPHAEL CUSHNIR, present moment awareness expert and author of *The One Thing Holding You Back*

RASANATH DAS, monk, former investment banker

DAVID HOULE, futurist, author of *Entering the Shift Age*

YASUHIKO GENKU KIMURA, founder of Vision-in-Action, former Zen Buddhist priest

CHARLES LAWRENCE, shaman

HIS HOLINESS SRI SRI RAVI SHANKAR, spiritual leader

DR. DAN SIEGEL, neuroscientist, author of *The Mindful Brain*

NEALE DONALD WALSCH, author of *Conversations with God: An Uncommon Dialogue*

All of these people were fascinating to talk to and I will introduce many of them in more detail in the pages that follow. My interviews with these people were all extensive, lasting an hour or more, and the transcripts would fill many volumes. I have only provided the fundamentals of their words in these pages to illuminate the main points I wish to make. If I have left anyone or anything out, I sincerely apologize because you all led me to a better understanding of the topic of consciousness, capitalism, Wall Street, and how we can change finance and the world by living and working more consciously. All the interviewees were welcoming, gracious, and more than willing to share their knowledge and personal stories for the benefit of my readers and the world at large.

PART I

CAPITALISM—A DEFENSE

Misconceptions About Adam Smith's Capitalism and Ayn Rand

Two of the most important theorists in history regarding capitalism were Adam Smith and Ayn Rand. Adam Smith is often known as the Father of Capitalism and Ayn Rand's opinions on capitalism have been debated for the better part of a century now. Unfortunately, both of these people have been misinterpreted by the media and teachers, often dismissed, and seldom read. People think they know what Adam Smith said from a short mention of him in a high school history book. More people know about Ayn Rand from what is said about her in the media than from actually reading her books. Both Smith and Rand would be appalled by how many perceive or understand capitalism today. It is time they be vindicated and we reeducate ourselves about their ideas. Countless books have been written about both Smith and Rand and I encourage my readers to read those books and more importantly, to go back to the source and read Smith and Rand themselves.

Before I share the interviews I had regarding Smith and Rand, I will briefly introduce them with a short biography and a few key passages from their works.

ADAM SMITH, THE FATHER OF CAPITALISM

PROFESSOR
Christopher J. Berry

MEET THE REAL ADAM SMITH

Christopher J. Berry, Professor of Political Theory at the University of Glasgow, is a leading expert on the life and work of Adam Smith. Here he gives an overview that describes the making of the man, the global significance of his writing, and explains why Smith's work still resonates with us today and why it's moral.[1]

---

1   More here: http://www.gla.ac.uk/about/history/fame/adamsmith/

CHRISTOPHER: Adam Smith was born in Kirkcaldy, Scotland in 1723. He entered Glasgow University at the early—but for the time not unusual—age of fourteen. He studied logic, metaphysics, math, and later Newtonian physics and moral philosophy under some of the leading scholars of the day. The seeds of Smith's two great books were sown in his professorial years. *The Theory of Moral Sentiments* appeared in 1759 and drew on his lectures, and his second great book *The Wealth of Nations* was published in 1776. If Smith of popular repute is the "Father of Capitalism," the advocate of "market forces," the enemy of government regulation, and believer in something called the "invisible hand" to produce optimum economic outcomes, then he would be a disappointed parent. All his work is deeply steeped in moral philosophy. Indeed, the simple fact that the final edition of *Moral Sentiments*, containing extensive revisions, appeared in 1790, the year of his death, tells us that Smith's commitment to the moral point of view endured alongside and beyond the publication of *The Wealth of Nations*.

The Theory of Moral Sentiments is a leading example of a particular approach to moral philosophy—one that regards it not as sets of rationally or Divine-ordained prescriptions but as the interaction of human feelings, emotions, or sentiments in the real settings of human life. In many ways, it is a book of social and moral psychology. What we can call economic behavior is necessarily situated in a moral context. But more than that, the key theme of the book is an opposition to the view that all morality or virtue is reducible to self-interest. Indeed, his opening sentence declares that everyday human experience proves that false; he writes:

> How selfish soever a man may be supposed, there are evidently some principles in his nature which interest him in the fortune of others, and render their happiness necessary to him, though he derive nothing from it except the pleasure of seeing it.

Our morality is founded on certain truths about human nature. Everyone is capable of sympathy, or fellow-feeling, and that ability enables us to imagine what we would feel if we were in the situation of another and, once we have made that imaginative move, we can then judge whether those feelings are appropriate. We have to learn about "situations" but Smith believes that happens because humans are social creatures. Smith illustrates the natural fact of human sociality by likening society to a mirror. It is this responsiveness to others—pleasure in their approval, pain in their disapproval—that Smith used to explain why the rich parade their wealth while the poor hide their poverty. The rich value their possessions more for the esteem they bring than any use they get from them, and it is this disposition to "go along with the passions of the rich and powerful" that establishes the foundation for distinctions of status. And it is this desire for esteem that explains the incentive we all possess to better our condition. This is one of the links between *The Theory of Moral Sentiments* and *The Wealth of Nations*. In many ways, the moral interactions Smith describes in *Moral Sentiments* bear on the practices that characterize his contemporary commercial society. The very complexity of that society meant that the bulk of inter-personal dealings were with strangers.

A "society of strangers" is a commercial society which Smith identifies in *The Wealth of Nations* as one where "every man is a merchant." A commercial society's coherence—its social bonds—do not depend on love and affection. You can coexist socially with those to whom you are emotionally indifferent. As Smith famously said:

> It is not from the benevolence of the butcher, the brewer or the baker that we expect our dinner, but from their regard to their own interest. We address ourselves not to their humanity but to their self-love and never talk to them of our own necessities but of their advantages. Nobody but a beggar chooses to depend chiefly upon the benevolence of his fellow-citizens.

Nothing in this means that Smith is denying the virtuousness of benevolence. When Smith came to write *The Wealth of Nations*, he made it clear that the "wealth" lay in the well-being of the people. This covered not only their material prosperity but also their moral welfare.

QUOTES

Man, according to the Stoics, ought to regard himself . . . as a citizen of the world, a member of the vast commonwealth of nature. . . . We should view ourselves . . . in the light in which any other citizen of the world would view us. What befalls ourselves we should regard as what befalls our neighbour, or what comes to the same thing, as our neighbour regards what befalls us.

—*The Theory of Moral Sentiments,* Book III, Chapter iii

Is this improvement in the circumstances of the lower ranks of the people to be regarded as an advantage or as an inconveniency to the society? The answer seems at first sight abundantly plain. Servants, labourers and workmen of different kinds, make up the far greater part of every great political society. But what improves the circumstances of the greater part can never be regarded as an inconveniency to the whole. No society can surely be flourishing and happy, of which the far greater part of the members are poor and miserable. It is but equity, besides, that they who feed, cloath and lodge the whole body of the people, should have such a share of the produce of their own labour as to be themselves tolerably well fed, cloathed and lodged.

—*An Inquiry into the Nature and Causes of the Wealth of Nations,* Book III, Chapter viii

All for ourselves, and nothing for other people, seems, in every age of the world, to have been the vile maxim of the masters of mankind.

—*An Inquiry into the Nature and Causes of the Wealth of Nations,* Book III, Chapter iv

PROFESSOR
Craig Smith, Ph.D   *Adam Smith, the Father of Capitalism*

MEET THE REAL ADAM SMITH

Dr. Craig Smith is the Adam Smith Lecturer in Scottish Enlightenment at the School of Social and Political Sciences at the University of Glasgow, Scotland.

CRAIG: When people have heard of Adam Smith, they've heard of the economist side of him rather than the moral philosopher, but they've also only heard a very partial version of the economist as well. They've heard the invisible hand setting . . . and that's it. I mean, if you pushed people even further than that, asking, "What did Smith actually say beyond that about how an economy operates?" Most people wouldn't know. They wouldn't have any real sense of what his argument was or anything like that. So he's become a kind of symbol for something which is kind of a caricature, I suppose, of what he really argued and believed in.

KIM: And I would say, the antithesis of what he really was trying to communicate.

CRAIG: Yes, yes. I'd agree with that. Particularly when you get people in the media writing things like, "Oh, Adam Smith said all we need to do is be selfish and everything will work all right, because of the invisible hand." Well, if you look at the first page of *The Theory of Moral Sentiments*, he tells you that people aren't selfish. That's the whole premise of the start of that book. It is to say, "Well, look. We're not selfish people. We're actually concerned about others and we have to try and understand why we're concerned about others and what the implications of that are." So it reveals that the people who make that kind of claim just have no awareness of, as you say, *The Theory of Moral Sentiments* at all.

KIM: I thought he was saying there are two things we need to pay attention to; first, that we as human beings are going to be concerned with our own self-interest first and foremost, because we are just going to be . . . and second, we will have a desire for social relationships and that mankind is sympathetic by nature. Are you familiar with Nonviolent Communication? In it, Marshall Rosenberg states that mankind is compassionate by nature as well. So I found it interesting to find them both in alignment. So we get the concept of, "We are interested in our self-interest, because our survival depends upon it, but we also experience compassion for our neighbors, and living in the balance of this." As though it's a scale that's constantly shifting, but finding the balance of these two sides Smith was not only advocating—advocating seems to be the least of it—that it was this he was trying to articulate and explain. Am I correct?

CRAIG: Yes. I think the metaphor or the image I would use isn't so much a scale though. One which is used quite often by Smith scholars is one of concentric circles. So what Smith recognizes is we are first and foremost concerned for ourselves and for those who are close to us. And then we're concerned emotionally for other people in a series of circles as they move away from us in terms of spatial distance if you like. So what he says is even if there is somebody we don't know, we can still be imaginatively concerned for that person. So it's not like we're not self-interested when it comes to our family, but we are more self-interested when it comes to other people.

What he is saying is that we're also concerned about other people, but our emotional investment in other people isn't quite as strong as in our family. How we approach them is different. So you might be, for example, willing to do something for your sister that you would be unwilling to do for somebody you'd never met before. And that's something Smith thinks is perfectly natural. And moreover, it's something that I, as somebody else, would recognize as being appropriate. I would recognize that it's appropriate for you to do something for your sister that you wouldn't do for me, for example. So what he wants to try and understand is how these different attitudes can have come together. At the beginning of the book, what he talks about is self-ishness. He says . . . well, some people, some philosophers in the past have said that human beings are always selfish and he has in mind here Bernard Mandeville and Thomas Hobbes. And he says, "Well, that's obviously not the case," because if you just think about your own feelings, you care about other people. You care about those close to you, but you also, to a certain extent, are interested in other people. You can sympathize with someone you've never meet before, if he's in unfortunate circumstances, but the amount of sympathy you can have with somebody like that is different from the amount of sympathy you can have with somebody close to you. And so what that means is there are different standards of appropriate behavior toward strangers and those close to you. That's not to say that the action toward strangers is selfishness; it's to say it's different from what you have to your family. So rather than it being a scale, it's like these concentric circles work-ing as different levels of emotional investment or concern with people depending on how close they are to you.

KIM:　Would you speak to how his version of sympathy is different than the way we understand sympathy. Is it possible that the appro-priate word is "empathy" that he was speaking to?

CRAIG:　Yes. The problem with sympathy is that in our use, it has a kind of association with pity and with feeling sorry for somebody. Whereas in Smith's language, it is the ability to have fellow feeling with any kind of emotion. So for Smith, you can have sympathy with somebody's happiness just as you can have sympathy with his grief. So empathy, I suppose, is quite a useful word to distinguish what Smith has in mind. He's also saying that you have sympathy or empathy with another person's experience; you, yourself, are having emotions generated in you by observing that. So you don't feel exactly the same feeling as those people, but you can look at them, you can imagine you being them and how you would feel in that circumstance, and so you can kind of recreate the emotional experience. And when you recre-ate the emotional experience of imagining yourself in their situation, you find yourself in a position where you can either approve of it or disapprove of it. So if you sympathize, if you successfully sympathize with somebody who's happy, you will feel a degree of happiness and you will also approve of him feeling happy, because of the situation he's in, but if you see somebody who's happy and you imagine yourself in his situation and you think, "No, I wouldn't be happy in that situation," then you'll disapprove of it. You wouldn't feel the feeling. Smithian Sympathy is actually a kind of a process. It's a mechanism, if you like. So empathy sometimes suggests in our language that you feel the same thing somebody else feels. But Smithian Sympathy is a bit more complicated because you can feel the same thing somebody else feels and approve of it, but you can also, through the sympathetic process, not feel the same thing and so disapprove of his reaction. So it's a little bit more than empathy, but empathy I think is a good word to describe the difference from our modern sense of sympathy.

KIM: Do you consider yourself a capitalist?

CRAIG: I don't like the word "capitalism." I had a big debate with colleagues about this before, because I regard myself as a classical liberal, an old-fashioned Whig, as Hayek would say. An old-fashioned Whig, kind of, eighteenth century liberal like Adam Smith was. So I don't really like the term "capitalism," because I don't think it really captures what Smith is talking about. One reason for that is historical. He's writing before Marx coins the term "capitalist." What he's talking about is probably better described in his own terms as being "commercial society" or "the market." In those terms then, yes, I describe myself as somebody who broadly supports commercial society or the market, rather than capitalism.

KIM: That's a great distinction. It's so funny that the Father of Capitalism wouldn't have identified himself as a capitalist.

CRAIG: No, no. I don't think he would have. In fact, if you read *The Wealth of Nations*, he is actually worried about the owners of capital because he sees them as being one of these groups of businessmen who gather together and then try and protect themselves from competition. He's more interested in the operation of the market than he is in the interests of those who hold large amounts of capital.

KIM: What's the most important thing readers need to know about Adam Smith and *The Theory of Moral Sentiments* and even *The Wealth of Nations*? In a nutshell, who is this man and what was he up to?

CRAIG: I would say the thing you have to remember about everything Smith wrote is he wants to understand and he wants to explain. So *The Theory of Moral Sentiments* is not a book that tells you how you should live your life. It doesn't provide you with an argument about what the good life is or what right is or what justice is. It's not that kind of philosophy. What it is, is an attempt to understand what actually happens when we make moral judgments. So when you read *The Theory of Moral Sentiments*, what you should be doing is actually thinking to yourself, "Do I recognize this? Can I see the feelings Smith is talking about in myself when I face moral decisions?" That's why he uses all these everyday examples to try and show you that the theory he's come up with is actually a better explanation for what you're actually going through when you make a moral judgment. If you read it in that respect, the book becomes something you can see touching your own life because it describes everyday things that go on when you find yourself in particular situations. You can recognize them. Smith also ties that together with the theory about sympathy, about the impartial spectator and conscience, and he gives you an account that brings it all together and explains it to you. In the second work, *The Wealth of Nations*, he's doing the same thing for the economy. He's saying, "We can look around the world as it is and we can recognize these different aspects of it." What we can then do is understand how trade operates and how nations have become richer. We can understand what the benefits of that are. And I think the key thing or one of the key messages in *The Wealth of Nations* is that the wealth of a nation is the wealth of its people. It's not the wealth of its government or the amount of gold it's got in the bank. It's the standard of living enjoyed by the people of the country. That in itself is a new idea in the eighteenth century. But what he wants you to do is also consider that the people he tells you about in *The Theory of Moral Sentiments*, people having that moral experience in their everyday lives, *are* the people who are acting in *The Wealth of Nations*. They are embedded agents; they're moral agents. They're people who have been socialized, who've grown up in society, who've learned how to be moral and how to judge other people and judge themselves. How to control their actions. How to make a decision over what is the right thing to do. But then in this one aspect of their economic life, they interact with other people through a whole set of institutions like the market. So he's not saying that when people go into the marketplace, they suddenly become selfish. They don't. They're still the same agents. They're still the same moral agents that existed in the story you get in *The Theory of Moral Sentiments*. But what happens is they're interacting with people who are on the outer edges of these circles of sympathy that they certainly don't know. They're strangers. And when you interact with strangers, you interact with them obviously in a less intimate fashion than you would do with your family and your friends. So you interact with them through institutions and laws and rules in the marketplace. That's not to say you couldn't sympathize with somebody you were trading with. You could because sympathy is an imaginative process for Smith. You could imagine yourself in that person's situation, but you couldn't do that every time you are involved in trade with somebody because it would just be inefficient and you're involved with so many different people in your everyday lives. So he's not saying you cease to be a moral agent and suddenly become selfish when you enter the marketplace. You don't. You remain a moral agent, but the way you interact with the vast number of people in an economic basis is by using a set of established rules or customs that ensure you can operate successfully in trade.

Often our mistake is to presume that Smith's account of the successful operation of the economy in *The Wealth of Nations* depends on the agents being selfish. He often uses phrases like "self-interest" and "self-regard" and all this kind of thing, but if you actually look at the analysis of what's going on, it's not so much that these individuals are nasty people out for their own gain. It's simply that they're following a set of incentives in a particular set of circumstances. And they're trying to maximize the benefit to them and their family and friends and so on from those circumstances. And that has led to the evolution of a set of rules and institutions that allow people to interact in that way which is the marketplace. So when two people come together to trade, they interact by appealing to each other's self-interest.

That doesn't mean either one of them is entirely motivated by self-interest or is incapable of any other kind of emotion or moral feeling. It simply means that in the case of this one aspect of their lives, it's more effective. People have learned it's more effective for them to interact in a bargaining scenario than through an emotional imaginative sympathy process. So I guess that's how I see it. It's tempting sometimes to think the sympathetic agents of *The Theory of Moral Sentiments* are different people from the agents in *The Wealth of Nations*, but they are not. They're the same. He's just focusing on a very particular aspect of their life in the second book.

KIM: It's like the facets of a diamond. I feel as though people have taken one facet of his many-sided diamond, and only focused on that. But to disregard all those other facets is to lose the heart of his message.

CRAIG: Yes. I think that's fair. Most of the people who think they understand Adam Smith have never read *The Wealth of Nations*, never mind *The Theory of Moral Sentiments*. What they've had is at some point in their lives, a college lecturer has said, "Adam Smith is free market capitalism." And that's all they know about it. And if you go even just beyond the surface of that, even a cursory examination of what it is that Smith is interested in, it becomes clear that there's far more to him. His interest was far more wide ranging than even just *The Theory of Moral Sentiments* and *The Wealth of Nations*. He's interested in so many different aspects of human experience in life. And you're not going to get a genuine idea of his—the depth and breadth of his thought—unless you appreciate that.

This might help make it clearer. I often say to students, "If you look at *The Theory of Moral Sentiments*, Smith is building it up in layers through the first four books, right? So each one of those books is about a different part of your moral experience, something you will recognize when you find yourself making a moral decision. And each part of it builds up to give you a complete picture of moral experience." So he talks about sympathy and imagination. He talks about how we judge other people, how we're judged by other people. He talks about how that then becomes internalized into the impartial spectator. So we start judging ourselves in making decisions about what's the right thing to do imaginatively before we act. He talks about where rules fit into this. The moral rules we come up with. And he talks about where the virtues or the character traits we admire fit into this. So the first four books are discussing almost every kind of conceivable situation, as many different parts of how we think about morality together and give us a kind of account that brings them all into the one thing. Instead of being a theorist who focuses on virtue or who focuses on rules or who focuses on sympathy alone, all of the different things are brought into the one account. And that's why he can appear to be repetitive—because he lays out one point; then he lays it out again and explains to you why it's connected to some other part of our moral experience. So often, when you find him apparently repeating himself, what he's actually doing is cuing up the next step in the argument.

KIM: We've heard about crony capitalism. What would Smith say about that?

CRAIG: The people Smith attacks as mercantilists in the eighteenth century were businessmen who associated together and lobbied politicians to protect their own interests. And that, to me, is a description of crony capitalism. Those were the exact people Smith was attacking. (Mercantilists were the big merchant companies in the eighteenth century.) So a theory developed in the eighteenth century that said the wealth of a nation is the amount of gold and trade generated by its big businesses, the merchants. And this came to be known as mercantilism. Smith's *The Wealth of Nations* is basically an attack on that idea.

The idea that Smith comes up with is the wealth of the nation isn't the wealth of these businessmen and the amount of gold they have in the bank and the amount of trade they do abroad; it's the standard of living of the people who live in the country. That's the true wealth of nations. So the mercantilist theory says governments should protect home producers against competition. The government should encourage or give bounties and support the companies who want to export goods abroad; they're always in competition with other countries on an economic level through conscious policy. Smith comes along and says, "No, that's just wrong." It's got the wrong understanding of what wealth is. And it's also bad for the economy because if you protect these big companies, what you're doing is you're effectively insulating them from competition, whether that's competition from abroad or from new producers at home. You end up actually hurting your own people by preventing them from getting cheaper goods just to protect the producers.

What I find staggering is all of these people in the contemporary press who criticize capitalism and then rail against big business and damn Adam Smith by association and have no conception that that's precisely what Smith was arguing against. And then the idea that banks should be bailed out, if you like. That's almost completely the opposite of what Smith would argue. The idea that big car companies, for example, should be protected by the government or subsidized by the government—that's what Smith is arguing against. So it strikes me that if you wanted to make an argument against crony capitalism, it's Adam Smith you would look to, not Marx or somebody like that. What strikes me is his analysis of the eighteenth century is actually a pretty appropriate analysis for what's gone on over the last eight to ten years in industry and in the relationship between the government and the banks.

KIM: If I give you a magic wand to wave over Wall Street, what would your magic wand do?

CRAIG: A good question. I'm not, by training, an economist. I am a historian and philosopher so I can't speak to the specifics of any regulatory regime or anything like that. That's not really my field. But I guess one of the things I'd stress would be that, often, what happens when regulators and lawmakers intervene is they actually create protections and even incentives for people to behave in a particular way, which doesn't, at the end of the day, end up being optimum. And one of the things Smith's quite keen on trying to get across is that it's not that you shouldn't have laws and rules, it's just that you need to be very careful about what those laws and rules are. And you can't expect those laws and rules to operate in the marketplace in a way that's in everyone's interest if they are decided by politicians who are influenced by businessmen.

What you're going to get if businessmen and politicians come together is a set of rules that meet the electoral interests of politicians and the financial interests of businessmen. And those two things are not the same as what's in the country's interest. Smith's argument is that the free market is actually what's in the interest of the country at large. The free market isn't what the politicians and businessmen in the eighteenth century were trying to construct, and it's not really what we are calling "crony capitalism." In Smith's view, if you are aware of that, what you have to do is ensure what he calls the operation of the simple and obvious system of natural liberties. And if you do that, then all the incentives that cause businessmen to act in potentially damaging ways and a lot of the loopholes they use would be closed to them.

So you can say, "But look, there may have been a financial disaster if some of the banks had been allowed to go bust during the financial crisis, and that may have affected a lot of people's lives." But the aftermath of that would then give you the question, "If you had gone through that, if you lost your money, would you ever again invest your money in a bank that did the kinds of things these banks were doing?" No, you wouldn't. "If you were a banker, would you ever again be able to run a bank that did the kind of things they were doing before that?" No, you wouldn't. So the discipline that comes from the system of natural liberty is lost when you try to intervene in that way. And Smith knew this because he wrote in *The Wealth of Nations* about the Ayr Bank in Scotland going bust. He knew what happens when banks go bust. He knew it was a very real economic problem. But if you try to deal with that by preventing it, by regulating it, and getting support for companies like that, you lose some of the discipline and some of the incentives that come from the market. So I guess if I had a wand to wave, I would probably have it do one thing: make regulators, politicians, and businessmen think twice before they did something and think about whether what they were doing was really in the interest of the economy as a whole, or whether it was just a way of protecting themselves.

AYN RAND, THE ADVOCATE OF CAPITALISM

My appreciation of Ayn Rand began in my late teens, and since then, I have watched her work, her words, and her reputation be wildly distorted as well as condemned, especially her views on capitalism. What she believed and advocated has rarely been accurately represented, especially in the media. I am going to try to set the record straight by explaining more about her early life and by quoting her directly from her writings so that you can determine for yourself whether what you've been told and taught about her is accurate. I also feature here two interviews that speak more about Ayn Rand and her work; one is with Yasuhiko Genku Kimur, one of my Teachers of Consciousness, and the other with John Allison, one of my Wall Street 50. I have found that there are usually only two kinds of thoughts regarding Ayn Rand, one that demonizes her as well as her philosophy, taking it out of context, and the other is using it to hide behind a sanctimonious neglect of honoring another's rights. Both of these views are in my opinion an exaggeration of what her philosophy advocates and misses altogether the point of her philosophy.

A CONDENSED BIOGRAPHY

Ayn Rand was born in St. Petersburg, Russia, on February 2, 1905. She taught herself to read at six years old, and at nine years old, she decided she would become a writer. In high school, she experienced the Kerensky Revolution, which she supported, and in 1917, the Bolshevik Revolution, which she denounced. Her family moved to escape the fighting, but she witnessed the Communists confiscate her father's business, and her family experienced periods of near-starvation. When she learned about American history, she took America as the model of what a nation of free men could be. When her family returned home, she entered the University of Petrograd to study philosophy and history. Graduating in 1924, she experienced the takeover of her university by the communists. In 1925, Rand obtained permission to leave Russia for a visit to relatives in the United States. Although she told the authorities that her visit would be short, she planned never to return. Rand arrived in New York City in 1926 and spent the next six months in the United States. Eventually, she obtained an extension to her visa, and she moved to California to pursue a career as a screenwriter. She began writing *The Fountainhead* in 1935. Depicting the ideal or heroic man, as represented by her main character, the architect Howard Roark, was the main goal of her writing—what she called man as "he could be and ought to be." *The Fountainhead* was rejected by twelve publishers before being accepted by the Bobbs-Merrill Company. When it was published in 1943, it made history by becoming a bestseller through word-of-mouth two years later, and it gained her lasting recognition as a champion of individualism. She began her novel, *Atlas Shrugged*, in 1946. Two years later, she moved back to New York City and worked full-time completing *Atlas Shrugged*, which was published in 1957. Some say that *Atlas Shrugged* was her greatest achievement. In that novel, she dramatized her unique philosophy. Although she considered herself a fiction writer, she realized that in order to create heroic fictional characters, she had to identify the philosophic principles that make such individuals possible. She wrote and lectured on her philosophy, Objectivism, which she characterized as "a philosophy for living on earth." All of her published books are still in print, and hundreds of thousands are sold each year.

The following is Rand speaking for herself about her Objectivist theories and what she means by the virtue of selfishness and how she views capitalism:

From *The Objectivist Ethics*, written in 1961:

- The Objectivist ethics proudly advocates and upholds *rational selfishness*—which means: the values required for man's survival qua man—which means: the values required for human survival—*not the values produced by the desires, the emotions, the "aspirations," the feelings, the whims or the needs of irrational brutes, who have never outgrown the primordial practice of human sacrifices, have never discovered an industrial society and can conceive of no self-interest but that of grabbing the loot of the moment.* (Italics mine)

- The Objectivist ethics holds that human good does not require human sacrifices and cannot be achieved by the sacrifice of anyone to anyone. It holds that the rational interests of men do not clash—that there is no conflict of interests among men who do not desire the unearned, who do not make sacrifices nor accept them, who deal with one another as traders, giving value for value.

From *The Virtue of Selfishness*, written in 1964:

- The meaning ascribed in popular usage to the word "selfishness" is not merely wrong: it represents a devastating intellectual "package-deal," which is responsible, more than any other single factor, for the arrested moral development of mankind.

- In popular usage, the word "selfishness" is a synonym of evil; the image it conjures is of a murderous brute who tramples over piles of corpses to achieve his own ends, who cares for no living being and pursues nothing but the gratification of the mindless whims of any immediate moment.

Yet the exact meaning and dictionary definition of the word "selfishness" is: concern with one's own interests.

This concept does not include a moral evaluation; it does not tell us whether concern with one's own interests is good or evil; nor does it tell us what constitutes man's actual interests. It is the task of ethics to answer such questions.

The moral purpose of a man's life is the achievement of his own happiness. This does not mean that he is indifferent to all men, that human life is of no value to him and that he has no reason to help others in an emergency.

There is a fundamental moral difference between a man who sees his self-interest in production and a man who sees it in robbery. The evil of a robber does not lie in the fact that he pursues his own interests, but in what he regards as to his own interest; not in the fact that he pursues his values, but in what he chose to value; not in the fact that he wants to live, but in the fact that he wants to live on a subhuman level.

From *On Capitalism: The Unknown Ideal*, written in 1966:

- Observe the paradoxes built up about capitalism. It has been called a system of selfishness (which, in *my* sense of the term, it *is*)—yet it is the only system that drew men to unite on a large scale into great countries, and peacefully to cooperate across national boundaries, while all the collectivist, internationalist, One-World systems are splitting the world into Balkanized tribes.

  Capitalism has been called a system of greed—yet it is the system that raised the standard of living of its poorest citizens to heights no collectivist system has ever begun to equal, and no tribal gang can conceive of.

  Capitalism has been called nationalistic—yet it is the only system that banished ethnicity, and made it possible, in the United States, for men of various, formerly antagonistic nationalities to live together in peace.

Capitalism has been called cruel—yet it brought such hope, progress and general good will that the young people of today, who have not seen it, find it hard to believe.

As to pride, dignity, self-confidence, self-esteem—these are characteristics that mark a man for martyrdom in a tribal society and under any social system except capitalism.

Capitalism demands the best of every man—his rationality—and rewards him accordingly. It leaves every man free to choose the work he likes, to specialize in it, to trade his product for the products of others, and to go as far on the road of achievement as his ability and ambition will carry him. His success depends on the objective value of his work and on the rationality of those who recognize that value. When men are free to trade, with reason and reality as their only arbiter, when no man may use physical force to extort the consent of another, it is the best product and the best judgment that win in every field of human endeavor, and raise the standard of living—and of thought—ever higher for all those who take part in mankind's productive activity.

Capitalism has created the highest standard of living ever known on earth. The evidence is incontrovertible. The contrast between West and East Berlin is the latest demonstration, like a laboratory experiment for all to see. Yet those who are loudest in proclaiming their desire to eliminate poverty are loudest in denouncing capitalism. Man's well-being is not their goal.

Capitalism cannot work with slave labor. It was the agrarian, feudal South that maintained slavery. It was the industrial, capitalistic North that wiped it out—as capitalism wiped out slavery and serfdom in the whole civilized world of the nineteenth century. What greater virtue can one ascribe to a social system than the fact that it leaves no possibility for any man to serve his own interests by enslaving other men? What nobler system could be desired by anyone whose goal is man's well-being?

I ask you now that you have read her own words, does Rand sounds like a woman who is advocating or even suggesting that each of us "*Do whatever we want and the hell with everyone else*"? I believe it's clear she most certainly was not. I hope this discussion will at the very least encourage you to read Ayn Rand's books and writings for yourself and then determine what her message really is and the perspective she would advocate.

CONSCIOUSNESS TEACHER
Yasuhiko Genku Kimura   *Capitalism: A Defense*

AYN RAND AND WHY BUSINESS IS SOCIETY'S GREATEST TRANSFORMING AGENT

Yasuhiko Genku Kimura is a mystic, philosopher, and a former Zen Buddhist Priest. He is also the founder of Vision-In-Action. His primary focus is trying to bring about an evolution in human consciousness. Here he speaks about whether or not the assumptions we are living under are correct for us.

KIM: You are a former Zen Buddhist priest from Japan. How did you come to advocate business as society's greatest transforming agent?

YASUHIKO: After my formal study of Buddhism in Japan, I went to India to study various schools of Eastern philosophy of the Indic origin. I also studied contemporary spiritual philosophy quite extensively. I was in my mid-twenties. What struck me the most about the Indian society was its pervasive abject poverty. One day while having a discussion with Mother Teresa's followers, a thought occurred to me and words just came out of my mouth: "*You don't need to be poor to be spiritual and you don't need to be an asshole to be rich.*" We can attain wealth both in the spiritual and material planes. The human dignity demands that we attain both. That was the beginning of my awakening beyond spiritual philosophy to integrate the material dimensions of life in my thought and action.

Shortly after I came to the United States, in 1984 a friend introduced me to Ayn Rand's work. Her philosophy was different from the kind of philosophy I had studied before, and it provided me with a critical key for integrating the spiritual with the material. Rand, in herself and in her work, integrates heightened rationality with heightened emotionality, and critical reason with creative passion. She and her heroes are deeply spiritual.

She was adversely impacted, even traumatized, by the communists, and therefore, she went to the extreme of anti-collectivism. And while I feel her philosophy was incomplete and insufficient to produce her "ideal man," her novels dramatically imparted an enduring vision of man and the world into which humanity can live.

After and along with Ayn Rand, I read the works of the Founders (Thomas Paine is my kindred spirit and most favorite) and Libertarian thinkers such as Lysander Spooner, Rose Wilder Lane, and Isabel Paterson, while Ludwig von Mises opened my eyes to the science of economics.

KIM: Please speak about the relevance of your integration of Buddhism and Randian, Painite, and Libertarian thought?

YASUHIKO: The primary value and contemporary significance of Buddhism is that it is a time-tested path of inner liberation, freedom, and self-realization. Yet because of its exclusive focus on the internal spiritual dimension, it provides no philosophical foundation for developing external societal liberty and freedom or achieving self-realization in the world. You see, one can be internally free in a prison while one can be internally imprisoned outside a prison. We can eliminate prison as such completely and be free internally and externally. A proper synthesis of the Buddhist and Libertarian approaches makes it possible for us to achieve such inner-outer integrated freedom and self-realization.

Also, Buddhism, especially Zen, is based not on belief but on self-inquiry and examination. This is in alignment with the basic orientation of Western philosophy as exemplified by the Socratic dialogue. Ayn Rand used to ask her students: Check your premise. Checking one's premises, examining assumptions, is the fundamental function of philosophy. Hence Socrates' famous statement in Plato's *Apology*: Life unexamined is not worth living.

KIM: What is the significance of all this to conscious capitalism and finance?

YASUHIKO: Conscious business, conscious capitalism, and conscious financing have all arisen as the result of business people examining their own assumptions and cherished beliefs and asking deep questions. They will continue to do so because to be conscious means to examine and ask questions. This consciousness, this examining and asking, will be the prime mover of the evolution of conscious business, capitalism, and finance.

Ayn Rand has a book called *Philosophy: Who Needs It*. Her answer was everyone because we are existentially all philosophers. Consciously or unconsciously you are a philosopher because you cannot live without having assumptions, without thinking. What is required is that you awaken your own inner philosopher consciously.

KIM: So the question is: are the assumptions you are living the right assumptions?

YASUHIKO: "Right" in the sense of proper or appropriate. The rightness of assumptions depends on the context or the purpose of the discourse, which you create or in which you are engaged. A right set of assumptions in one context or discourse may be wrong in a different context or discourse. What is called a "paradigm shift" usually involves a radical shift in assumptions because assumptions are the foundation of a paradigm.

One of the distinguishing paradigmatic features of conscious business, capitalism, or finance is the emphasis on stakeholder values as opposed to merely shareholder values, and inclusion of the whole (society, ecology, etc.) in the signification of prosperity and success. There is a shift in assumption vis-à-vis the purpose of business from profit making for the company to value creation for the whole.

One of the fundamental assumptions of humanity is scarcity, which engenders the scarcity mentality that pervades throughout the world, including the business, corporate, and finance communities. Elimination of the scarcity assumption and mentality is one of the challenges that conscious business, capitalism, and finance face. Once eliminated, we will have a different kind of world on the face of the Earth.

WALL STREET 50
John Allison   *Capitalism: A Defense*

CRONY CAPITALISM, AYN RAND, GREENSPAN,
AND FUTURE BANKRUPTCY

John Allison is the CEO and President of the Cato Institute and was the longest serving CEO of a major bank in the U.S. when he was CEO of BB&T Bank. Allison is a major contributor to the Ayn Rand Institute and has said that *"Atlas Shrugged* was the best defense of capitalism ever written." Here he speaks about how Greenspan was the number one person responsible for the '08 crash, and that he was not acting consistently with Ayn Rand's Objectivist principles. Furthermore, if we don't change our ways fast, we are looking at national bankruptcy.

KIM: I am seeing a collapse between capitalism and corruption and that's daunting to me because I feel that's what the media has spun it as, and those who are less educated won't be able to separate the two. They aren't the same thing, and what is wrong on Wall Street is not capitalism, but the antithesis of it.

JOHN: I think you are very correct. In fact Ayn Rand calls it a spiral down—the government passes destructive laws, the laws don't work, the economy goes down, the government blames business, they pass more destructive laws, the economy goes down, they blame business, and it becomes a circular downhill process. As they pass these laws, a bigger and bigger percentage of the business community becomes crony capitalists (i.e. crony socialists). Goldman Sachs is the ultimate crony capitalist. It is a firm that should have failed in the financial crisis. However, it wasn't the main cause of the crisis; government policy was really the cause of the financial crisis—but it is easy for everyone to see that these crony capitalists were receiving favors from the government and then to call that capitalism, but it is really crony socialism. The more rules and more laws get passed, the more crony capitalists there are because all of these laws allow exceptions, allow favors. The Obama administration is doing this to solar energy. Bush was doing it to oil. It is the same principle left and right—encouraging government interference, which in fact, spurs more crony capitalism. So the average Joe sees capitalism as crony capitalism, which he is right to reject, and he doesn't really grasp what a true, free market would really be about.

KIM: One of the things I hear from people is that Greenspan followed Ayn Rand's philosophy, and this is why and how this all happened. And I feel ill-equipped to answer them properly, but it pains me. I am curious how you would respond to that?

JOHN: This is a very interesting story. I was the longest serving CEO of a major financial institution in the U.S., so I knew and observed Greenspan's behavior from the time he got to be head of the Fed until he retired. Absolute power corrupts absolutely. When Greenspan joined the Fed, he had written in *Capitalism: The Unknown Ideal*, which he co-authored with Rand, that we ought to get rid of the Federal Reserve and we ought to go on a gold standard. I honestly believe that when he went to the Fed, this is what he believed. But he loved being the maestro, and he became very corrupted and ended up acting totally inconsistently with his pre-Fed philosophical beliefs, which you can see in the decisions he made. Greenspan is probably the number one person who caused the economic misallocation. But it is not true that he was acting in a way consistent with Ayn Rand's principles; he wasn't. His Randian principles were to get rid of the Fed and go to a gold standard, so unless he got rid of the Fed and went to a gold standard, he didn't do what his principles required him to do. The other myth—he deregulated—is just not true. The financial industry was not deregulated during Bush. For example, there were three really bad laws passed: the Privacy Act, the Patriot Act, and Sarbanes-Oxley. There was a massive increase in regulations during the Bush administration executed through Greenspan. There was no deregulation of the industry. I have written a book, *The Financial Crisis and the Free Market Cure*, which clearly proves the financial crisis was caused by government policy, not market failure. We don't live in a free market. We live in a mixed economy. The big culprit is the Federal Reserve. Greenspan wanted to be the hero and he didn't want to have an economic correction during his term, so he kept pushing it out into the future by holding interest rates below market rates, which incentivized massive mis-investment. The mis-investment ended up in the housing market because of government policy through Freddie Mac and Fannie Mae, these giant government-sponsored enterprises, which when they failed owed $5.5 trillion, including $2 trillion in sub-prime mortgages. They drove the credit standards down in the sub-prime market, which they absolutely dominated, because Congress was putting huge pressure on them to do affordable home lending. So, yes, some of the Wall Street people did some dumb stuff, but it was trivial compared to conscious government policy, which, by the way, goes all the way back to Lyndon Johnson to try to increase home ownership with low-income people, including a lot of people who can't afford to own a home.

The anti-capitalist argument that capitalism causes many booms and busts is not factually correct. Government policy causes most booms and busts. This is intentional government policy that was based on the belief that they could overcome market reality—that everybody could have a wonderful home and there would be no consequences to it, but that's not true. There are real economic constraints and the politicians wanted to wish them away, and you can't do that. The government made too many promises, in this case, it promised too many houses, and the economy can't afford what it promised.

I think we are probably going to have some temporary economic recovery, but I think that if we don't change directions, it's almost a mathematical certainty that in twenty to twenty-five years, the United States goes broke. If you look at the unfunded liability under Social Security, Medicare, and government pension plans, along with massive annual operating deficits, a dysfunctional foreign policy and a dysfunctional education system combined with the retirement of baby boomers, it is extremely probable the U.S. will suffer severe financial problems if we do not change direction. Now, countries don't file bankruptcy. What they typically do is default on some of their debts or hyper-inflate their currency so you get paid Social Security, but it is not worth anything. They ration medical care. If you need your knee replaced, you can't get it replaced. So it's a funny kind of default. It's not that the government files bankruptcy and cleans things up. We die a slow death and become a Third World economy.

So the question is: Do we have the political will to change direction? I don't know how to answer that question. What is the risk of a further crisis? My experience in business is that things take much longer than you think to go badly, but when they go bad, they are worse than you think they are going to be. So, I don't know how imminent it is. We've got another twenty to twenty-five years before the financial position of the U.S. becomes unsustainable. How far markets will discount back is not clear. My own gut feeling is we've probably got another ten years or so of slow growth, but certainly not optimal growth, before there is a crisis. Right now, if we were really aggressive and we were willing to take some pain, we could fix our government financial problem. However, we can't fix it without chemotherapy, but we can fix it.

Ten years from now, it will not be fixable without severe economic pain. Typically, under financial stress, the country ends up moving toward some form of statism. Unfortunately, Congress promises serious reform and its members end up arguing over the insignificant issues and being elected based on short-term considerations, which destroys the will to deal with the long-term issues.

KIM: Do you feel, philosophically, people need to first understand what has happened as opposed to just the facts?

JOHN: I really do. In the closing part of my book, I spend a lot of time talking philosophy because I think people have to grasp the philosophical issues. And the fact is that philosophical ideas are much harder to change. Even when people get the facts, many evade. People may see something intellectually, and then they'll somehow evade the facts. Good intentions are supposed to produce good outcomes, by fiat. Affordable housing was a "good," altruistic idea. People who are libertarian understand the issue. But for the average person, who is philosophically ignorant, it is hard to grasp that something that was intended to be good (affordable housing) could cause so much destruction. It is so much easier to believe that greed, which is defined as bad, caused the problem. It wasn't greed, it was altruistic good intentions that caused the financial crisis. People do not understand that altruism is economically destructive. Individuals acting in their rational self-interest lead to better economic results. That is what is philosophically hard for people to accept.

Shared Value Theory

The reason I interviewed Professor Michael E. Porter is because of the *Harvard Business Review* article he co-wrote with Mark R. Kramer titled *"Creating Shared Value: How to reinvent capitalism—and unleash a wave of innovation and growth."* Erika Karp (one of my *Wall Street 50*) shared the article with me. In it, Porter and Kramer articulate how the connections between societal and economic progress have the power to unleash the next wave of global growth. They say that an "increasing number of companies known for their hard-nosed approach to business such as Google, IBM, Intel, Johnson & Johnson, Nestle, Unilever, and Wal-Mart, have begun to embark on shared value initiatives." They tell us there are three key ways companies can create opportunities: 1) reconceive their products and markets, 2) redefine productivity in the value chain, and 3) enable local cluster development. They also say that if firms look at their decisions and opportunities through the lens of shared value, new approaches, greater innovation, and growth will occur not only for companies but society will also benefit.

What I enjoyed most about Professor Porter was his enthusiasm. His passion for this topic was infectious, and I was completely enrolled in how powerful shared value is for our economy, communities, and other nations as well as in alignment with what Adam Smith spoke of in *The Theory of Moral Sentiments*.

PROFESSOR
Michael E. Porter   *Capitalism: A Defense*

CAPITALISM IS MAGIC

Professor Michael E. Porter is the Bishop William Lawrence University Professor at Harvard Business School and a leading authority on competitive strategy; the competitiveness and economic development of nations, states, and regions; and the application of competitive principles and strategic approaches to social needs, such as health care, innovation, and corporate responsibility.

MICHAEL: If I talk to most of the smartest people in finance who are in very senior positions in the field, they are still repeating the same old story about how finance is about providing liquidity and mitigating risk and . . . no, no, no. It's not about that. Capitalism is about meeting customers' needs.

KIM: When you hear me speak of consciousness, I'm curious what that word personally means to you.

MICHAEL: Well, I have many, many feelings and reactions. In a certain sense, people in finance just have to learn some basics. The CEO of one of the leading regional banks in America would tell you, "Our industry created products whose success was dependent on the failure of our customer." The example he likes to use is free checking accounts. "We don't make any money on free checking accounts. We make all our money on overdraft charges." At some level, there is a kind of threshold a society needs to honor, and also a consciousness about society and societal impact such as "Do no harm." And yet here's an industry that has cleverly invented products and services that actually don't serve the basic purpose capitalism is supposed to serve.

So when you view capitalism as meeting customers' needs, then you can see that these products and services are not doing that. You can expand that definition to giving a person a loan when there's no way he can ever pay it back. Or getting him into a credit card that you know has escalating costs if he gets behind on his payments. So I think at some basic level in finance, there's been this massive failure to confront what the real purpose is of their organization.

I think if one starts to infuse a sense of, "Wait a minute. We should care about what happens to society. We should care about our customers as individuals. We should care about whether we are behaving ethically and in ways we can be proud of." I think that's a threshold to live up to. I think the irony of all the shared value work is that it's actually capitalism, and what people in the finance world who are capitalists do is indeed the most powerful way in society for doing social good.

You talk about awakening capitalists. One of the ways we have to awaken capitalists is not just to get them to stop creating products that depend on the failure of the customer. That's Threshold Level I. But what I found is we have to awaken capitalists to what capitalism really is, *this enormously powerful vehicle for meeting human needs that has massive benefits.* The first benefit is that it's self-sustaining. If we can use capitalism to address poor nutrition, we don't have to depend on giving and generosity. If we can use capitalism to deal with nutrition, we can scale it to hundreds of millions or billions of people. Whereas, if we use the NGO (non-governmental organization) or government model, we're constantly strapped for resources. We're constantly strapped for the next donation or the next fundraising cycle, and fundamentally, if we look back in history, capitalism is and has been the tool to make the world better. Some of the bad in the world may have been created by capitalists, but pretty much most of the good in the world had been created by capitalists who provide services and meet the basic needs of people, whether they're food needs or security needs or housing.

I think many capitalists have lost this insight. What's capitalism really all about? The making money part of it is actually sort of the gate that a capitalist has to go through, which is critical of capitalism, because as I like to say, capitalism is magic. It's where all wealth in society is actually created. The government can't create wealth. NGOs can't create wealth. Only capitalists can. And it's the active making of a profit that unlocks all that wealth creation in society because if you can actually figure out how to make that profit, then you get into the world of sustainability and scalability. And it's the ability to make that profit that makes all those people you hire permanent employees, not temporary employees. It makes all the things you buy from suppliers to be things you can keep buying forever. So capitalism is this enormously powerful, almost magical phenomenon where you have nothing and then somebody comes up with a way to meet a need efficiently that you can make a profit at, and all of the sudden, you have vast value—a vast wealth in society plus all those needs are met.

I think what we've somehow lost at some deep level is what capitalism is really all about, and as a result of that, a lot of people in finance have kind of failed to understand what their role is. The fundamental role of finance is to provide capital to enable these investments that create all these values for society, but instead, the financial field has gotten sort of inward-looking, and they thought the goal was to create financial instruments that allow them to make a profit as opposed to seeing their core role as actually providing the fundamental feedstock to the magic of capitalism.

For example, now an investment bank doesn't view its core customers as the companies it's providing capital for and it doesn't perceive its core function as enabling that capital to the right company and creating all the circumstances it can to help that company win in building a profitable business. I actually have this somewhat radical view that risk hedging is part of our problem today, because everybody's risk hedging rather than actually doing the homework, so that they get the money into the fundamentally right investments. So, all of a sudden, you can do quick and dirty. The fundamental role of capitalism is to get capital in the right place and then to provide the monitoring, governance, and pressure to enable whatever organization is using that capital to use it well to meet needs. And somehow, finance has gotten so far removed from that.

KIM: What do you think made that happen?

MICHAEL: When Harvard Business School and other business schools used to talk about "finance," what we meant was "corporate finance." And the core training at business school was: How do you fund a company? How do you decide how much debt to have and how much equity to have, and how do you allocate capital within the company to make sure the company is using capital well? That was the core of finance at business schools. But then with modern economics and so forth, this whole notion of capital markets popped up. And capital markets have overwhelmed finance. Finance is all about capital markets, and capital markets are about efficient markets, stocks, movement of stocks, how you create derivatives from this and that. Way back at the beginning of every single derivative is some business that's investing money and generating cash flow. And so for me, the cash flow is the dog. And the derivative is the tail. The long, long end of the tail. But somehow, finance is focused on the tail and not the core activity of finance, which is actually the use of capital to generate profit through capitalism.

I don't think it's evil or a consciously evil strategy, but it's kind of how the field has evolved. I think people have just been lulled into thinking a bank's purpose is to provide liquidity. No, no, no. That's good but that's not the fundamental purpose. The fundamental purpose is to get capital to people who are going to use it to meet needs profitably. And we've lost that purpose. And now, if you go one step beyond that, we have the issue that there's been an inability to see that same engine of capitalism is an enormously powerful vehicle for dealing with every single social problem we have.

People have not seen the connection between the social and capitalism. They said, "Capitalism is this and social is that. And social is something you do with donations and philanthropy and being a good guy and being generous and all that." And what we've lacked is the understanding that there's really a profound connection between capitalism and meeting social needs. And now if we go one step beyond and ask, "What's the role of an investor?" then we've had this evolution about socially responsible investing and ethical investing and all this kind of stuff and that's fine. But that stuff is really more about values and screening out companies that are doing harm, but they miss this fundamental opportunity for investors really to drive this process of mobilizing capitalism on societal issues.

Right now, our big campaign, and Erika Karp of UBS (now of Cornerstone Capital Inc.) has been very helpful with this, to start to help investors see and understand that they've missed the biggest part of investment analysis . . . the core investment analysis that is going to determine where real money is made over the next twenty or thirty years, and it's going to be with the companies that figure out and tackle these big societal problems; that's where the biggest market opportunities are. I mean, middle class people don't need more food. We have all the food we need. Too much in fact. Middle class people need these new ways of dealing with the problems of their health and their nutrition. The capitalists who figure out how to do that are going to be the growth companies. Just like all the conventional food retailers in North America were pretty much ho-hum, which is why Whole Foods became the rocket ship—it figured out a way to tap this unmet need for healthier and more nutritious products. But that wasn't good values. That wasn't ethics. All those people may have ethics and values . . . and that may have helped them see the opportunity, but fundamentally, that was capitalism.

I've become a born again capitalist in a sense. I mean I always have been. I'm a Harvard Business School professor, and yet I used to think that capitalism is over "here." But then I started this work with Mark Kramer on foundations in philanthropy. And it started out completely divorced from business. And it was all about, "Well, gee. We got these foundations. They're giving all this money. How do we apply rigorous, strategic thinking and value thinking to a non-profit foundation?" And that led to the first article. From there we wrote an article on corporate philanthropy and began to apply the general theory of value from philanthropy to a corporation, and to do that you start asking yourself, "Okay. What can the corporation bring together with money to add value?" And then out of that came the strategic society article, which was a way of thinking more strategically about how a company was going to engage in society. One of the major conclusions of that paper was that the ability to connect to your business is fundamental. And from there it was actually not that big a leap to have this phenomenal aha moment where we said, "Wait a minute, actually, the biggest opportunity of all—that would infect society—is just to be a capitalist."

KIM: That must have been a very profound moment.

MICHAEL: It was very profound. I have to tell you, Nestlé brought us along. Because Nestlé had read this Strategy in Society article

and they had this deep sense of, "Oh, my gosh, we've got to be connected to these communities of ours" because it was sourcing milk in
India and buying coffee beans in Costa Rica. They understood that,
so after Nestlé read the Strategy in Society article they latched on to
that and said to us, "Look. This is big." The company actually came
to me and said, "Would you write another article on this?" So they
gave us a lot of help and support, and out of that came the shared
value article. And then we were kind of off to the races, but it's
interesting how I, as a Harvard Business School professor, started
out thinking very differently about how we affect society. I started out thinking the way you affect society is through philanthropy
and foundations, and I was very concerned that our philanthropic
institutions were not delivering the value they could. And I still
believe that today. And I believe many NGOs are not delivering the
value they could. One of the key items in shared value is that there's
not a tradeoff between social and economic. There's not a tradeoff
between good environmental performance and good economic profitability. So all these things raise my consciousness. I started seeing
more dimensions; that you had to wrap around your understanding
of how a company competed in its industry. And, again, out popped
the shared value article, which took about two-and-a-half years to
write. It was very hard to write because in a sense, it gets at the very
basic underlying premise of what is business and why is it there and
what does it do.

KIM: What do you think when you hear the word "consciousness"?

MICHAEL: Well, consciousness is somehow the awareness of a
broader set of things that matter in affecting one's worldview of how
progress is made. To me, there are higher forms of consciousness,
where you have a greater awareness of a set of factors that are in-
fluencing what you fundamentally care about in what you do. In
that sense, I'm a classic case that my consciousness about business
and capitalism has been fundamentally transformed through this
journey.

KIM: Your story to me is: If a Harvard Business professor were able to have his consciousness raised as he continued on this journey and continued to stay curious, then how can we not ask our CEOs maybe to consider that their consciousness can also be raised. Right?

MICHAEL: Right. And they can be. I think that is happening in more and more companies now. Of all the things I've ever written— and I'm very proud of many, many of them and their impact for the good—our article on shared value has resonated with a lot of leaders and given them a way of thinking about social impact and their company's role in a way they can wholeheartedly embrace. Asking a CEO to fill out a bunch of ESG indicators and publish his social responsibility report, he'll do, but because he feels he has to. But this gets them excited. All of a sudden they are proud of running their company. It's all about your business, your value chain, your surrounding environment, your supplier base, what your product is, who your customers are. Shared value requires much more tailored thinking. You can't just get the general idea. You've got to say, "How do I apply it to me?" It is about capitalism because capitalism is fundamentally that each case is different. That's been raising the bar. That raises the bar for shared value. Whereas, I think getting people to do some of the basics of sustainability has been easier. Because they have to think. I think the sustainability movement has been really positive. It's sort of a foundation. It's a platform. It's stuff that you should be doing. But let's not think that's the same as the opportunity if we can go that next step. The next step will blow the ceiling out. Muhammad Yunus, creator of Grameen Bank, is a great example of shared value.

Capitalism is magic. But those of us who are capitalists, in capitalist businesses, don't understand just how magical this really is. We've kind of lost it. Fifty years ago, when you had Hershey Corporation in Hershey Pennsylvania, Hershey Corporation made everything good, as I saw it happen in that community. Everything came from Hershey and that was because there was nothing else there. There were no other corporations and they just sort of intuitively accepted responsibility for building up the supplier base and improving the health of their workers because it was good for them, and in the old, old days, capitalism. The great capitalist understood this intuitively and did it. But as we got a more modern society with more institutions and more government entities and more non-profits, all of a sudden, businesses kind of slipped away from this. It wasn't that they actively said, "No, we don't want to do this." The real blow recently has been globalization. That an American based company says, "Oh, I'm not an American company anymore. I'm a global company." It was a slippery slope to, "Okay; therefore, I don't have to worry about my American communities." But worrying about the American communities actually was, in many cases, one of the reasons why they were successful—because of the cluster they built.

KIM: Maybe they thought they weren't needed anymore?

MICHAEL: I think that's partly the view—there are other people who do that; that's not our job. And so a lot of businesses will tell you that our responsibility is to maximize profit, full stop. But ultimately, the shared value idea says, "But wait a minute guys, if you want to maximize profits, you've got to see these connections."

And now, it's interesting to interact with you because you come at this from a different world, with a different set of experiences. We're learning from that as well because we have to find a way to imbed this thinking in other lines and strains of thought and start to see how these things come together. I think the problem is our intellectual foundations of capitalism really come out of economics and out of a relatively stylized view of what the firm is and what competition is. And I think it has got driven out a little bit by the scholarly work.

The Myth of Shareholder Value

I found Professor Lynn Stout by accident. I was doing research on how to develop one's conscience in business and stumbled upon her first book, *Cultivating Conscience: How Good Laws Make Good People*. In it, she shares my conviction that every day we as humans behave selflessly and usually overlook that in favor of fixating on the bad things that mankind does. Then I discovered her second book, *The Shareholder Value Myth: How Putting Shareholders First Harms Investors, Corporations, and the Public*, which was hands down one of the most important and powerful books that I read in the three years of research for this book. In my interview with her, she discusses how this myth came into being, who started it, and how we can and must transform this misinformation as soon as possible for all of our sakes.

PROFESSOR
Lynn Stout   *Capitalism: A Defense*
<hr>
THE SHAREHOLDER VALUE MYTH/FRIEDMAN'S
MISUNDERSTANDING OF THE LAW

Professor Lynn Stout is the Distinguished Professor of Corporate and Business Law, Clarke Business Law Institute, at Cornell Law School. Here she explains how businesses' favorite and most famous mantra, "maximize shareholder value" is in actuality not in their (nor our) best interest and has almost destroyed our economy and is based on a mis-reading of corporate law.

LYNN: In my first book, *Cultivating Conscience: How Good Laws Make Good People*, I talk about how our conscience needs "breathing room" to work. You need to feel it is okay for you to follow your conscience; that you're not hurting anybody and you're not going to hurt yourself, at least not too badly, if you follow your conscience. In the second book, *The Shareholder Value Myth: How Putting Shareholders*

First Harms Investors, Corporations, and the Public, I try to create that breathing room by explaining to business executives why it's okay for them to do what many of them already intuitively know they should do, including taking care of their customers, suppliers, and employees, and, in general, being good corporate citizens. I explain why that's actually the best thing for the business and for shareholders. There isn't this supposed great conflict between taking care of shareholders and what you feel is ethical in life.

KIM: Where does the adage/edict come from, "maximizing shareholder value?"

LYNN: In my book, *The Shareholder Value Myth*, I explain that shareholder value ideology was invented by the Chicago school of economics in the 1970s. It's not the way we ran business for most of the twentieth century. It comes out of academic theory and it gets picked up in the 1980s by some corporate writers, and at the activist hedge funds; then it gets the support of CEOs in the 1990s when we changed the tax code to tie executive pay to share price performance.

A lot of people think that shareholder value thinking has always been around. Actually, it's kind of a new invention. And one of the things I point out in the book is that it's not required by law and it's not consistent with the American historical business experience, nor supported by the data. The irony is I actually am a little Hayekian[2] myself. And what we've done to corporate governance is very anti-Hayekian. The shareholder value thinking comes from academics and bureaucrats, not from business. What we've attempted to do, instead of letting the business world develop its own practices, is have top-down central planning by governments and would-be reformers from outside of business.

---

2   Referring to Friedrich August Hayek (1899–1992), an Austrian, later British, economist and philosopher best known for his defense of classical liberalism. In 1974, Hayek shared the Nobel Memorial Prize in Economic Sciences (with Gunnar Myrdal) for his "pioneering work in the theory of money and economic fluctuations and . . . penetrating analysis of the interdependence of economic, social, and institutional phenomena."

The shareholder value stuff is not originating, and never originated, inside corporations. It came from the outside, from changes in the tax code and changes in the SEC rules and from (hopefully) well-meaning, but unfortunately "loaded with unintended consequences," reforms. The story, ironically, is that if you're really a Hayekian or into free markets, you would never buy into what's happened. Shareholder value thinking doesn't come from business experience but from Milton Friedman and those guys. Mike Jensen and William Meckling wrote a very famous paper in 1976, called *The Theory of the Firm*. It's the most cited paper in all of management literature. It's probably the most influential paper in business schools and economic departments that have studied the firm for the past thirty years.

But the problem was these economists got the law *wrong* in this paper. They're economists, not lawyers. They analogized the corporation to a sole proprietorship, and they said, therefore, that the corporation had to have an owner and the owner had to be the shareholders and that's legally . . . flatly wrong. Corporations are not owned by shareholders. They own themselves. That's what Citizens United is all about. They're independent, legal entities. And what shareholders own is a contract with the corporate entity, just like bondholders and employees and suppliers have a contract. And it gives them certain governance rights, but it doesn't make them the owners. And it clearly does *not* mean the corporation has to be run only for their benefit. Or even worse, for their short-term benefit. And for their benefit, read only share price. By the way, the idea that shareholders care only about share price implies shareholders are sociopaths. The good news is, I don't actually think most investors and shareholders are sociopathic. I think they care about things other than share price. But the way we teach corporate purpose right now, there's no room for that. My book goes into this in great detail.

I have a chapter where I talk about how the rise of economic theory basically drove people to stop paying attention to ethics and conscience. It sort of explains how we only teach half of Adam Smith. Most people in business want to feel good about what they're doing. They want to feel they are a positive influence on the world. My *Shareholder Value Myth* book is very consistent with that.

KIM: Going back to the idea that shareholder value thinking came from academics and bureaucratic central planning, isn't central planning, more along the lines of what socialism and communism is?

LYNN: It is. And actually, that's the incredible irony—the Chicago School of Economics and the way their ideas ended up being applied was absolutely the opposite of a free market. It is crazy. I made that point in one of my articles. I said, "If you're really a free market economist, then you're going to say, 'We're going to let the business world figure out how to do this on their own.'" And instead, what we did was change all the rules to force executives to focus on shareholder value where they hadn't been doing it before because they didn't, based on their experience, think that was the best way to run a business. But we changed the law and we changed the rules and made them do it and advised them to do it.

KIM: I thought the Chicago School was supposed to be an offshoot or an Americanized version of the Austrian School, so how did it get twisted up so badly?

LYNN: I think a lot of it comes down to basically this misunderstanding about what a corporation really is. I tell this story in one of my chapters, but there is a real puzzling element to it. Because what it did was it led all these economists to conclude that some of the natural practices the business world had evolved are all wrong. It led a lot of economists to conclude that the natural business practices that had evolved in the business world on the basis of experience were incorrect. And that economists were smarter than business people and knew better about how to run a business. The Chicago School, in the corporate governance area, said, "Economists are the really smart guys. We know how to run the business so just listen to us and we'll tell you the best way."

KIM: Now, here's a question: If you had a magic wand and were able to wave it over Wall Street, what would that magic wand do?

LYNN: We need to do three things.

First, we have to repeal Section 162(m) of the Tax Code, which requires corporations to tie top executive pay to so-called "objective performance metrics." Most people don't know this, but the Tax Code was changed in 1993. What we did was we basically made it so that CEOs and managers who, beforehand, had breathing room just to focus on running the business in the way they thought best, suddenly were told that their pay was going to depend directly on whether they got the share price up. So we have to get the government out of the business of telling business how to compensate executives. I mean, it's good to make them report it, and it's good to let investors react, but we shouldn't have government regulation of executive compensation. I know that's counterintuitive to a lot of people. But back in the days when we didn't have regulation, executives actually got paid less and did a better job.

Second, we have to make it so investors hang on to their shares for a longer period of time, so they care more about the future. Today, the holding period for a share of stock is, on average, four months. It used to be eight years. So I would like to reduce the trading on Wall Street. I would basically like to tax short-term trading. You can do it by changing the capital gains rules. You can do it by enacting a financial transaction tax. I want to get the opportunistic short-term traders and the hedge funds out of the market because right now corporations are being run to please them. And they really are short-term in focus, and they really don't show a lot of evidence of caring about anything other than making as much money as possible tomorrow.

Third, we have to do what you're doing. We need to educate people that, in fact, there's no legal requirement that corporations maximize shareholder value and that's not the best thing for business, society, or investors over the long-run. So there, you gave me a magic wand. I just used it.

KIM: When did this hit you? When did you begin to notice this? How did it all come about?

LYNN: Basically, I'm one of those people who changes her mind without a funeral once I see the evidence. I was taught that corporations were owned by shareholders and the legal obligation was to maximize shareholder value and this is good for society. That's how I was taught. That's what I taught my own students for the first ten years. But I have this problem. I read the newspaper and pay attention to what's going on. And I read case law and it became really apparent to me that what I was seeing didn't match with what I had been taught and what I was teaching. And that focusing on shareholder value, if you actually read the cases, is not a requirement and didn't seem to be working out very well. I had an epiphany when I had a talk with an economist, Margaret Blair. She's great. She's at Vanderbilt Law School. She convinced me in five minutes that there was another way to think about corporations.

She and I had a conversation. She had just read this other paper about understanding what corporations do and the light bulb went on over my head. I said, "If we are willing to adopt this other understanding of what corporations are for, not to maximize shareholder value but to bring together all of these groups and try to maximize the surplus generally . . . then all of this stuff I'm seeing in corporate law cases and in the business world makes sense now." That's why corporate law is the way it really is. That's why business people, if they're left alone, do things the way they do, and all of this stuff I'm teaching and the Chicago school of economists is teaching doesn't work. Because we didn't understand what corporations really are. They're really legal entities. Their job is to aggregate assets to pursue large-scale, long-term, highly uncertain projects for society's benefit. That's why they're there. They're not something shareholders own and they don't exist only for shareholders. They have a social function.

KIM: Now, when you got that, was there a part of you that thought, "Oh, my God! Nobody knows?" It's like suddenly realizing the emperor has no clothes.

LYNN: It was exactly like that. Margaret and I just looked at each other and I said, "We've all been doing it wrong. Let's see if we can convince people to do it right." She and I wrote a paper together called "A Team Production Theory of the Corporation." It's really famous among law professors now. And you know, it's fifteen years later, but you have to be patient in this business. Fifteen years later, it's amazing to me how people are getting on board now. So there's a real paradigm shift going on. There's no question in my mind.

KIM: Fifteen years . . . it's like discovering gravity and having to wait fifteen years for people to get with the program.

LYNN: Fifteen years is pretty good. I'm taking it. For humanity to change its mind about something, it usually takes longer than fifteen years.

CONSCIOUSNESS TEACHER
Patricia Aburdene   *Capitalism: A Defense*

CONSCIOUS CAPITALISM

Patricia Aburdene is a world leading social forecaster, the author of *Conscious Money and Megatrends 2010: The Rise of Conscious Capitalism,* and one of the earliest members of the Conscious Capitalism community. Some say she was the first to coin the term "conscious capitalism." Aburdene believes, "We the people have the power to transform capitalism as investors, consumers and managers and capitalism has the power to change the world." Here she speaks about the holistic approach of conscious capitalists.

KIM: As an early advocate of Conscious Capitalism, tell us a little bit of what the movement advocates.

PATRICIA: I think it's a new vision of what capitalism can be. In my book *Megatrends 2010: The Rise of Conscious Capitalism*, which came out in 2005, I described conscious capitalism as best I could. John Mackey read the book, liked it, and invited me and several other people to come together and talk about whether this could be a movement. So we did, and then we've moved forward. Out of the many meetings the group has sponsored over the years has come what I call the trademarks of conscious capitalism. They include Purpose, Values, and the Stakeholder model of capitalism, rather than the shareholder model of capitalism.

The shareholder model of capitalism is what I would call traditional capitalism, which says basically, that at the end of the day, investors are the most important stakeholders. Milton Friedman, wrote this very famous article in the 1970s, entitled "The Social Responsibility of Business Is to Increase Profit," the idea being that business does not have any social responsibility; its only responsibility is to create profits and return that profit to its investors.[3] The irony here is conscious capitalists fully want to and intend to earn a profit. But the way they go about it is a little different—they take a holistic approach to business. Conscious capitalism looks at the business as a whole: What are the employees contributing? What are the customers contributing? What are the suppliers contributing? What's the community contributing? What does the environment contribute? So it looks at all of the stakeholders. That is to say everyone who is a party to or has an interest in the business. Conscious capitalists consider the impact of a decision on all of the stakeholders; they don't favor one stakeholder particularly over another, but they consider the whole. Surprisingly, this conscious approach often beats traditional capitalists at their own game—earning profits. How so?

John Mackey speaks about it as the paradox of profits, meaning when you take the whole picture into consideration, when you manage as if customers, employees, as well as investors and all the rest, have a vital role to play in the organization, you can actually make more profit. In the book *Firms of Endearment* by Raj Sisodia, David Wolfe, and Jag Sheth, the authors found that eighteen public companies that

---

3   *Author's note:* Friedman's opinion on this topic is what Professor Lynn Stout says in the previous chapter was Friedman's misunderstanding of the law.

observed and honored the stakeholder model of capitalism, which is now also called "Conscious Capitalism," outperformed the S&P 500 by a factor of nine-to-one over the ten-year-period from July 1, 1996 to June 30, 2006. In subsequent years, as the study was updated, conscious capitalists increased that profitability to a factor of 10 or 11.

Two more trademarks of conscious capitalism are **Purpose** and **Values**:

- **Purpose**: Business needs strong earnings to reward investors, fuel compensation, and fund the R&D that delights customers. But Conscious Capitalists insist that business exists to fulfill a deeper purpose, such as to "make a difference" or "contribute to life." Sunny Vanderbeck, cofounder of social equity investor Satori Capital, describes purpose as "the non-financial reason a company is in business." Profit is essential, but profit is a business result. It is not the purpose of business.

- **Values**: Positive values create an inner compass that gives a business direction and focus. Online retailer eBay was built on the value of trust. Early on, founder Pierre Omidyar posted this on eBay's website: "We believe people are basically good." Trust became the core of eBay policy, and technology later reinforced that trust. As a result, only a fraction of 1 percent of eBay transactions end in fraud.

Sure, some might argue, "Capitalism is capitalism," but that is not the case. Free enterprise was not set in stone during the Industrial Revolution; it's a living, breathing, dynamic philosophy of business that expands over time to reflect the values, awareness, and aspirations of its followers. The reforms of the New Deal sanctioned labor unions (which business opposed) yet built a middle class that could afford automobiles, appliances, and televisions, thus solidifying the success of free enterprise. Similarly, the Securities and Exchange Commission, deemed unfriendly to business, stabilized markets, attracted middle-class investors, and sustained capitalism until the recent crises. When people change, so does capitalism. Today, business is reinventing free enterprise and reversing the errors that threaten its future. Government intervention alone, however well intentioned, cannot achieve the moral rebirth of capitalism. Regulation can foster a culture of compliance, but it cannot create a culture of commitment; that requires a change of heart in the individual capitalist.

THE CONSCIOUS CAPITALIST CREDO

We believe that business is good because it creates value, it is ethical because it is based on voluntary exchange, it is noble because it can elevate our existence and it is heroic because it lifts people out of poverty and creates prosperity. Free enterprise capitalism is the most powerful system for social cooperation and human progress ever conceived. It is one of the most compelling ideas we humans have ever had. But we can aspire to even more.

Conscious Capitalism is a way of thinking about capitalism and business that better reflects where we are in the human journey, the state of our world today, and the innate potential of business to make a positive impact on the world. Conscious businesses are galvanized by higher purposes that serve, align, and integrate the interests of all their major stakeholders. Their higher state of consciousness makes visible to them the interdependencies that exist across all stakeholders, allowing them to discover and harvest synergies from situations that otherwise seem replete with trade-offs. They have conscious leaders who are driven by service to the company's purpose, all the people the business touches and the planet we all share together. Conscious businesses have trusting, authentic, innovative and caring cultures that make working there a source of both personal growth and professional fulfillment. They endeavor to create financial, intellectual, social, cultural, emotional, spiritual, physical and ecological wealth for all their stakeholders.

Conscious businesses will help evolve our world so that billions of people can flourish, leading lives infused with passion, purpose, love and creativity; a world of freedom, harmony, prosperity and compassion.

www.ConsciousCapitalism.org

Summary—Capitalism: A Defense

To discover that Adam Smith was the first to argue against crony capitalism, hear a Harvard business professor say his journey has made him a "born again capitalist," and that Milton Friedman got it wrong, certainly was not what I expected to learn when I began this book.

What do all these statements have in common? That things aren't always what they seem and that smart and educated people don't necessarily know everything and are not infallible.

When I first started to read Smith's *The Theory of Moral Sentiments*, I couldn't help but think I was missing something; here was a man who cared about his brother and community yet all I had ever heard about him was that he was an advocate only of self-interest. I hadn't studied economics so I doubted myself. Yet as I read and re-read Smith's own words, he spoke to a much more complex belief system that was built on man's inherent ability for empathy for others. I remember the relief I felt when I interviewed Professor Smith. His comments affirmed my suspicions that Adam Smith had been misrepresented and misaligned. It was also a pleasant surprise to hear Professor Porter speak of how capitalism is "about meeting customers' needs" and "getting capital to people who are going to use it to meet needs profitably." While I sat there in his office on what has to be the most beautiful and intimidating campus in the world (Harvard Business School), I felt I was listening to him prove my long-held belief that one could be profitable while improving the world, and in fact, he was saying they were interdependent. Hearing Professor Stout then reiterate in her interview what her book *The Shareholder Value Myth* declared—that Milton Friedman had been incorrect—taught me, and I hope it teaches you, that no matter who someone is, an expert or not, no matter his or her education or experience, do your own due diligence, read everything yourself, and don't surrender your own mind to the "authority." Trust your own conclusions if you have done the homework and have put it to the test. You may very well see something no one else had ever noticed before.

Let me share with you a story from MSNBC[4] to illustrate this point:

> A 28-year-old economics graduate student has rewritten a study led by Harvard economists Carmen Reinhart and Kenneth Rogoff that has been widely cited as the intellectual basis for worldwide government austerity measures. The Harvard study argues that higher public debt slows down economic growth when the GDP rises above a 90% threshold. But after an attempt to duplicate the Harvard study's findings, Thomas Herndon, a Ph.D. student at the University of Massachusetts-Amherst, ended up debunking Reinhart and Rogoff's economic theory and found that the Reinhart-Rogoff study was incorrect due to spreadsheet coding errors and selective data.

Even experts make mistakes and misinterpretations. Trust yourself.

Consciousness and the quest to attain more of it seems to be everywhere. From John Mackey's Conscious Capitalism organization to his NY Time's best seller by the same name. Business magazines are even featuring this topic in print and online at least once a month. H&M has a *Conscious Clothing* line. I've seen a successful jewelry company use the word in its title, promising its jewelry will assist you in attaining more of it, and there is even a *Conscious TV* station and a place online from which you can order your food called *Conscious Box*.

What's going on? As the futurist David Houle says in the next chapter, we are in the midst of the Age of Transformation. As we transform, we become hungrier for more authentic and real connections, and this desire will continue to grow stronger and take even more precedence over time.

In the midst of our multiple social media platforms, and our having more "friends" than ever before, not to mention our ability to

---

4   Taken from http://www.msnbc.com/the-last-word/debunked-the-harvard-study-republicans

attain almost everything we "want" with the swipe of a finger, we still find ourselves feeling disconnected, lonely, and empty. The Transformation Age may be happening, but as it's just getting started, I think it will be messy for a while. The realization that having our *wants met* is not the same as having our *needs met* is a great place to begin. We may *want* a BMW, but having one isn't going to meet our *need* for respect.

Now, while I see friends and families out to dinner with everyone looking down at their cell phones, I can't help but think, "Why is it that they expect a connection will occur on their phone more readily than with the person sitting across from them?" Yet if it weren't true to some extent, they would put their phones down. If we want to improve the connections we have with our family and our friends, our clients and colleagues, it begins internally with the relationship we have with our self. If we don't know the answers to some basic questions like, "Who am I?" and "What am I doing?" or "Why am I doing this?" then we must be willing to sit in the unknowing until we do. In many ways, our addiction to social media is simply our hunger for connection, our hunger to be seen and known. We are all hungry and it's consciousness we are starving for.

In her interview, Patricia Aburdene deftly states that, "When people change, so does capitalism." We are changing and as we do, the relationship we have with ourselves will change as will our yearnings. If the hunger for more consciousness has begun in your own life, know that you are not alone. It's happening for many people right now.

So where do you begin so that you may become more conscious? You begin by starting new practices and new habits one at a time. In the next section, I outline what I call *The Five Practices*, which will help you do just that.

If you get the inside right, the outside will fall into place.
—ECKHART TOLLE

PART II

BEING A CONSCIOUS CAPITALIST

Becoming More Conscious

Consciousness means living a life that is awake, being aware of your action and your inaction, understanding what motivates you and knowing you are connected to the effect your behavior and thoughts have on yourself, others, and the world. It means living with integrity and having a set of values you strive to adhere to. Not so you can impress anyone but because you honor who you are. Of course you make mistakes, but you are able to acknowledge it when you do without shame, course correct, and make amends when necessary.

When Ray Anderson, the founder and chairman of Interface, Inc., was interviewed in the 2004 Canadian documentary *The Corporation*, he spoke about the moment he became "awake." He was preparing to do a talk about the environment, which he readily admits he didn't give a damn about, but as he read Paul Hawken's book, *The Ecology of Commerce*, he experienced what he described as a "spear in the chest" moment. From then on, the way Anderson ran Interface was completely different. He implemented what he called "Mission Zero," which was the company's promise to eliminate any negative impact it may have on the environment by the year 2020 through the redesign of processes and products, the pioneering of new technologies, and efforts to reduce or eliminate waste and harmful emissions while increasing the use of renewable materials and sources of energy.

Wow. Anderson had a big change of heart. Awakenings like this one can be as piercing as a spear. Awakenings can also come gradually over time, but often they rush in—in one moment and when we least expect them. But the good news about expanding one's consciousness is: it can also be sought out.

This awakening of consciousness is happening all around us according to David Houle, the author of *Entering the Shift Age*. Houle speaks about our world being in the midst of a global shift as the Information Age now gives way to the Transformation Age. "Conscious Capitalism is going to be much more of a congruent definition of capitalism in the next twenty years," says Houle. "It will be mainstream by 2020. Any major change in human history has almost always been preceded by an economic factor leading the way before the change reaches politics and culture," Houle said.

Further evidence of our moving into more consciousness is found in the book *SQ21: The 21 Skills of Spiritual Intelligence* by Cindy Wigglesworth, where she discusses how our culture has now advanced from valuing not just IQ, but also giving equal importance to our EQ (Emotional Intelligence), and we are now moving into a world where SQ (Spiritual Intelligence) is going to be necessary. Wigglesworth defines this intelligence as having "the ability to behave with wisdom and compassion while maintaining inner and outer peace regardless of the situation." This statement comes from a twenty-year veteran of a Fortune 50 company working in Human Resources—not the place you'd expect to hear about it, and yet there it is. In our interview in this section, I ask her to give us a further definition of spiritual intelligence and how it relates to consciousness.

If there is one common quality I see in all of *The Wall Street 50*, it is their spiritual intelligence. I'm certain they would all score well if they took Wigglesworth's spiritual intelligence assessment. They each have displayed the ability to act with these very skills no matter the circumstances, while maintaining their equanimity.

The following are only snippets of lengthy conversations with those I call the *Teachers of Consciousness*. I asked them to define consciousness and explain how it can be applied to business and Wall Street. They had much to say, but the following quotes are only a sample of what I found to be the most eye-opening.

CONSCIOUSNESS TEACHER
His Holiness Sri Sri Ravi Shankar   *Becoming More Conscious*

His Holiness (HH) Sri Sri Ravi Shankar is a renowned spiritual leader and global humanitarian. His vision of a violence-free and stress-free society has united millions. He is the founder of The Art of Living Foundation. Here he speaks about how, even in just a few minutes a day, we can become more self-aware.

HH: You know when someone is carrying money to the bank? And then the way they feel when they have come out of the bank after having made that deposit? They feel completely different . . . Imagine someone is carrying more than two pounds or more of pressure . . . how conscious they are all the way through? When you make an investment or when you're at work doing your job, you're in a different state of consciousness than when you go home and you have finished working for the day. Our consciousness changes from morning to evening. In the morning, as soon as you wake up, you're in a different state of consciousness. In the afternoon, it is different. In the night, it's different. Generally, when you are really in the depths of your being, when you are really yourself, you are an authentic expression of consciousness. Whenever you say you're authentic, you are in a higher state of consciousness, where you are straightforward and you are honest. These are all the qualities you expect others to have. The state of consciousness that you're expecting from others when you're dealing with them should also exist within yourself. Sometimes people expect these things from others, but don't exhibit the same qualities they expect from others.

KIM: What would your advice be to someone who has not investi-gated that authenticity? For those people who have not yet begun that journey of consciousness, where would you advise them to begin?

HH: I really don't believe that any one has not done this at all, be-cause in day-to-day interactions in everyone's life, constant learning is happening. To some degree, these things are already happening if you begin to look for them. So, it's just a matter of becoming aware of: Who am I? Where am I in life? What is it that I want in life? Even if people take only a few minutes, take a little time every day, for them-selves. Just ten or fifteen minutes to ponder on their own life. Think— you have spent so many years doing this and that, so think about how you would like to spend the rest of your years. Ponder about what it is that you want clearly in your life. Take a couple of minutes of com-plete silence, such as meditation. For the intellectual, it brings and forces a mix of emotions which are very positive.

CONSCIOUSNESS TEACHER
Neale Donald Walsch   *Becoming More Conscious*

Neale Donald Walsch is a modern day spiritual messenger and the author of *Conversations with God: An Uncommon Dialogue*. Here he speaks about how our pure intention for discovering who we really are can open us up to serendipity.

NEALE: What is consciousness? It's the state of living with awareness, deep awareness of who we are. That is, our true and complete identity rather than the limited identity that some people assume is ours and with an intention to place that awareness into expression in our daily life in a way that advances our true agenda. Our true awareness of who we are, and the embracing of that identity generally sponsors a true agenda. It almost always alters our priorities, our life priorities, and causes us to experience all the activities of life in a brand new way because it changes the contextual field within which those experiences are encountered and created.

KIM: For someone with what you call a "limited identity" who is stepping into who he or she truly is for the first time, what would you suggest that person do to live with more awareness?

NEALE: I would encourage them to go within and find a space of willingness to truly encounter the question and allow it to be answered by all the devices of life itself. And by that, I mean that when we go within with such purity of intention and such cleanliness of purpose, then the outer world tends to draw us and bring us in contact with the exact and perfect people, places, and events, allowing us to use the exterior world as our personal encyclopedia, our personal Google machine—attracting *us to* and attracting *to us* the right circumstances and events, and in exactly the right order. To provide us with the next step in our journey of self-discovery. If it's our pure and honest and true intention, energized by a deep willingness to know what our true identity is and what our actual purpose on the planet is, we will find ourselves going from that innermost place into outer experiences; the right book will just fall into our hands, and a magazine article will suddenly show up in a six-month-old publication we find at the hairdresser's on the table while waiting for an appointment. We will meet somebody on the street who will recommend something to us. We will be drawn to a particular circumstantial experience that will expose us to exactly what our mind is calling for. And if we remain open to that, we will begin to find that we are leading ourselves right to the information we seek, to that which can expand our consciousness.

I have the wonderful experience of producing books that really have flowed through me; they've touched the lives of fifteen million people in thirty-seven languages, and I don't think that's either an accident or a coincidence. It didn't happen by chance, but rather because there is a yearning among the people, a growing yearning and an increasing hunger among the people of the world to find larger answers to the questions that loom before all of humankind in this first quarter of the twenty-first century. So I think that it's not at all surprising that my *Conversations With God* books would have touched so many millions of people so rapidly. In my latest book, *The Only Thing That Matters*, I encourage the reader to join in a bit of a mental process in which he imagines himself to have written the book he is reading, and to allow the book to speak to him in the voice of his own mind. People are responding to that with an amazing reaction. They write me letters and emails telling me how they experienced it. We see that all the mind does is bring us the information we have called forth. That information itself tends to come at us much more powerfully and affect us with a much higher level of impact because we all feel someone is talking to us. But rather we are truly speaking to ourselves; we are speaking to the self-capitalist we are and allowing life to speak to us—through us. Life is a process that informs life about life through the process of life itself. And when we engage that process on a personal level in the ways I am describing, it can be transformational.

CONSCIOUSNESS TEACHER
Yasuhiko Genku Kimura   *Becoming More Conscious*

Yasuhiko Genku Kimura is a mystic, philosopher, and a former Zen Buddhist Priest. He is also the founder of Vision-In-Action. His primary focus is trying to bring about an evolution in human consciousness. Here he speaks about how logical is not the same as rational.

YASUHIKO: In a narrow sense, consciousness is the mental activity with the use of language to reflect upon itself, so self-consciousness is when we bring consciousness to reflect upon ourselves, our activities, our past, our relationships, our thoughts by objectifying within our mind space to see—that is the primary function of consciousness; it is a self-reflection, a self-observation, a self-introspection. Julian Jaynes said, "Without language to actually objectify himself there is no such thing as consciousness." That is his thesis, that human consciousness did not begin far back in animal evolution, but instead, it is a learned process that came about only three thousand years ago and is still developing.

I'm a philosopher and Buddhist symbolist priest scholar so sub-consciousness has been the subject of my study all my life. One could say that Buddhism is the study of consciousness. What do you do in meditating? You just watch yourself, so a function of consciousness is actually to self-reflect. So if you start to reflect on yourself while you're thinking, then you cannot think normally. You see, the moment when you are thinking, the moment you want to observe yourself thinking, you can't think—either you can observe yourself or you can think. That reflection stops when you start to think, so when you say conscious financing or conscious capitalism or conscious anything, consciousness means reflection and introspection, and so people who are in finance, they are all smart people and they think, but they may not be reflecting upon themselves. I'd say it is self-introspective and self-reflective. You want to be able to see the consequence of your action and also understand why you're doing what you're doing. The Japanese word for "thinking" is *khangairu*, which comes from the ancient Japanese *kammi kairu*, which means "a return to the inner divinity." So what happened is ancient people had an awareness of this thinking activity, which includes this conscious activity of returning to the source of your thought.

KIM: If someone wanted to become more conscious, where would you recommend they begin?

YASUHIKO: First they need to see the consequence of their action. They may have become rich doing what they're doing, but in the process, many people may have been hurt by their actions, and there are social consequences as well. Second, they really need to ask of themselves why they're doing it. So on a smaller scale, if you're married and have a family, maybe you're working sixteen hours a day neglecting your family; you may be rich, but you may not have happiness—and wealth without happiness is not really wealth for most people.

Consciousness and conscience are very connected, so the people who have consciousness also develop their conscience and become more connected to their actions. Many people come to the point where they have succeeded in their lives and in their career, and they have what is called a mid-life crisis and say to themselves, "I have succeeded in whatever I had been doing and have money and everything and yet feel somehow empty." And they want to know how to increase their own net-happiness and the net-worth of society. Always one needs to ask the question to oneself, "Why am I doing what I'm doing?"

I was a very bright kid when I was young, and I had a lot of expectations from my parents and my teachers. I carried that heavy expectation, so my original purpose in life was to be the best student, number one in the class and then number one in the whole school, then number one in the whole city, number one in the state, number one in the Tri-State area. Tri-State was as far as you could go then. I scored the perfect score in every exam, and I was number one in the whole Tri-State examination, and after a few moments of euphoria, I was like, "I don't want to do this anymore." It was not fun.

You see, when you're a child, there is a lot of pressure academically, especially in the Japanese educational system—as it is here in the United States. You see it as a win or lose competition, so if you're number one, everybody else is a loser, basically. So every time you win, you're creating losers right there, and being the number one student, you don't become very popular in school. If anything, you lose your peers.

At that point, having accomplished whatever it was that I was supposed to accomplish, I found myself not at all happy. I was miserable and lonely and I didn't want to continue. That was the bottom line. So I began to think about life's purpose at a very early age and began to read philosophy, and eventually, I had some kind of insight into my life and begin to meditate. That's what started it. This was a long time ago, and my life was so far removed from business, so I went into a Buddhist Seminary and then I went to India to study philosophy at University. When I was in India, in Mumbai/Bombay, I took a break and went to Calcutta. Three days before I arrived, the new Pope at the time, Pope John Paul, had visited there. The *India Times* said it had cost three million dollars for him to visit Poland. I thought that was interesting. At some point during my stay, I went to visit Mother Teresa's Mission in Calcutta. While there, I spoke my mind and said, "Look, Mother Teresa is Catholic, and the Catholic Church has so much money; why not ask them to just invest some money here? There is no need to worship poverty; you don't need to be poor to be spiritual, and it seems like you guys are worshipping physical poverty here and there are a lot of people dying here, and while you may feel good about that, these people can be cured. Why don't you just ask the Vatican to invest money here in Calcutta and build a hospital, a school, and make those ill people healthy and then let them study and become self-sufficient? Why continue to worship poverty?" That was the first thing that I saw and thought to myself—there is something wrong with this whole thing. After I expressed my views, I was no longer a welcomed guest there.

The beauty of Sun Tzu's *The Art of War* is that it's rational. It is written not to encourage war; it is actually written in an exceptional way to dissuade you from ever even going into war, but if you have to, then "do this" it says, and you'll not lose the war. Being conscious also means being rational, and rational means way beyond being logical; it means you have a sense of the whole. Then being conscious and being rational in that sense are the same. So it is like rational capitalism; rational financing is the same as consciousness, and in a way, it's probably better to use the word rational. People say, "What do you mean? I'm rational." No, often they are not. They might be logical, but that's not the same as being rational.

CONSCIOUSNESS TEACHER
Dr. Dan Siegel   *Becoming More Conscious*

Dr. Dan Siegel is a mindfulness expert, clinical professor of psychiatry at the UCLA School of Medicine, Executive Director of the Mindsight Institute, a neuropsychiatrist, and an interpersonal neurobiologist. Here he speaks about the accuracy of Einstein's observations regarding mankind.

DAN: If the ship of the human family is sinking, then everyone—people who make money by services, goods, sales, the "capitalists," people working at schools, people raising kids, people working on farms, everybody—has to work together to turn the ship around; so we don't hit the iceberg, we all will need to work together. For-profit and non-profit worlds need to work together. Part of the dilemma of the human species is that we have a human brain that has a tendency to believe that the self is defined by the skin, and the self believes it's separate from the larger world in which it lives; it believes it's a singular noun rather than what I call a plural verb, where I believe I'm separate from you and you are separate from me. There isn't "you as a separate self," "me as a separate self." We can be differentiated in our self experiences for sure, but there is an inter-self experience, and for that, we don't really have a good word, but we need one.

The inter-self experience says there is a larger membership. It's somewhat similar to when people in a company work collaboratively.

Yes, they differentiate and honor each other's different skill sets, but then they draw together to let the whole be larger than the sum of its parts. That's what integration creates; that's what collective intelligence is. That's what I mean by inter-self—you realize when you are a member of a group that is creating something collaboratively that the stewardship of the project is not based on one person's idea. This is what we need as a human family; we need this inter-self reality.

Einstein called for the solution to what he said was the "optical delusion of our separateness." I'm really optimistic that conscious capitalism can work together with other efforts to bring awareness into the world. That effort, for us in interpersonal neurobiology, is awareness of the importance of integration.

Einstein said, "A human being is a part of the whole called by us 'the universe,' a part limited in time and space. He experiences himself, his thoughts and feelings, as something separate from the rest—a kind of optical illusion of consciousness. This delusion is a kind of prison for us, restricting us to our personal desires and affection for a few persons nearest to us. Our task must be to free ourselves from this prison by widening the circle of understanding and compassion to embrace all living creatures and the whole of nature in its beauty."

CONSCIOUSNESS TEACHER
Chip Conley
Becoming More Conscious

Chip Conley is Head of Global Hospitality and Strategy for Airbnb and Founder and Former CEO of Joie de Vivre. His prescription for success is based on Abraham Maslow's Hierarchy of Needs. Here he speaks about his organizing principle for beginning his first company to "create joy" instead of money, but that by creating joy, he knew the company would do well financially too.

KIM: When you hear that phrase, living consciously, what does it mean to you?

CHIP: I think the opposite is what comes up for me—unconscious. And to be unconscious, in some ways, physically, means that you're dead . . . not dead but that you're just breathing but not aware. You don't have awareness. And conscious means aware; consciousness means to be aware. In the context of business, the awareness of the systemic impact of what you do. Yes on the ecological, environmental side of things and even on the sustainable side, I think that's one piece of it. But to me, awareness is even more important on the personal relationship side, like how do you affect people? I hear a lot about the ecological systems, but from a business perspective, it's more about the nature of what a company can do to you on a bad day and the physical effects it can then have on your family. So I would say a conscious organization is one that is aware of its ecological footprint and its emotional footprint on its people.

When I started my company, I intentionally called it "Joie de Vivre"—that's "joy of life" in French. My whole philosophy was why not create the whole organizing principle for the company to be creating joy, instead of creating money, with the idea that by creating joy, we would do well financially. I would say there was definitely some push back from people who thought it sounded like some alien ship from California or San Francisco had landed. I definitely felt resistance—talking about emotions and relationships and psychology and joy. It sounds really soft. I had gone to Stanford Business School, which is a little more liberal business school, but it's still all about the analytics. But what I saw over time was that people saw the domino effect and the positive impact.

We had a great culture; it led to employee satisfaction, which led to great customer satisfaction, then market share. As I explored that further, I was able to show how, empirically, things were working in our companies, and it was easier for me to convince outside investors. Over time, there was a huge shift. When the *Harvard Business Review* story came out January/February 2012, there was a cover article with a happy face about the super value of happiness, and there were six articles inside about how happiness drives success within a company. You would have never expected an article like that in the *Harvard Business Review* ten years ago.

Joie de Vivre had two once-in-a-lifetime downturns during the last decade, especially in the Bay Area, which is where we are based, and one of them was the dot.com bust, which was very Bay-Area central and very painful. It forced me to really ask: How do I apply psychology to leadership? And I used Abraham Maslow's hierarchy of needs, which is what led me to write the book, *Peak: How Great Companies Get Their Mojo from Maslow*. But the real fundamental shift I had was asking whether we could create a self-actualized workplace? Could we create an environment where even in the worst of times, when people are focused purely on survival, they can still thrive? And we've proved that we could, and further, we tripled in size.

Usually the biggest issue around conscious capitalism goes beyond just that you're sometimes having to do things that are just against the norms; it's usually long-term versus short-term. That is the biggest fundamental factor. When someone is extremely short-term oriented, it is easier to be unconscious. When you're long-term oriented, you're looking more at systems and effects, and you have a tendency to look at the bigger picture.

And there have been times where I've had to make the hard calls, where it's not what I want to do, but it is what would be best for the company and it's necessary. So it doesn't mean that you don't make the hard calls, but every day there are great opportunities to be conscious or unconscious.

The question I asked myself during the downturn was: What do I want my company to look like during the downturn? That's a really great question for a CEO or any leader within any company to put next to their computer, so they can see it every day.

We need to figure out how to get beyond quarterly earnings and have more stock analysts who focus on the long-term. Bill George, who was CEO of Medtronics, who created the most value increase for any company on the stock market, once said, "We get the investors we deserve." If you take a long-term perspective as he did when he said, "We're not going to have quarterly earnings mean that much," what matters most is that if you get investors who believe in that, you're not going to have decisions that are short-term oriented. So I'd like to see analysts take a longer term view at how they value things.

CONSCIOUSNESS TEACHER
Cindy Wigglesworth *Becoming More Conscious*

Cindy Wigglesworth is the Founder of Deep Change, Inc. and the creator of the SQ21™ a Spiritual Intelligence self-assessment, the first competency-based spiritual intelligence assessment instrument.

KIM: Will you explain to us about spiritual intelligence and how we can acquire it?

CINDY: Spiritual intelligence is an innate human capacity that is made available to us if we are willing to develop it. And although spirituality seems like a personal thing and doesn't have much to do with business or work, take a look at Jim Collins' book *Good to Great* where he speaks about the key characteristics of visionary companies and exceptional leaders including: consistent focus on vision and values, ability to embrace paradox, and humility. These characteristics are directly related to spirituality. Hence, as individuals (at all levels of the organization) develop greater personal spiritual intelligence, they experience increased personal satisfaction, improved job performance, and become more effective team players and leaders. All of these enhancements improve the bottom-line. Spiritual intelligence skills are also strongly positively correlated with higher stages of adult development—which are themselves highly correlated with increased leadership capacity. The ability to hold multiple perspectives and to develop systems thinking are related to the ability to relax the ego and hold a wider view—a spiritual intelligence skill set.

KIM: When there is push back around the word "spirituality," how do you think people are defining it? What does spirituality in that context mean for you and for the person who would be curious about it?

CINDY: I make a comparison between emotions and emotional intelligence. We all have and experience emotions. But we are not all emotionally intelligent because emotional intelligence is a set of skills. Those skills are developed over time with practice. The seminal work for me in this field was the Emotional Competence Inventory model Richard Boyatzis and Daniel Goleman created, which has the eighteen skills of emotional intelligence laid out in four quadrants.

The difference between spirituality and spiritual intelligence is the same. I believe all people are born innately spiritual. I define spiritual in a way that echoes Abraham Maslow. It's an innate human hunger to be connected with something larger than ourselves, something we consider divine or sacred or extremely noble. So if you think about the hierarchy of needs, it would go above self-actualizing. In fact, Maslow's final book talks about the level beyond self-actualizing; he calls that "self-transcendence." People who feel self-transcendence have this desire to be of service and this commitment to move beyond their contracted ego self into this larger sense of who they are. So I very much tapped into that—Maslow's sense of needs. We have this innate hunger (spirituality), but being spiritually intelligent takes time. Spiritual intelligence, like emotional intelligence, is a set of skills that is learned through practice. So "spiritual intelligence" is a very deliberate choice of words. I don't go into corporations to teach spirituality; I go in to teach the intelligences people need to meet the challenges they face. And those intelligences will be some combination of physical, intellectual, emotional, and spiritual. So the spiritual intelligence skill set is what I teach.

KIM: And how does that relate to the idea of consciousness?

CINDY: I think what people who use the word conscious in this context are talking about is awareness and being self-responsible. So it's like I am self-aware and I'm owning responsibility for my own stuff and I'm owning responsibility to grow up. I need to go grow up because conscious leaders are grownups. In the adult development sense, they have matured past the childish blame game of "It's not my fault, it's everybody else's fault."

Conscious people really see life and humanity as far more complex than the earlier stages of ego development typically want to see it. In the earlier stages of ego development, and we see a lot of this in corporations (I will use Susanne Cook-Greuter's model here), you see people at the expert stage of development; this is a peak level of IQ, a real deep specialty in their field. They may know more about their particular kind of derivative transactions or how the laws work in the banking industry or whatever. When they know more than almost anybody else in their field and they are very proud of it, they will stand up in their expertise area and go to battle over their expertise area. The world is a right or wrong world; either they are right or you are right. The delineation between right and wrong is crisp and clean. As you move past the expert stage to the achiever and beyond, you start realizing that crisp and clean boundaries barely exist. Even when people point out that you should never kill another human being, they will say "except in cases of self-defense."

The world is a complex place. So how do you respond effectively to the world we see? It requires stages of development that help us match our interior complexity to the exterior complexity we have to deal with. We talk about this in the world of Spiral Dynamics theory (based on the work of Dr. Clare Graves). Life conditions drive adult development. So when life conditions demand, we have to develop the internal neural complexity, new brain patterns, whatever you want to call it, that allow us to more correctly perceive the challenges. If you oversimplify challenges and insist on putting things into either bucket A or bucket B, and think "I like bucket A, so I am going to search and find all the data that supports my theory that it is actually bucket A," you can create a self-comforting bubble, but the self-comforting bubble could be your destruction. You might feel better in the short term, yet you could be the *Titanic* waiting to hit the iceberg, because you are really not reacting, responding to the full data set—to what's going on in the world.

KIM: When did you become aware of these limitations?

CINDY: I became aware of the limitations of my worldview in my twenties when I was probably hard-core in what I would now see as the expert stage of adult development. At that stage, there was a right or a wrong for everything and if I just applied my IQ and learned enough, I would be able to figure out what was right and wrong about everything. And as I started my career it became clear that this approach just wasn't working. It was really frustrating. What do you do when you realize your world view isn't working? Initially, you try to do it better. I am just going to be a better expert; I am going to be more expert than anybody else in the room, because clearly I am not expert enough or I would have the right answers. And eventually you get frustrated when you realize that the solutions you propose logically seem like they should work, don't work.

I can't remember the specifics but I was in the field of human resources and I remember finding situations where although I would win and I would get to influence the outcome of a meeting or a choice, that choice then backfired. And it would leave me completely stumped and I would say "How is that possible?" When we run into these limitations, we are forced either to reevaluate growth or close down and get toxic. People will tend to grow if they have a supportive structure around them. Without the right support or with too much stress, people will tend to contract and get even self-delusional, thinking if the world would just go back to the way it used to be, it would all be all right.

KIM: How do we take the next step?

CINDY: Robert Kegan, who is one of the developmental psychologists I love, talks about what it is that helps people take the next step developmentally. His basic advice requires the right balance of challenge and support. "Challenge" meaning somebody or something is in your face creating the irritation, like the sand in the oyster. And "support" meaning you have the educational tools, the mentors, the coaches, the teachers, the friends around you who are role-modeling a more complex behavior that seems to be better suited to the time, that allows you to try on something new in a fairly safe way. And this is the essence of coaching, of course. Ideally, if you find the right coach, someone who's developmentally at the right stage, far enough ahead of you, they can help you see what you can't see and they can do it in a safe environment. A good coach helps somebody take a safe next step, a low risk next step.

KIM: Support is important, then?

CINDY: I think it's good to get cognitive support. If you are having this idea in your head that something's wrong here and I am not sure what it is, but I am really not happy with the current model of how we are handling banking or how we are handling stock trades or how we are handling derivatives, then look for books or articles or groups online or someplace where you can stimulate your mind to give it an opportunity to stretch in a safe way. There are plenty of people out there who are asking the same questions; the problem is finding them and being able to have a conversation with them in a safe container. So an online group where you are anonymous, you know you use an alias or whatever, can be a way to have a conversation.

Attend a conscious capitalism event or some other event where this is a topic of conversation with other people from finance who are likely to show up. It's a place where you can maybe meet over lunch, a breakfast, or dinner, have a chat with somebody who is in your field, and say, "Well, I am really feeling like there is a moral disconnect between who I am and how I am asked to be at work."

If we are going to innovate whatever is next, there is some courage required, and yet we also need enough safety. So where is the challenge, where is the safety? Find safe places. Obviously, books are safe because you can buy them and read them at home. Read articles, join online chat groups, but then take the next step and meet with people face to face. Find a group to meet up with or find a conference you can attend. You can start by just showing up and listening. You don't even have to risk anything other than your physical presence, but see what gets sparked in you. I have found that my inner knowing knows when I find pieces of information I need to hang on to.

CONSCIOUSNESS TEACHER
Alan Cohen *Becoming More Conscious*

Alan Cohen, MA, is an author, speaker, and leader in the personal growth movement, encouraging outer change through inner awakening, and is a featured presenter in the documentary *Finding Joe*, which celebrates the teachings of visionary mythologist Joseph Campbell. Here he speaks about how in the midst of the difficult there is opportunity for transformation.

KIM: Living a life consciously. What does that mean to you?

ALAN: It means each of us is searching for quality of life. We're all searching in different ways, but we all want the experience of happiness . . . of being happy, of being whole, of being expressive, creative, and successful. Another word for consciousness is mindset. It's the lens through which you view the universe. Psychologists, scientists, and quantum physicists have told us for ages that life is not anything in particular; it's more what you make of it by the vision you're using to see it. So my understanding is that as we shift our consciousness, we shift the way we see the world, and as a result of seeing the world differently, we get different results. That's why if we want any significant change in life, whether it's our finances, our relationships, or with our health, it must be associated with a change in consciousness or mindset; otherwise we'll revert to the conditions that prompted us to think about it or wonder is there anything more?

KIM: How can people who don't have anyone to support them navigate through this?

ALAN: They should reach out for anyone and anything that matches where they're headed. And, you know, when you choose a goal, you become keenly aware of two factors. One is everything that matches the goal and two is everything that opposes the goal. And so, you know, even if you're coming from a family or a business or a religion or history or dysfunctional system that is putting pressure on you to stay small and old and limited, there usually is at least one person or one company or one friend or one book or one seminar or one class that lights you up and ignites you and reminds you of how good it could be if you stayed with it. So at that point, you have to cling to that person or path like a lifesaver because it truly represents the life you're going to step into as opposed to the life you're trying to get away from. No one is ever wrestling alone—no matter how dark it seems or how weird it gets, there is always a book or a friend or a teacher you can lean on to help pull you through that difficult time.

Also, tell the truth . . . the impeccable truth about what you're doing that's not working for you. What hurts? Is it the hour-and-a-half commute in both directions? Is it working for tired employees? Is it loss? Is it selling things you don't believe in? Is it working with people who have shallow values? I mean, what is it about your current work that is not working for you?

So the next question is: What do you fantasize about? What career or people have you seen that lights you up to think about it? Almost everybody has something they'd rather be doing. And even if, at this point, it's just a fantasy or just a vague idea, it's really healthy to explore because vague ideas turn into strong ideas or strong ideas turn into reality. In the Twelve-Step programs they call it a "feel in searching moral inventory." I suggest people do a feel in searching vocational inventory and just tell the truth. That's usually the first step of transformation.

The second piece is that, if you, indeed, do have to stay where you are at least for a while because of financial obligations, find aspects of the job that you could expand and magnify and appreciate and work with that make it better. In other words, shine the light on what is working even if it's a small piece of the job, and see what you can do to maximize that. Take what you have and make it what you want. The other way to look at it is that your job might be a seminar of personal transformation. If you feel stuck or irritated or bored or victimized, here's a chance to do some good in your work and say, "Well, am I really stuck?" And then maybe you need to do some tolerance work. Ask yourself what choices do I really have before me and whom can I communicate to that could actually help me?

So even in the midst of the difficult, there may be a tremendous opportunity for transformation that you would not have if you were in an easier position. Lots of people say that was what it took for them finally to get out of their job or to get themselves promoted or get out of a bad marriage. The muscles they built in that process were so powerful they serve them for a lifetime, and that, in a way, they are glad it happened, because it really moved them to another round of consciousness which is so much more valuable than even if I just got a different job.

WALL STREET 50
Robert A.G. Monks   *Becoming More Conscious*

Robert A.G. Monks is a shareholder activist and corporate governance adviser, as well as an author. Monks founded the Institutional Shareholder Services (ISS), LENS Investment Management, Trucost, and Governance for Owners. All of the aforementioned firms specialized in achieving efficiency, sustainability, and informed investing for their clients. Monks was appointed by President Reagan as the Director of the United States Synthetic Fuels Corporation as well as to the founding Trustee of the Federal Employees' Retirement System. Monks pioneered the practice of shareholder activism, which is an attempt by a person to use his or her rights as a shareholder in a company to effectuate social change or to change a company's direction or behavior. This approach to ethical business first dawned on Mr. Monks after a trip to Maine in the 1970s where he witnessed firsthand the gross pollution floating down the Penobscot River. Upon learning that this was the result of local paper companies, in which his trust company was a shareholder, he had an epiphany. He reached out to other trust companies and mutual funds with stakes in the company, so they could use their combined majority share to influence positive change in the company. This experience led to his pioneering the concept of corporate governance, which emphasizes the importance of balancing both the wants and needs of corporate executives and stakeholders and those of the customers and the general public. Monks has been a major advocate for this business paradigm.

ROBERT: As you were speaking just now, about what your book is about, I was reminded of the work of a very distinguished scholar, a woman named Dr. Marcy Murninghan, who was then head at the Harvard Divinity School. She put together a series of interviews with people, one of whom was John Whitehead and another was me. She has a blog site now. I worked with her a lot, about twenty years ago. I myself have been a TM meditator over thirty years so I have been very much in the world of "consciousness." I think the saddest element that I have encountered in recent times arose out of an initiative I did about three years ago. I looked at a testimony before a Congressional committee by the CEO of Goldman Sachs, Lloyd Blankfein, whom I didn't know. And I wrote him a letter and I said underneath the carapace of CEO of Goldman Sachs, I detected a human being, and it was the human being I was addressing. He replied, and we ended up talking for several hours at his office. And what I was struck with was that he was a very fine man, but he was very limited in the sense that he explained his framework as being that of *a trader* and he said, "All I do is make a market; that is what my job is," and "These complaints are misdirected because they have to do with a failure to understand the dynamics of the marketplace." I was not successful in being able to persuade him in the words of Shakespeare, "There are more things in heaven and earth, Horatio, Than are *dreamt of* in your philosophy." (*Hamlet:* 1.5.167–8.) [The emphasis here is on "dreamt of" since Hamlet is pointing out how little even the most educated people can explain.] What was missing was his sense of holism and a sense of consciousness. I think the difficulty is really illuminated by that simple encounter between myself and Lloyd Blankfein. I consider him to be a very decent human being. Lloyd Blankfein is not invested in breaking the law or trying to transgress public sensitivity; it is simply that he is living in a context where being a trader is the entire explanation for why people do things, and it is something that people feel is a satisfactory organizing energy for their content.

KIM: Yes, that's a powerful example. The challenge for all of us in this is how do we stand in the face of these people who are decent human beings and try to communicate to them successfully what consciousness is? You did this, but it sounds like you were unsuccessful.

ROBERT: Yes I failed in that instance. I had a good chance and I felt very badly about it because I have seen Lloyd go on, and he has basically said the same thing to a variety of additional authorities who are higher than me. I think it is just sad because it is not helping the resolution of the question of the interests of humanity.

KIM: What does consciousness mean to you? When would you say you became aware of the concept?

ROBERT: It is curious. Frankly with me, it was always in my stomach. I always had the feeling that something was right, and no matter how much I could argue and rationalize, I couldn't triumph over the feeling in my stomach, whether I was doing something right or not; it is kind of simple. I enjoyed a thorough education; there wasn't any educational institution that authenticated people as being rationally fit to be unleashed on society that I didn't attend. The fact is that none of that produced a sense of consciousness with me; It came from a very powerful physical response that would not allow me to ignore it. Essentially, most people in society derive a sense of correctness from the credentialing of their education. I have said I was credentialed by everybody as being very rational and reasonable and everything else, but that didn't produce the right answer; the right answer was something that came truly from my stomach lining and a feeling of whether I did the thing right or not.

KIM: Did you find that you were listening to that all the time, or did you find there was a particular age that you hit when you thought, "You know what, I have to surrender to this stomach feeling because when I don't . . ."

ROBERT: Well, for a long period when I was an apprentice, which I would say lasted until I was about thirty, I wasn't terribly worried about my stomach because I was really equipping myself; I wasn't really acting as a principal in the world. Also by that time, I had been married for about ten years and, fortunately, my wife was very helpful.

KIM: The reason I was drawn to you was because of your interview in the documentary *The Corporation*, where you talked about that river being polluted and how it troubled you for years, and then you realized when that proxy came across your desk . . . Can you say a bit more about that?

ROBERT: Yes, that was, to use a grandiose word, a sort of *epiphany* for me because I put together that the waste material being shipped down the Penobscot River at night with subsequently having a proxy on my desk, as the head of a trust company, and shareholder of Great Northern Paper, which was the company sending the trash down in the first place. It became very clear to me that the capitalist system could very well be harmonized with human welfare. In order to do so, the owners in the modern world, major trust institutions, not individuals, could require that their companies conform with particular standards of conduct compatible with human welfare. And so that has become really the work for me in the last thirty years.

KIM: When you first thought to yourself, "I have to speak up," was that when the sense of trepidation, the sense of "Nobody does that" struck you?

ROBERT: I have always been conscious of being over-privileged, and the way in which I expiate the sense of being over-privileged has been to feel obligated to take up subjects that other people choose not to because the consequences of incurring this disfavor from the great and the good is too inhibiting. I have been able to support myself pretty well all my life and have for one reason or another not been worried about whether I displeased the great and the good, it has just been a sense in me that it is sort of a mission that I should raise issues that need to be raised, which most people for understandable reasons are reluctant to raise.

KIM: Thank you for doing so. And also, I am curious; what would you say to somebody who is not in that position, somebody who is thinking, "My gosh, if I speak up here in this meeting or in this company or even in this one-on-one encounter, I put myself financially at risk, I put my family financially at risk." What guidance would you give that person?

ROBERT: To get another job. Because you really cannot live as a questioning fulfilled human being in a way that makes you deny your capacity to require integrity from your employer.

KIM: In your book, *The New Global Investors*, you talk about how corporations can change and that they are still better than state-run entities. What would you like to say to a corporation today? If you were able to tell it, "This is how you want to pay attention," would it be to have an improved sense of consciousness?

ROBERT: It is the sense of consciousness. I was just reading yesterday a book written by a man named Sachs, a prominent economist, and Sachs writes, "How did we get in the dreadful situation in which the federal government is in the lap of the corporate lobby?" That's about where we are today. The greed has been taken over by the government, and the government is not capable now of functioning independently for the public good. So we are in a place where the challenge is that the corporate interest has taken over the government. That's a very bad situation, and the only alternative to it is if the owners of the corporations assert their human interests. The owners of corporations essentially are a hundred million people—because people own mutual funds, people own employee benefits plan interests, and this ownership is in the form of trust for the benefit of a hundred million Americans. The problem that I haven't been able to answer is how to enlist the constructive involvement of those trust institutions on behalf of a hundred million of Americans, to, in effect, represent the public interest because it is, after all, the public who own these companies or have a beneficial interest in the companies. Unhappily, the enforcement of the trust responsibility on these major institutions has been deficient, and they continue to act in their own interest as institutions rather than in the interest of the public.

KIM: I think there are some who ask "Where does one even begin?"

ROBERT: It is very, very difficult. I have become more selfish and I just say, "Look, all I can really do is be responsible for myself and do as well as I can and express what it is that I have that may be valuable," and it is possibly because I was lucky enough to have a father who was a clergyman so I understood the limits of trying to preach to people.

Robert Monks poses a powerful question: How do we enlist the constructive involvement of those trust institutions on behalf of our country? How do we persuade them to act keeping all of our interests in mind? If we elaborate on what Monks says at the end of his interview, that all he can do is be responsible for himself and do as well as he can and express what he has of value, then we have the map to where these answers lie. Because we can only seek the answers to these big questions *after* we have answered these first: "How do we do this (be responsible for ourselves, do as well as we can, express what we have of value to offer) with those closest to us, and deeper still, how do we do this on our own behalf when our own actions frequently betray our own self-interest?"

When Mr. Monks realized he was a stockholder of the company that was polluting the Penobscot River, he could have looked away. But he knew who he was, and when you know who you are, you are less likely to betray yourself and, therefore, everyone else.

One of my favorite lines is from the movie *Moonstruck* when Olympia Dukasis' character Rose Casterini turns down Perry's proposition with this sentence, "I'm not going to invite you in. Not because I'm married, but because I know who I am."

Becoming more conscious begins with knowing who you are and the life you choose to live and what you stand for—even when the temptations tempt and the storms rage. If you don't know who you are and what you live for or stand for, then you must be willing to be still long enough to figure that out. His Holiness Sri Sri Ravi Shankar suggests spending even a few minutes a day pondering your life. Yasuhiko Genku Kimura suggests you ask yourself, "Why am I doing what I am doing?" Dr. Dan Siegel suggests contemplating that we all really are connected, and Cindy Wigglesworth suggests you find cognitive support as you engage in the inquiry.

My suggestion is that you focus first on what you are not. You are not your past or the title you hold, nor the body you have, nor the ethnicity, skin color, age, or sexual preference you claim. You are not the money you make, have, or don't have, nor your education, your religion, or your beliefs, nor the car you drive, the clothing you wear, nor the political party you belong to. "What's left?" you ask. Only what is real. You.

The Five Practices to Become More Awake

Professionally and personally, I have read, studied, practiced, listened, and experienced more books, classes, courses, workshops, seminars, lessons, and "experiences" from so many professors, teachers, coaches, instructors, holy men and women, shamans, healers, and gurus than you would even believe. I've studied theology at a Roman Catholic Seminary, taken classes on Judaism at a synagogue, and studied at St. Bartholomew's School of Religious Inquiry. I've spent time with a Shaman, done deep work with a Taoist Master, studied Human Design, learned from a Hawaiian Kahu, and spent weeks on retreat developing a full-time meditation practice. I've studied the work of Marshall Rosenberg's NonViolent Communication in depth and undergone Psych-K sessions, participated in a Soul Retrieval ceremony, completed the Landmark Forum and the Advance Course. I've participated or experienced multiple religious, pagan, and spiritual ceremonies from a Goddess Circle to a Space Clearing of my home. I've witnessed a Shinto Priest ceremony, practiced zazen with Buddhist Monks in Japan, toured Israel with a priest and a rabbi, and studied mythology for over twenty five years through the work of Joseph Campbell and beyond.

Over time, as I began to weave a tapestry of all the learning and teachings I discovered, I began to notice that five fundamental threads repeatedly showed up. They are what I have defined as **The Five Practices**. These practices are the ones that I attribute to my own awakening. They are also the ones I strive to practice in my life on a day-to-day basis, and what I advocate and encourage with my clients.

The Five Practices are:

- Practice One: Self-Responsibility
- Practice Two: Self/Other Empathy
- Practice Three: Emotional Non-Resistance
- Practice Four: The Internal and External Journey
- Practice Five: Self-Awareness/Mindfulness

These **Five Practices** heal, empower, and elevate one's consciousness, not to mention improve one's quality of life and, yes, increase
one's wealth. As these five repeatedly showed up in my interviews
with *The Wall Street 50*, I decided to build Part II of this book around
them.

In the following pages, we look at each one in more detail. First,
I ask the *Teachers of Consciousness* to define these **Five Practices**, and
then I share bite-sized stories from *The Wall Street 50* that are examples of the essence of each practice. Some of the people interviewed
speak to how they became aware of the importance of a practice,
while others talk about how they live from one or more. Some are
featured more than once. And while they may not call the practice
what I call it, I saw evidence of them living in each practices' milieu.
You will also see some contradictions because these people don't all
say the same thing nor hold the same opinion. *The Wall Street 50* as
well as the *Teachers of Consciousness* include those with many different experiences, viewpoints, and even faiths, including atheism. I
don't expect you to resonate with each and every one. Some will
land and others won't. It will help if you view this section as a buffet,
where a selection of ideas, perspectives, stories, and viewpoints are
presented for you to experience. And if any one comment or story
really gets under your skin, then I would encourage you to be especially curious about it. When a great deal of resistance comes up,
it's more often than not a red flag that one might very well be too
attached to a particular perspective.

PRACTICE ONE: Self-Responsibility

Let me be very clear; self-responsibility is not about blame or self-reproach. It's simply a way of saying to oneself, "I am responsible for how I respond to what shows up in my life." This is challenging for a lot of people because they've been raised in what I call "the swamp of blame." Blaming themselves and blaming others. Everything shifts when you take responsibility for your life and everything that shows up in it. It certainly did for me.

My taking self-responsibility began in what I describe as the first of my many awakenings. In 2005, I participated in the Landmark Forum, a personal development course created by Werner Erhard in the 1970s. It's a three-and-a-half day intensive course about learning how to live from a place of complete personal responsibility and, by doing so, finding yourself living in the land of limitless possibility. It is one of the most powerful experiences I've ever had. It is also the reason I became a coach. That course woke me up and increased the level of consciousness from which I operate. It showed me that I had been keeping myself from possibility simply by the story I told myself about who I was, the family I had, my upbringing, and my life. I learned in that course that the story I had made up kept me small and powerless. When I awoke, my feelings of powerlessness were transformed into empowerment and I began to live a new story, one filled with the freedom to create a life I loved and the ability to live more powerfully than before, all while embracing the possibility that was right there for the taking. It was the hardest and easiest thing I've ever done.

Werner Erhard defines how we become self-responsible as follows:

> Responsibility begins with the willingness to take the stand that one is the cause in the matter of one's life. It is a declaration not an assertion, that is, it is a context from which one chooses to live. Responsibility is not burden, fault, praise, blame, credit, shame, or guilt. In responsibility, there is no evaluation of good

or bad, right or wrong. There is simply *what's so*, and the stand you choose to take on *what's so*. Being responsible starts with the willingness to deal with a situation from the view of life that you are the generator of what you do, what you have, and what you are. That is not the truth. It is a place to stand. No one can make you responsible, nor can you impose responsibility on another. It is a grace you give yourself—an empowering context that leaves you with a say in the matter of life.

Now we will hear *The Teachers of Consciousness* define or articulate what **Self-Responsibility** means to them. Then stories from *The Wall Street 50* will provide an example of what **Self-Responsibility** looks like in practice.

CONSCIOUSNESS TEACHER

Raphael Cushnir   *Practice One: Self-Responsibility*

UNDERSTANDING THE LAW OF ATTRACTION

Raphael Cushnir is an author, speaker, and a leading voice in the world of emotional connection and present moment awareness. He's a faculty member of the Esalen Institute, the Kripalu Center for Yoga and Health, and the Masters Program in Organizational Systems Renewal at Pinchot University. Cushnir speaks here about the missing piece in the Law of Attraction and how we can't will ourselves out of our feeling.

The Law of Attraction, as I understand it, simply says that what you focus on expands. The universe doesn't give you what you say you want, but the universe gives you what you are energetically attracting. So, for instance, if you are depressed, if you are having negative emotions, then you want to shift to a more positive state of being because a positive state of being attracts more of itself. If you want more stuff, if you want more love, focus on those things, and over time, that focus will bring you more in alignment with the universe meeting you at that place.

And so I think that there is one element of that, and that is very important and definitely rings true for me, which is that we create our reality to some degree and we do that through the quality of our feelings and our belief. But fundamental to my own approach is that you can't will yourself out of what you feel. So if you actually are feeling low or down and you try to push yourself into a positive state, that's what I call resistance and resistance just persists and also what it does is it sabotages your ability to achieve. So you might be standing in front of a mirror looking at yourself and saying a Law of Attraction type affirmation you know like my body is beautiful and a great expression of the divine, when underneath what you are really saying as you look at your 100 pound overweight body is, "I hate what I am seeing."

If you try to use the Law of Attraction to stop that hate, you will be at war with yourself and nothing you do in accord with the Law of Attraction will actually bring you what you want. So my perspective is about going through that feeling because when you go into and through a feeling, you naturally expand into a more peaceful presence. And the peaceful presence is the place from which all the good things come. So first I say if you want to start aligning with what it is that you want, keep in mind that when you expand in the present, you don't grasp and cling for things like you might otherwise.

So rather than asking for stuff or thinking your happiness is going to come from certain kinds of achievement or acquisitions in life, you end up feeling peaceful already where you are, and then that's ultimately the greatest gift, which allows you to work in collaboration with life to bring about, for instance, financial well-being if that's what you want. But the pearl beyond price, as it is sometimes referred to, is the recognition that I don't need anything to feel peaceful and fulfilled. I can do that here in this moment no matter what else is happening and therefore there is nothing missing, there is nothing wrong. And I am not reaching, I am not grasping or clinging, and therefore, I am free.

CONSCIOUSNESS TEACHER
Alan Cohen   *Practice One: Self-Responsibility*

BEGINNING WITH WHERE YOU ARE AND MAKING IT BETTER

Alan Cohen, MA, is an author, speaker, and leader in the personal growth movement encouraging outer change through inner awakening, and is a featured presenter in the documentary *Finding Joe,* which celebrates the teachings of visionary mythologist Joseph Campbell.

Everything is an exercise in awakening. No one is anywhere by accident, whether you're in a wonderful position or a horrible position. Because we are conscious, thinking, aware beings, our position and experience in life are never simply a result of external conditions. Our experience is a result of *how we are processing* the circumstances and what we make of them. Optimally, we employ our circumstances in our favor to elevate our experience.

One evening I was exiting the Chicago airport parking lot with some friends. It was a cold winter night and there were long lines of cars waiting to get out. Finally, we arrived at the tollbooth and the toll collector, a handsome Italian man, took our payment. As he gave us our change, he sang us a verse from the opera *La Traviata.* All the women in the car swooned, we applauded, and we went off into the night. The toll collector sang to all the cars passing through his gate. He was a pretty good singer, at that!

Soon after, I read the results of a poll in which people were asked, "What is the most boring job you can imagine?" The most common answer was "toll collector." That man took what most people consider the most boring job in the world, in the cold, where he was smelling car fumes and dealing with tired commuters, and he turned his toll booth into an opera house. This locus was his laboratory for self-expression, where he uplifted the people he touched. That toll collector was a master of the principle, "Take what you have and make what you want." Now, whenever I feel bored or bugged about my work, I remember that toll collector and I remind myself, "If he can make a heaven out of a hell, I can do that in my domain."

CONSCIOUSNESS TEACHER

Peter Block   *Practice One: Self-Responsibility*

REPLACING THE SCARCITY MENTALITY WITH ONE OF ABUNDANCE

Peter Block is an author, consultant, and citizen of Cincinnati, Ohio. His work is about stewardship and the restoration of community. Here he speaks about our need to create more awareness of the abundance that's already all around us.

Let me go behind the question of, "Can Wall Street be conscious?" You see Wall Street doesn't reside on Wall Street; it and we all are participants of Wall Street. Every privately held or publically traded company is Wall Street. I don't make a distinction, I don't demonize Wall Street. They do what Wall Street does, and every private business owner does what a private business owner does, which is try to accumulate surplus. For example, there we are in the wilderness . . . where God gave us manna, and as soon as we try to have too much, overnight it spoils. So we are all deep participants in accumulating surplus. Some people do it with buying too many sweaters at Wal-Mart. Some people do it with the excess food they put in their stomachs. Obesity is the anxiety of "I don't have enough; I need more." My daughter lived in an Ashram which had lousy vegetarian food and I have never seen people pile their plates so high because they knew that nothing about that meal would be satisfying. All the private sectors are designed to live life according to the current business perspective. The current business perspective is the accumulation of surplus, the belief in speed, scale, and cost. So in actuality, this is a scarcity mentality. The private sector, the business perspective is actually organized around scarcity. Things then only have value in that world if they are seen as rare, and then we are willing to abuse or mistreat the commons in service of our attaining that which we have deemed rare. So if I pollute a river or the sky, or consume the land, well that's the collateral cost of the perspective I'm living from: scarcity. So consciousness is a choice to organize your life around abundance instead of scarcity. That's not what most business people do. They're not paid to do that. So conscious capitalism is trying to compensate for the scarcity mentality of the private sector. So just stay with consciousness, just stay in the abundance of God, abundance of the world, and abundance of the spiritual life.

EXAMPLES FROM THE WALL STREET 50

WALL STREET 50

Joseph Perella   *Practice One: Self-Responsibility*

BE AROUND PEOPLE WITH HIGH STANDARDS

Joseph Perella is the co-founder of Perella Weinberg Partners; prior he held several senior positions at Morgan Stanley, including Vice Chairman, Chairman of Institutional Securities and Investment Banking, and Worldwide Head of Morgan Stanley's Investment Banking Division. Previously he had co-founded Wasserstein Perella & Co., Inc. Mr. Perella's investment banking experience consists of more than forty years.

It's important to surround yourself with high achievers and people who are smarter than you. This was something my father instilled in me. He always said, "If you surround yourself with people who aren't on the same level as you, they're going to drag you down." He didn't mean this in an arrogant way. He was trying to illustrate a point: If you are around people with high standards, people who are smarter than you, they may pull you up to their level. If you surround yourself with people whom you respect, people you would like to emulate, and people you can learn from, you too will grow as a person. That's a lesson I've kept with me throughout my life.

WALL STREET 50

George Schwartz   *Practice One: Self-Responsibility*

TAKING DELIBERATE CONTROL OF YOUR LIFE

George G. Schwartz is the Chief Operating Officer and a Director at Boston Private Bank & Trust. He has over twenty-five years of experience in the financial services industry.

There was one moment in particular that really got me much more focused [aware of my self-responsibility]. From an early age, I was influenced by eastern philosophers. Joseph Campbell was intriguing to me and Jung and all the other sort of people who intersect with awareness or consciousness of position and being. The main catalyst that got me extremely focused was my sister died young. Because we were very close, she and I had similar challenges growing up in terms of our family environment. I came to believe the trauma of that environment was part of what led to her early death. As a result of that, I saw the difference between being a victim as opposed to being responsible. I think some people don't know how not to be a victim. That realization gave me much more of a sense that I need to take a more deliberate control over my life and focus on the mindfulness aspect of being.

WALL STREET 50

Glen C. Dailey *Practice One: Self-Responsibility*

SEIZING THE OPPORTUNITY

Glen C. Dailey has spent over thirty years managing the prime brokerage business of several firms. Most recently, he was a Managing Director and founder of Jefferies Prime Brokerage which he joined in 2006 and led through 2014. He previously founded Bank of America Prime Brokerage in 1995 and led the business for eleven years; he was Head of Prime Brokerage at Furman Selz for the prior twelve years.

I don't make a conscious decision when I wake up to be a good person or a fair person. I was taught growing up that if you do the right thing by people and tell them the truth, you will never have to worry about covering your tracks. That attitude comes from my father who was a New York City Police Officer for twenty-two years. There are always issues that arise in the course of doing business. It may be an error on a trade with a customer, a problem with an employee's performance, or the level of service you receive from a vendor. I always believed that if something was wrong, I should do whatever was needed to make the situation right. Sometimes that cost money, and other times, it may have hurt someone's feelings, but people always appreciated when I told them the truth and treated them fairly. A colleague once told me that problems never go away until you deal with them. The longer you wait, the worse it usually got. Dealing with the issue, solving it quickly, and moving on have served me well over the years.

Wall Street is the land of opportunity, which I have certainly benefited from. When I think about capitalism, I believe it is about working hard, giving 100 percent, and doing the right thing. I always believed that the only constant was change. In the course of a career, your circumstances will be constantly changing; if you give a 100 percent effort in your current situation, you will be prepared for a great opportunity that inevitably arises.

Capitalism is about seizing the opportunity when it knocks at your door.

WALL STREET 50
Alex Green   *Practice One: Self-Responsibility*

DON'T ENVY THOSE WITH MORE

Alexander Green is an author and the Chief Investment Strategist of The Oxford Club and Chief Investment Strategist for Investment U. A Wall Street veteran, he has over twenty-five years' experience as a research analyst, investment advisor, financial writer, and portfolio manager.

When I was a young man I had a college degree, but I didn't have anything else. I couldn't afford to live on my own, so I lived in an apartment with some other guys and I couldn't afford a nice car so I drove a beat up junker where the stereo was worth more than the vehicle. I didn't have any health insurance and I didn't have any savings and I didn't have much of anything, because, surprise, I hadn't earned anything. And yet at that time, even though I had nothing, I didn't envy Ted Turner and Warren Buffet. I never for a minute supposed that they owed me a dime just because they had money and I didn't. I figured that what they had, and earned it legally, was theirs and the reason why I didn't have anything was because I hadn't done anything.

So I think this idea that wealthy people "having more" somehow means that you have less—as if because Bill Gates has tens of billions and I don't have what I should have—I mean how does that even work? How can it be that Bill Gates has more because I have less? Bill Gates has affected me as he affected billions of people on this planet because I've used computers with operating systems that run MS-DOS. I've used Microsoft Office. You know he's changed the way people live in many ways, so I just reject this whole notion that we should somehow be envious and disdainful or accusatory toward the great entrepreneurs and successful business men and women.

I know it seems crazy to some people that some have so much and so many have so little but I will back that up by saying in United States . . . this is something that I think everyone should be aware of . . . in the United States the majority of the people who are living under the poverty line have telephones and televisions and air-conditioning and running water and microwaves and DVD players—the richest robber barons 150 years ago could never have dreamed of such wealth—so we are moving in the right direction. I'm not saying that there aren't people in this country who are hurting, but it's my own personal feeling that you don't raise up the wage earner by dragging down the wage payer. I've worked for a lot of wealthy individuals and I've never thought that sticking it to them would be a good thing. Maybe I needed to work harder, needed to work smarter, needed to work longer, and in many cases I did. So I think it really falls on individuals no matter where they're born or what circumstances, to try to raise themselves up because we live in a free enterprise system that gives you the opportunity if you're willing to pursue it.

WALL STREET 50
Cynthia DiBartolo   *Practice One: Self-Responsibility*

BE PART OF A POSITIVE CULTURE

Cynthia DiBartolo, ESQ. is the Founder and Chief Executive Officer of Tigress Financial Partners. She has thirty years of corporate and securities experience with Merrill Lynch, Smith Barney, Citigroup, and Bear Stearns. In 2009, in the prime of her career, she was diagnosed with Head and Neck Cancer. The extensive surgery left her with a reconstructed tongue, tracheostomy, and significant limitations in speaking. So she took leave and spent the next two years learning how to talk again. Her disability also sidelined her career on Wall Street; as a result, she decided to found Tigress Financial Partners, a woman owned and operated investment bank and broker dealer sensitive to people with disabilities and dedicated to the principles of diversity and inclusion.

Forty years ago, the whole purpose of Wall Street was to build up small business, provide capital to small business. Now think about that. Today, a small business can't find capital. But as a country, small business is what grows prosperity. They employ many, many people but small business is really without that support now. When Wall Street became a kind of conduit for bankers and businessmen's benefit as opposed to their clients' benefiting, that was the beginning of the fracture. Unfortunately, when you have a small number of high profile firms doing bad things, it changes the industry as a whole. It affects everybody. We all get lumped into it.

I had the chance to decide what I wanted to do after my surgery. I questioned what I saw then asking myself, "Do I want to go back to being part of a culture that I wasn't proud of?" Culture drives behavior. Behavior drives performance, and performance drives result. So the culture is key. For me, it was about how could I be a part of culture that espouses that and be aligned with my own values? By creating an entity around me that held a value set equal to mine was the answer.

Tigress is that. I was passionate about creating something I'd be proud of. It doesn't have to be wildly successful right away, but it has to be something that we love. And then the rest of it comes. I also wanted to provide an environment that was extremely positive. I think the best decisions that really happen embrace diversity, inclusion. And diversity, not just in gender, or in race, but diversity of thoughts and diversity of approaches. I have to say, my impetus was to ensure that morality shone.

PRACTICE TWO: Self/Other Empathy

Self-empathy is one of the most life-changing paradigms available to all of us today. Self-empathy is something we need to practice if we are going to be able to do any of these practices. Expressing internal empathy to oneself in the face of unpleasant feelings that we might have (when our needs are not being met) is key for us to navigate through. As I said earlier, all human beings are driven by need, and when we don't have our needs met, we experience unpleasant feelings. For example, if your need for respect, security, and purpose aren't being met, you might be feeling frustration, resentment, and/or anxiety.

When others don't meet our needs or when we ourselves don't meet our own needs, unpleasant feelings occur. To assist us in *not* resisting these feelings, we need to practice self-empathy. That allows us to process the feelings that show up and then we can begin to move *through them* and out of them instead of just pushing them down deep inside ourselves—which may rid us of feeling them in the moment, but I assure you, they won't go away until we do process through them.

Can you remember a time when you were expressing yourself and your unpleasant feelings to someone and perhaps the person responded, "Oh, that's nothing—you know what happened to me?!" Remember how that felt? It probably pulled you up short. It may have even stopped the flow of you feeling your own feelings. The other person may very well have meant well, but you walked away not feeling any better. In fact, maybe you even felt worse. We are all guilty of responding this way, especially if the person is someone close to us. We may even do this with ourselves—express our impatience internally. The gift of empathy is very rare—most folks haven't been taught how to "be with someone," without trying to "fix" them or their pain or challenge, nor have most people learned how to be with what is *hard to be with*.

Martin Buber, the Jewish philosopher, says the most precious gift we can give one another is our presence. And Marshall Rosenberg, creator of NonViolent Communication, says that "being present to another" is the first step in empathic connection. To make ourselves fully present to *what is alive in the other person now*, in this moment, means we can't think about what we're going to say next. In an interview he gave to Dian Killian, titled *Sympathy and Empathy*, he elaborates:

> Having strong feelings inside and being aware of them is sympathy, not empathy. So, if I say to someone who's hurting, "Gee whiz, I feel sad when you say that," that is an example of sympathy, not empathy. If you can remember when you had pain in your body and you got lost in a good book—that is empathy. The pain hadn't changed but you were no longer aware of it. You were sort of out visiting, "visiting" the book. With empathy, we're with the other person. Not that we feel their feelings, but that we are with *them* while they are feeling their feelings. If I take my mind away from the person for one second, I may notice I have strong feelings. If so, I don't try to push my feelings down. I say, "Go back to them." My own feelings tell me I'm not with the other person. I'm home again. "Go back." If my pain is too great, I can't empathize. So I can say, "I'm in so much pain right now hearing some things you've said—I'm not able to listen. Could we give me a few moments to deal with that so that I can go back to hearing you?" It's important not to mix up empathy and sympathy, because when someone is in pain and then I say, "Oh, I understand how you feel and I feel so sad about that," I take the flow away from them, and bring their attention over to me.

Most of the time when it comes to our feelings, we've not been taught to have understanding, never mind empathy for ourselves, so how could we have learned how to have it for others? We have grown up with a John Wayne mentality that says we need to get "over it" and move on with our lives. No doubt there is a time and a place when we might need to move forward, but I have found that the fastest way to move forward is when we allow ourselves to really feel our feelings and emotions all the way through to the other side by practicing empathy for ourselves when we have them.

When dealing with others, bringing your "presence" to them first and foremost will be a rare treat for them since very few people do this. Additionally, if you silently incorporate empathy while listening to them, you will see a remarkable and powerful shift in them.

You can even bring empathy into negotiation. Marie R. Miyashiro, author of *The Empathy Factor: Your Competitive Advantage for Personal, Team, and Business Success*, says:

> Contrary to popular opinion, negotiation doesn't have to involve sacrifice or compromise. In fact, the dynamic can be one of mutual giving and receiving, in which all parties in the negotiation end up feeling satisfied that their needs were valued and addressed. This may seem like a fairy-tale outcome, but the power of empathy makes it possible.
>
> Basically, empathy, or empathic connection, is the skill and practice of identifying and connecting to the needs, or deep values, of another individual, or a team or company as voiced by individuals. It's a skill for "getting" what matters to others so they feel seen and heard. I use needs and values interchangeably. Many people confuse needs with wishes, wants, or strategies, whereas needs go deeper and, as defined in this process, refer to *universal human needs,* such as trust, respect, autonomy, understanding, meaning, progress, collaboration, and contribution. We may *want* to double our market share, for example, but market share is not a need; it's a strategy to meet needs as growth, viability, contribution and progress.
>
> Needs-based negotiation is highly effective, and this skill or the lack of it can make or break a manager's career. In fact, William Ury, bestselling author of the business book *Getting to Yes* and co-founder of Harvard Law School's negotiation program, says, "NonViolent Communication is the most important process you'll ever learn."
>
> Why is connecting to needs so important? Because *conflict only occurs at the strategy level, not at the need level.* When we really get what matters to other people and they get what

matters to us, we've greatly increased the probability we will arrive at a strategy to satisfy multiple parties' needs.

Your awareness of yourself and others will exponentially increase when you practice empathy. Learning how to practice self-empathy and empathy for others is one of the most profound experiences I have ever had, and I find it is one of the most powerful gifts I can give to others, from clients to strangers not to mention to myself.

As Tenzin Gyatso, the 14th Dalai Lama, states:

> This, then, is my true religion, my simple faith. In this sense, there is no need for temple or church, for mosque or synagogue, no need for complicated philosophy, doctrine, or dogma. Our own heart, our own mind, is the temple. The doctrine is compassion. Love for others and respect for their rights and dignity, no matter who or what they are; ultimately these are all we need. So long as we practice these in our daily lives, then no matter if we are learned or unlearned, whether we believe in Buddha or God, or follow some other religion or none at all, as long as we have compassion for others and conduct ourselves with restraint out of a sense of responsibility, there is no doubt we will be happy.

Now we will hear *The Teachers of Consciousness* define or articulate what **Self/Other Empathy** means to them. Then stories from *The Wall Street 50* will provide an example of what **Self/Other Empathy** looks like in practice.

CONSCIOUSNESS TEACHER
Raphael Cushnir   *Practice Two: Self/Other Empathy*

BRINGING EMOTIONAL AWARENESS TO THE
BUSINESS AND POLITICAL SPHERE

Raphael Cushnir is an author, speaker, and a leading voice in the world of emotional connection and present moment awareness. He's a faculty member of the Esalen Institute, the Kripalu Center for Yoga and Health, and the Masters Program in Organizational Systems Renewal at Pinchot University.

Whenever we talk about things like Wall Street and consciousness, it is really easy to slip into some kind of us versus them. And I don't believe in my heart that there is an us and a them. I believe that as we start practicing awareness more and more, we come to see we really are all connected. And I don't mean that in a wishy washy, new age-y way, I mean literally all connected. And so I know that there are, let's say, honest disagreements people can have about the way forward or how to approach our challenges. But it seems to me that completely apart from that, we don't choose to see all we can, whatever side of an issue or debate we are on.

What if we could bring more emotional awareness into our political sphere? We would change everything so that if two leaders were sitting down and one said, "I want you to know that I just had a fight with my teenage son, so I am feeling a little bit on edge today." And the other person said, "Yes, I hear you. By the way, my wife has been sick and I am feeling a little bit fearful." If they talked like that before they ever talked about the treaty that they were to address, no doubt it would have a very different outcome. So similarly, if we all decided that before we got into the argument we would first address all the commonalities, all the things we share, all the things that are valid in our points of view, and put that in the middle of the table, then only when we finish that step and find ourselves on some kind of threshold, could we begin to try to hash out our differences, if we had that kind of goodwill, then I think something really different could happen.

And it doesn't matter whether it's the Occupy Movement vs. Wall Street or Republicans vs. Democrats. That choice is a choice that is a yes to life, it is a yes to inclusion, and it is a yes to all of our connectedness. I think anything that brings us closer to that would make a difference. What would make a huge difference? It isn't even what is so often spoken of in political circles of the United States, bi-partisanship, because usually that means compromising and starting from the perspective of compromise. Because I know that you want different things than I do, so let's try to see if we can meet in the middle. That's not what I am talking about. What I am talking about is even before we begin to negotiate let's look at everything that we share and then begin.

Yes, the common need, but also the common humanity. This may sound to business people like some kind of idealism or a pie in the sky way of looking at things, but I think there is nothing more courageous than to start from this place. Begin to start from a place of collaboration and choose to collaborate from the perspective of what we already share. It's hard because our brains (as a result of evolution) literally have a negative bias. They are looking for threats and so we start most of our conversations from a place of trying to protect what is ours from those threats. What changes that approach is consciousness and so bringing consciousness to places where we otherwise would be working from an evolutionary disadvantage is really the fundamental challenge right now for human beings at the beginning of the twenty-first century. What happens in the next 100 or 200 years will determine the fate of our species, ultimately, on the planet and life on the planet itself. So we have an invitation, we have a possibility to look at and to work with those challenges from a place of consciousness. And if we don't do that, if we continue looking from that place of threat, then all will definitely be lost.

EXAMPLES FROM THE WALL STREET 50

WALL STREET 50
Andrew Scheffer   *Practice Two: Self/Other Empathy*

WEALTH MANAGEMENT IS ABOUT LISTENING TO PEOPLE'S NEEDS

Andrew Scheffer is a meditation teacher and a Private Banker/Wealth Manager with an MBA from Wharton. He has trained extensively, as a monk and as a layman, for more than twenty years with Sayadaw U Pandita, the world's leading expert of Mindfulness meditation. Scheffer has worked as a Financial Advisor, Sales Manager, Investment Consultant, and Team Head at Morgan Stanley, UBS, ANZ, and Bank of

Singapore in New York and in Singapore. Scheffer is working to establish a Panditarama Meditation Center in the greater New York area.

I was asked during my Goldman interview: Why would somebody who is a Buddhist monk want to make rich people richer? And my response was, "It's really not about making rich people richer." I spent eight years in a monastery learning that I'm not the center of the universe. And instead—and as a result of that, I'm able to focus on other people a lot more. And private wealth management is about listening to other people's needs, understanding, and making recommendations based upon what is best for that individual, not what's going to drive you the most revenue. I've trained in that for eight years at this point, and that's why I wanted to do this training in the first place because I knew if I had not done this training, I would be like a number of other people. When faced with that dilemma and faced with bills to pay and things to buy, I might make a decision that would inevitably start a chain of similar decisions and cognitive dissonance that then would be my life. So I wanted to do this mindfulness practice to the point where I could return to a normal life with the strength and the clarity to make decisions that maybe when I was younger I wouldn't have been able to have made.

WALL STREET 50
Mori Goto   *Practice Two: Self/Other Empathy*
TREAT OTHERS THE WAY YOU TREAT YOURSELF

Morihiko Goto is the CEO of Goto Capital Markets, Inc. and has worked on Wall Street for over twenty-eight years. Goto is a Vestry member for St. Bartholomew's Episcopal Church, in New York City and volunteers often at its Crossroads Homeless Shelter, preparing dinner and staying overnight.

I always go back to—the Ten Commandments. It's not really spelled out, but they imply that you should treat others the way you want to be treated. Would you like to be cheated on? No. So don't cheat other people. And do you treat yourself well? Okay. Then you're going to treat others well too. And you know, that's the thing, the day-to-day thing. If you conduct inappropriate business, you are violating one of the Ten Commandments. If you're making inappropriate profit, you are cheating. I mean that's basically stealing. So you don't do that.

Matthew 7:7 says, "Ask and it will be given to you. Search and you will find. Knock and the door will be opened to you. For everyone who asks receives. And everyone who searches finds, and for everyone who knocks the door will be opened." As a Christian, my role model is Jesus Christ. He did not say that you shouldn't ask for money. He never said that. And actually, I have a mysterious reason to believe that He had enough money. And I feel it's okay to be abundant. Remember, He was able to share five fishes with 5,000 people and had some left over! It is okay to be abundant. I mean, there is no place in the New Testament that says "Be rich. Go out and make a lot of money on Wall Street and save people." It doesn't say that. But the bottom line is: My faith does not teach me that the Creator wants me to be poor.

What would a Father be like? I have a kid. Do I want my daughter to be poor and unsuccessful? Hell no. I want her to be and do very, very well. So, what do you think He wants for us? He wants us to do very, very well. And what makes you happy? Because I happen to be a father, every time she really nails something and then gets something done in an amazing fashion, I feel very good. So I have this take that our Creator would be very happy if we each reach full, maximum personal potential. That's something I believe in. So am I going to be a billionaire? Well, if I do become a billionaire, what am I going to do? I will gradually retire, but I'll make sure I have half a dozen successors who understand how to do things and how I would run things. I'll train them; that's my responsibility. Then I'll quit one day. And then after, if I save that money, and have a 10 percent return, that's $180 million every year. That's more than enough to pay rent. That's more than enough to pay the mortgage, no matter how big the house is, and I don't live in a big house. I ask myself now, "How can I put that money to work in a community?" How can I do that? I think about these things, and I really feel that if I really want to do it, then somebody created me this way in the first place.

WALL STREET 50
Carla Harris   *Practice Two: Self/Other Empathy*
IF YOU WANT TO GROW YOUR POWER, GIVE IT AWAY

Carla Harris is a Vice Chairman of Global Wealth Management, and Managing Director and Senior Client Advisor at Morgan Stanley. For more than a decade, Ms. Harris was a senior member of the equity syndicate desk and executed such transactions as initial public offerings for UPS, Martha Stewart Living Omnimedia, Ariba, Digitas, and others. Harris is also a speaker, gospel singer, and author. President Obama appointed Harris as the chairperson of the National Women's Business Council.

My spirituality is very important to me, and it does govern everything I do, so when I make a decision about anything that involves somebody else—it can be as small as spending a half an hour with a kid I don't know very well who is going to college but there is nobody else in his family who has ever gone to college—who I am spiritually will definitely drive that decision because I will say to myself, "Do I have another half an hour in my day?" If I do, I need to squeeze it in because this kid needs some help, and he is reaching out to me because I have the ability to help him, so I'm going to do that. And it could show up the same way in a boardroom where I think somebody is really not being a good guy. "Am I going to behave badly because he is behaving badly, or am I going to take the hard road to understand the power of who I am and what I bring to the table because of who I am?" I am going to drive the point home in a different way so I don't descend to his level of behavior. So my spirituality is very important; that's where I find my value. I believe also that whatever you are going to do, do it to the best of your ability no matter what. You may win; you may lose; you may succeed; you may fail. But at least you have the satisfaction of knowing you gave it your very best. So always do your best no matter what you are doing. Always distinguish yourself to other people because that's the whole point of having the gift, whether it's a tangible gift, physical gift, or financial gift. Part of my value is knowing that if you want to grow your power, give it away. Power grows if you give it away, you multiply it. Keeping it does absolutely nothing for you; it makes it finite, limited, and it will run down over time. But if you want to keep it growing and keep it manifested, give it away.

WALL STREET 50

Mayra Hernández   *Practice Two: Self/Other Empathy*

CORPORATE SOCIAL RESPONSIBILITY—A FAMILY LEGACY

Mayra Hernández is Head of Corporate Responsibility for Grupo Financiero Banorte, the third largest financial institution in Mexico. In 2009, she assumed the position of Corporate Director of Social Responsibility and Sustainability. Prior to her current position, she founded two companies: Entrelínea, a design firm in Mexico City, and IMPACTOMH, a company with a focus on branding and sustainability. She headed the design of the "Mujer Banorte" (Banorte Woman) product, the first of its kind in Mexico aimed at the economic empowerment of women.

My job is corporate social responsibility for a bank. So to me, it all has to do with profits. So the more profits the bank makes, the more I can help.

The bank is a fascinating story because my grandfather was a chairman of the board. My grandfather is a self-made man. When he was about five or seven years old, he was a shoe shiner. He had to shine shoes to help his family. He was an entrepreneur from the get-go because one day he was taking a break and a friend asked him if he could borrow his box and he said, "You know something, I'll rent it to you." And then he realized that he could make more money if he bought more boxes and had to work less.

Then one day with his father, they started a mill for corn. In Mexico, the staple is tortillas, which are made out of corn flour. So with this mill and an engineer refugee from Cuba, they industrialized the whole process of flour . . . to make corn flour or to make tortillas. So, that's how he became a very important and huge entrepreneur and took the business global.

Then when he was sixty-two, the banks were taken by the government, and then in '92, the banks were being privatized again. He bought the second to last bank in Mexico, which was very small, the regional bank in the north of Mexico where my grandfather is from. And nineteen years later, it became the third largest bank in Mexico and the only one that's still Mexican-owned. I asked him, "What inspired you to get a bank? I mean, you are already very successful with your business and a bank had nothing to do with what you knew." He said, "You know, I was successful worldwide, one of the top ten Mexican businessmen, but still, for a lot of people, I was like a tortillero, a man who makes tortillas. And I always wanted the prestige and I was lacking the prestige. So, I thought, well, with a bank this is a very good opportunity."

Something that I really admire is that he was very humble. Because he knew that he knew nothing about banks. But he had his vision and his ability to convince the set of investors to get the bank with him. And he was very conservative in his business . . . in his business dealings. So, the rest of the banks had to sell the Mexican banks to foreign operations either out of mismanagement or out of greed.

KIM: How did the social responsibility focus come about?

MAYRA: Since I was very young, he used to tell me that when he founded the food company with his father, they spent a lot of time figuring out how they could take care of the environment. Let's say, waste less energy. And then, recycle the water they would use. I'm talking back in the '50s and '60s, a very long time ago. That's one part, and then my great-grandmother was always very interested in their employees' wellbeing. And then a few years later, they realized that those things they were doing were actually helping the business. So I used to listen to those stories since I was a very young kid growing up. So maybe ten years ago, I started bringing about corporate social responsibility. So for me, it was something very easy to understand and then to start doing. So, I started doing it in my own world with my small graphic design business. But I also always had this desire or dream of being able to contribute to my grandfather's businesses. And contributing to the greater good through his business. So, the funny thing is that when I said to him, "You know, I want to do corporate responsibility for one of your companies," he said to me, "Mayra, I have no idea what you're talking about" because he never called it that. It was just a natural extension for him.

His legacy, especially for Mexico, is a very big one because I see him as a true example of how dreams can come true—if you really believe in them and are willing to work hard at them. He was also a visionary. I mean, he always had very big goals, he always had an eye on the future, although he was grounded in the present. His recent passing has allowed me to see just how much of an impact he has had on his fellow Mexicans. He really is an inspiration for other people to follow.

WALL STREET 50
Aaron Smyle   *Practice Two: Self/Other Empathy*

BEING A MEDIATOR

Aaron Smyle is the Founder of Smyle and Associates, LLC offering his expertise in the areas of taxation and compliance. He holds a B.S. in Finance, an M.B.A. in Professional Accounting, a Masters in Taxation, and is an Enrolled Agent (EA). He currently sits on the board of the American Institute of Wine and Food, a non-profit organization to advance the understanding, appreciation, and quality of what we eat and drink.

In fifth and sixth grade, I was a peer mediator. So if kids got in trouble, they would come to me in a structured environment, a table like this. One there, one here, and myself. And we would hammer out what was wrong, what caused the fight, what caused the argument. What could we do to fix it. So if we could come to some decision, some resolution to the problem, then they wouldn't get in trouble with the school.

I think that may have been a turning point for me as far as experiencing empathy—in order to do this work I had to put myself in the shoes of these two people that were arguing, I had to ask myself: What does this person want from the discussion? What does this other person want from the argument? What's the common ground? Doing this as a ten-year-old really encouraged my problem solving skills, in addition to helping me develop empathy. I can see today how that experience influenced me.

WALL STREET 50
Eric Carangelo   *Practice Two: Self/Other Empathy*
EMPATHY FOR THE LOSING TEAM

Eric Carangelo is a Vice President at State Street and has worked in finance for over twenty years. He specializes in large portfolio trades as well as interim asset management for institutions such as pensions, endowments, and foundations, and is active in several charities.

ERIC: You know, my team just won. We're going to the Super Bowl again (2012). I'll be honest with you though. I feel a little bit bad for that kicker because that guy's life is about to suck for quite some time.

KIM: Whose life? Who is this?

ERIC: The kicker for the Baltimore Ravens had a thirty-two-yard field goal. It's a chip shot in the NFL. It's like—he's supposed to make that shot. A chip shot is supposed to be a real easy one. I mean you make that maybe 98 times out of 100 and yet he missed it. He missed it to tie the game and send it into overtime. So you know what happens then, self-doubt creeps in and it's the downward spiral from there. You're just—oh, you're hating life. Your teammates hate you for denying them a chance to go to the Super Bowl. It's like, holy cow. As a Patriot fan, I'm glad to have won the game, but to win in that fashion is . . . oof, man. I feel for the dude. That's a tough way to lose.

KIM: Why do you feel you can even be empathetic to that? How can you even relate to what that guy is probably going through right now?

ERIC: Oh, I don't know. I mean, everybody has self-doubt. How will you perform under pressure, right? When the chips are down, are you going to rise to the challenge or are you going to fold like a house of cards? And I think especially people who played sports at some point in their lives, you always worry about that, right? I mean, even non-sporting type events you just want to know, "Geez, how am I going to respond when I'm under pressure." That guy obviously did not respond to the pressure. It's a tough situation to be in and, you know, if you've ever failed once in your life or even been in that situation, and it doesn't have to be for a trip to the Super Bowl, it could be simple and as small as an intramural basketball game or something like that. And if you fold under pressure—I remember being in a summer league basketball game twenty years ago and we were down one point and I went to the free throw line with, I don't know, five, six, seven seconds left to play in the game. And the first free throw that I shot, I bank it in. I was so nervous. Now, the shot was on line and it was straight but it was obviously long, I had too much adrenaline flowing. And it hit the backboard and went in. And it was such a pressure-packed situation that I started laughing because I couldn't believe the ball went in—even though I hit off the bank; I mean, you're not supposed to see that. My teammates were ripping me, you know. But then, after all the pressure was off and we had tied the game, the next free throw I took was a swish and we went on and won the game. I mean, it is laughable now. It could've easily gone the other way—that was a positive experience but it could have easily gone the other way.

WALL STREET 50

Misha Rubin (Lyuve)   *Practice Two: Self/Other Empathy*

HARVESTING POTENTIAL IN YOURSELF AND OTHERS

Misha Rubin (artistic pseudonym Misha Lyuve) is a partner at Ernst & Young and an artist. He released his first album *Are We Ready,* and is donating all profits from his album sales to Worldwide Orphans Foundation.

I just got back from Haiti and I visited a lot of orphanages, and one thing that you see around, when you look at the little kids, you think about the potential that's not being harvested. I think when you look at the kids, it's very obvious, yet when you look at adults, even adults for instance in New York, or adults who work on Wall Street, there is a particular potential that they have as well. They could be very successful at their careers and they could make a lot of money and be very effective with their jobs. But there could be a whole world of potential that's not being expressed and explored inside of them. So when I think about consciousness in relation to myself, I actually think about maximizing my potential as a human being and allowing others to maximize their potentials. And for me, it's really an exploration or a journey. I know there is a particular exploration inside that exploration, the moments when I get out of my routine self and see a bigger puzzle.

WALL STREET 50

Glen C. Dailey   *Practice Two: Self/Other Empathy*

HELP SOMEBODY ALONG THE WAY

Glen C. Dailey has spent over thirty years managing the prime brokerage business of several firms. Most recently, he was a Managing Director and founder of Jefferies Prime Brokerage which he joined in 2006 and led through 2014. He previously founded Bank of America Prime Brokerage in 1995 and led the business for eleven years; he was Head of Prime Brokerage at Furman Selz for the prior twelve years.

There are people who helped me when I was young, but you know, they didn't have to. And now I do that for people, I take meetings with people that most other people wouldn't, and you know, the funny thing is as I get older I hear people say, "Oh, you met with me back then and gave me some piece of advice and I took it to heart and I did this or that, and now I have a new life." There were people who were nice to me when I was a kid and gave me time they didn't necessarily have to, and so now I try to do that for people at this point in time. If I can help somebody along the way, I will. I'm grateful for what I've been given, all the opportunities, and I've had more success than I certainly ever dreamed of as a kid. I'm grateful for what I have but I don't forget that where I came from were humble beginnings.

WALL STREET 50
Don Seymour *Practice Two: Self/Other Empathy*

BE THE SOLUTION

Don Seymour, the Founder of DMS Offshore Investment Services Ltd., is directly responsible for the creation of the regulatory framework of the Investment Services Division of the Cayman Islands Monetary Authority (CIMA). In 2007, he created "The Joanna Clarke Excellence in Education Award" to honor local educator Ms. Joanna Clarke—a teacher who made a critical difference in his life—to encourage and recognize the efforts of other people and organizations that contribute to education in the Cayman Islands.

As you may know today, the Cayman Islands are the dominant leader in hedge funds. With 200-plus possible hedge fund jurisdictions in the world, more than 80 percent of the world's hedge funds are domiciled in the Cayman Islands. It is an extraordinary accomplishment. Just how did that happen and why did Cayman excel? Ralph Waldo Emerson said, "If you develop a better mouse trap, the world will beat a path to your door." In that spirit, I believe that we understood what the market wanted and exceeded that need.

But with any success comes some failure. While we were attracting so many excellent funds, we were also attracting some bad funds. Those were my responsibility as well. In 1997, I was hired as the chief regulator of hedge funds and was directly responsible for the creation of the regulatory framework for hedge funds in the Cayman Islands. I developed the policies and procedures, hired the staff, and set the strategic direction. I was responsible for the entire spectrum of regulatory activities: authorization, supervision, and enforcement. In 1998, there was a global financial crisis precipitated by the default of Russian government debt. Many hedge funds blew up in response and the entire industry was stressed. When hedge funds such as Long-Term Capital collapsed I was at the helm working with them, U.S. Federal Reserve, and others to find solutions to maximize investor value.

Back then, being a fund director was simply a sinecure and directors didn't take their roles in safeguarding investor interests seriously. I would repeatedly implore them to do a better job safeguarding the interests of their investors. Investors would continuously make complaints to me at CIMA about the poor performance of directors. What we found was unfortunate. In many instances I couldn't even contact the directors, much less work with them to find a solution. There was an appalling lack of professionalism.

Meanwhile, investors would call me constantly and I would listen to the often intense, personal stories of these people who had invested in these funds—funds that didn't do what they were supposed to do. People were being hurt—hard working people who earned that money and trusted it to these fraudulent funds. They trusted, and ultimately, they were devastated. I listened to story after story and I was moved. For me, it became personal. We can never forget that real life human tragedy is a part of these stories. And I decided, "This just has to stop."

Regulatory intervention is always the last resort but it was time to resort to that in order to redress investor complaints. As the chief regulator, I took enforcement actions against those bad funds, and in taking those actions, I observed that the common thread throughout many of the failures was really a lack of good fund governance.

I thought this would be an easy fix, but surprisingly, few in the industry wanted to hear this. I was told it wasn't necessary and got little support. So I said, "I will do it myself." In 2000, I resigned from CIMA—leaving a prestigious, high paying position at the apex of the financial industry—with the notion that I was going to take action not just to change governance but to transform it for hedge funds. I set up shop at a desk in the back of a shoe store in a strip mall. My mission? Build a professional fund governance firm that investors would love.

I never imagined that action would lead me to where I am today, and to the level of success that DMS has achieved. At the time, industry observers thought it was positively crazy and my former boss—who is also one of the most brilliant people I've ever met—told me that it was "the worst idea he had ever heard."

Today, DMS is the worldwide leader in fund governance—more than 200 people strong. We've revolutionized the entire industry and now fund governance is a very serious issue—not just for us, but for our investors.

We have been at the front lines of the fund governance debate. We set out on this path to find a solution to a problem—to do the right thing. And in the course of doing so, we not only created positive change for the industry, we found financial success. Earlier I quoted Ralph Waldo Emerson and here's more wisdom from him—wisdom that I think rings true in our industry and certainly within DMS: "We are rich only through what we give."

PRACTICE THREE: Emotional Non-Resistance

Emotional non-resistance means to be able to "be with" any and all of our emotions, including the ones that are unpleasant to be with, like anger, grief, and shame. We don't have to like them or enjoy them. I'm simply suggesting that we do not deny them. Learning how to feel all of your feelings so you are not ruled by them is what this technique is about. Instead of labeling your feelings good or bad, begin by welcoming them—knowing that to do so facilitates your release from them. We've been taught that feelings mean something, when actually they don't mean anything. So when the unpleasant emotions occur and we make ourselves wrong for having and experiencing them—we get caught and stuck in the swamp-of-self-blame.

Raphael Cushnir's work around emotional connection and present moment awareness transformed my life. I highly recommend his book, *The One Thing Holding You Back: Unleashing the Power of Emotional Connection*, which goes into more detail on the subject than I will provide here. Raphael taught me how to be a *feeler of my feelings*. He taught me that denying my emotions kept me from freedom.

What happens with emotions when they aren't felt is that they burrow deep into our psyche. And guess when they burst out? When we are triggered by something that "looks like," "sounds like," "feels like" an experience from our past.

Learning how to let our feelings be felt and allowing them to wash over and pass through us so we can be free of them can be daunting at first, but with practice, it can be achieved. And what happens on the other side? Freedom. Freedom from the repetition of a feeling repeating itself countless times because the "emotion" is just in need of completing its cycle of being felt.

Five of the so called deadly sins are just feelings (wrath, sloth, pride, lust, envy). And guess what? We have no control over them. Feelings just happen—they come and go like the wind. Human beings don't have any control over them at all. Most of us have been taught by religion, culture, society, and family that to experience our emotions, especially the ones that are unpleasant or unexpected, means we should be ashamed of ourselves and the feelings we have. It's imperative we untangle ourselves from this belief.

To allow ourselves to feel our feelings, we first really need to understand that we don't have the ability to control them. I repeat: no control over *feeling them*, but let me be very clear about what we do have control over: what we *do with them*. We will get to that in a moment, but for now, we need to understand allowing ourselves to be a feeler of our feelings is the beginning of emotional non-resistance and a critical part of expanding our consciousness.

The next step is understanding that feelings arise from our needs being met or not met; depending on whether or not they are met determines whether we experience pleasant or unpleasant feelings.

So how does one feel the feelings that are challenging to feel? One baby step at a time. First, recognize what is happening in your body. It may take you a while to recognize what is happening because we have conditioned ourselves not to be very connected to our body. Say to yourself, "I'm experiencing _____ (a particular sensation or feeling)." It might show up in your chest, or stomach, or heart, or head, or legs, etc. Instead of pushing it away, allow it to continue and, if possible, turn the volume up on it, while neutrally observing it. The experience of it may last for only a few seconds or a few minutes; just stay there as long as you are able to, feeling the feeling and letting the sensation be. What you will discover is that as you stay with it, it will begin to change. It may move to another part of your body, or it may change in intensity. The fact of the matter is that it will move. What happens over time is that allowing feelings to be felt releases them. What makes feelings move or change? Only one thing: Feeling them.

In the beginning, this process can be very challenging, especially with very intense emotions that we haven't allowed ourselves to process before, so it is best to proceed slowly. In the midst of this process, there are two parts of our brain wrestling. The limbic area is asking us to "feel this," whatever "this" is, and the reptilian area is demanding that we stop because it perceives these unpleasant feelings as a mortal threat.

We aren't always going to be in a place where we can do this, so we should put the sensations/emotions/feelings up on the "shelf" to revisit them when we are able to have the privacy and the space to do so. Raphael says that when we "resist" emotions, they don't dissipate; they actually get stuck or lodged within our body. The unexpected truth is that our resistance to them is the reason they persist. The key is to feel them, or as he says, "surf" them. When we allow them to wash over us and move through us, they are finally felt, and like a wave that breaks on the shore, they dissipate. Feeling them might be difficult, but freedom awaits us on the other side.

Now we will hear *The Teachers of Consciousness* define or articulate what **Emotional Non-Resistance** means to them. Then stories from *The Wall Street 50* will provide an example of what **Emotional Non-Resistance** looks like in practice.

CONSCIOUSNESS TEACHER

Raphael Cushnir   *Practice Three: Emotional Non-Resistance*

Raphael Cushnir is an author, speaker, and a leading voice in the world of emotional connection and present moment awareness. He's a faculty member of the Esalen Institute, the Kripalu Center for Yoga and Health, and the Master's Program in Organizational Systems Renewal at Pinchot University.

Consciousness has always been *in* me. And I have been never separate from consciousness and that's true for every human being . . . but I wasn't living in alignment with it. I had an inner drive toward it even as a very young child, and as a teenager, I had a kind of mystical bent. But here is the thing: I was such a high achieving kid and had it so easy in that way. I really thought the world was my oyster and I could make it however I wanted to make it. And I had so much hubris about that. . . . I wanted to be an artist or filmmaker, which is one of the hardest things to do and actually make a living at. But in my teen years, as I saw myself evolving toward that career, I thought money was never even going to be an object for me in my life—that I was going be so successful, as I had been in my early days, that money would just be granted to me as a result of how fabulous I was and what I made and brought to the world.

So I was blinded to a certain aspect of consciousness and really believed somehow in my own story about myself (and the story that had been given to me because I was told at an early age I could do whatever I wanted to do as long as I put my mind to it). I didn't see the shadow side of that story, I only thought, "Cool, maybe that's why I don't have to do homework like other kids. Maybe that's why I can ace all of the school stuff, because I am so awesome," and so the gift of my abilities also came with a certain kind of willful blindness.

And the spear in the heart that you are describing was definitely what made the fullest transition because my personal and professional life fell apart. And it fell apart in such a way that it became a problem I couldn't solve. That was the first time that all of my so called "awesomeness" could not find a way out, could not fix the situation. So I was laid low, so to speak. Sometimes if your heart is not shattered, then the light can't get in. And for me, it was that great shattering and humbling that allowed me to take my own exploration to a deeper level—that really led to a healing and a transformation that became essentially what you could call the second part of my life.

I came to the recognition that the only thing I could hold on to was that there was nothing to hold on to. I had a mentor at the time who said, "I have an idea of what you could do with all this pain that you are experiencing." And I said "What?" And he told me very placidly, "How about nothing? How about doing nothing at all to try to change the way you feel?" Which had first sounded like torture, but it was also better than what most people were telling me, which was, "It's good to keep busy." Since I knew that distraction wasn't the road for me, I just went with his invitation and so I wasn't holding on to anything. I just allowed myself to let all of this pain arise, come into my awareness, and then I would move through it and let it depart until the next wave came. So it was a practice of not attaching, not holding on to anything, not interfering with what was arising. And then a little bit later, I said to this mentor, "You know, right now it feels like I am completely adrift; I don't belong anywhere in the world; there is nobody who really is connected to me in such a way that I know I need it or depend upon it. It seems like on the one end, I could be anything or nothing, and so I feel like I am just sort of spinning in the wind." Surprisingly, he said to me, "Aha, this is really good, this is excellent." It's so rare in people's lives that they have an opportunity not to be so enmeshed in relationships and situations such that they can come to a deeper understanding of who they really are . . . and what is important to them? What is meant to come through them? So again, his invitation to me was to look closely but gently; instead of *looking to control, look to discover*. And so without holding on to the idea of, "I am supposed to be this way or that way," or "My life should be this way or that way," I was able to open up to new possibilities that so intuitively were truer to me than I would have been able to get to without that kind of conscious letting go.

EXAMPLES FROM THE WALL STREET 50

WALL STREET 50

Jason Apollo Voss   *Practice Three: Emotional Non-Resistance*

TUNE IN TO THE TEMPERATURE

Jason Apollo Voss is Content Director at CFA Institute and author of *The Intuitive Investor*. He previously retired at age thirty-five after being co-Portfolio Manager of the Davis Appreciation & Income Fund, where he bested the NASDAQ, S&P 500, and DJIA by staggering percentages. He has studied the ancient martial art of ninjutsu and Eastern healing techniques. Voss also teaches meditation.

I begin every single one of my speeches with, "Tune in to the temperature of the room. Just spend thirty seconds tuning in to the temperature of the room. Tune in to the temperature . . . the feeling of the temperature of the room." Now, if I ask an audience, "How many of you, by a show of hands, gave it a number? Seventy-three degrees. How many of you did that?" Usually, most of the hands go up. Most people have given it a temperature; they've given it a number, right? If they haven't done that, and this is the second set of hands, "How many of you thought, well, it's a little chilly in here. I wish I brought a sweater," or "It's a little hot in here, I should . . . you know, I wish I brought another layer so I could take it off, that kind of a thing." Usually, the remainder of hands go up. Very rarely does someone say, "I just felt the temperature."

People have argued with me and said, "Well, you said to feel the . . . or to tune in to the temperature." And I say "No. I said tune in to the feeling . . . not the temperature of the room." And they'll say . . . "You told me to give it a temperature." "No, I did not. I said feel into it." For many people, every single decision up until that exercise has been about developing a preference around that. Most people have preference around everything that happens in their lives. Whether it's the color of the room that they're in or the attractiveness of the man or woman they're sitting across from . . . there's preference of absolutely everything processed, and as soon as you're in preference, you know, you're not really processing the truth of any situation.

You're not present. You can't be present because you're in the middle of all those . . . prejudices. And by the way, I make a distinction in my book between prejudice and judgment. And I think a lot of the spiritual teachings, in my own opinion, have been mis-taught. They'll say, "Don't judge." Well, that's not true. Every decision you make, there's a judgment and assessment involved. I think what they're admonishing is the pre-judging, right? You want to assess the truth of a situation and you want to respond to it, if you choose to respond to it, with your free will.

WALL STREET 50

Arnaud Poissonnier   *Practice Three: Emotional Non-Resistance*

EXPERIENCING POVERTY

Arnaud Poissonnier is the founder and CEO of Babyloan. He was, as he says, comfortably settled as a banker when during his visit to Tajikistan

with the NGO ACTED, he discovered microcredit and how those who lived there faced bank exclusion. He was inspired by what he calls "useful finance" and decided to launch Babyloan after this experience. He says he will never forget the first microfinance beneficiary he met—Satarova, a woman living in Dushambe, who was extremely proud of showing him she was able to pull through without being assisted by charity.

I fell in love with poor people and microcredit and what can be done for people, during the time I was traveling and when I chose to live in the slums. The best way I think to motivate people to help others is not to make them read books or talk at them and tell them what they *should* do; instead if they experienced the slums in South America, Brazil, or even the Philippines that would have more of an impact. If you are willing to sleep a few nights in the slum, your life will not be the same afterward. You will discover positive human energy exists in the slums. When you meet people in slums, they don't seem to be less happy than you and me; it is just another way of living, there is huge solidarity in the slums. They have very interesting ways of living. They are not less rich in terms of quality of life even though they have nothing in terms of material goods. I think the best way to be conscious about one's own life is to really experience a poor area or a slum and live among those who live there. I am very happy that the new pope, Francis, has worked many years in the slums. Wealth is not where we think it is, actually. I think human wealth can be found much more in the slums than on the fancy side of any town.

WALL STREET 50

Brad Katsuyama *Practice Three: Emotional Non-Resistance*

CREATE A LEVEL OF AWARENESS ABOUT YOUR JOB

Brad Katsuyama is the President, CEO, and Co-Founder of IEX Group. Katsuyama and his team are also the focus of *Flash Boys*, a book by Michael Lewis about high frequency trading (HFT) in financial markets. After Katsuyama discovered HFT's unfair trading practices, he decided to challenge fundamentally the business of the stock market, leaving RBC in 2012 to start-up a fair and transparent stock exchange. He also has created www.IamAnInvestor.org, which educates and informs us on how each of us is an investor and how to reclaim our rights as one.

There's a part that's referenced in the book *Flash Boys* where a small group of us sat there in a room before we decided to take a chance and start IEX. And we said, "Okay. What percentage of chance do you think that this particular idea is actually going to work?" The highest anyone said was "25 percent," and everyone else was lower, so I said, "Hey, good. So we are all on the same page." The point of that exercise was to make sure no one had this preconceived notion that we had an 80 percent chance of succeeding on that one idea. We all had a very good feeling that we would figure it out, so we learned quickly that we were all making a bet on each other and not a single idea. So that conversation actually gave me more confidence that IEX would be successful because I felt like everyone was going in with eyes wide open.

One of the greatest things that came out of this process of working with Michael Lewis was that he forced me to answer questions I had never considered about my role in the world and why I did certain things, and it just made me very introspective because I think over the last number of years, it's kind of like you wake up and put one foot in front of the other and you just keep going. But I think awareness is so important, and the best way to get that awareness is to ask yourself some really high-level questions: "What is my job? What is its function? How does that fit in with the economy? How can this job be done better? Who is the best person at this job? What do they do that is different?" Those kinds of questions, I think, are really important. And then asking those same questions to other people who do the job as well. I got a ton of ideas out of Steve Jobs's biography and related them to IEX, not directly but just in terms of understanding what problems he was trying to solve and how they related to the problem I was trying to solve. I'm sure a bazillion people have read that and said the same thing, but just trying to understand and relate to other people and then just try to relate that back to what you're doing is helpful. There has to be this level of awareness of what it is that you're trying to accomplish in your job.

PRACTICE FOUR: The Internal and External Journey

Becoming more awake and more conscious usually occurs after going on a journey of sorts. Everyone experiences his or her journey differently. Where our journey takes us is usually a combination of an internal and external adventure. It can be a metaphoric knock on the door that we have heard for many years about starting our own business or leaving a dead-end job or moving to Hawaii, and have refused to listen to. Sometimes, it may arrive without an option to refuse such as a health crisis or an unexpected severing of a job or a relationship. Some sort of unexpected or challenging event occurs and we are forced to begin a new path. The mythologist, professor and author Joseph Campbell called this the "Hero's Journey," and in his 1949 book *The Hero with a Thousand Faces*, he puts forth his theory that all the heroes and gods found in the world's mythologies and religions share the same fundamental structure or pattern, so even though their stories look and sound unique, the underlying structure beneath each of them is the same. These stories, he tells us, are there to inspire and encourage each of us to embrace our own heroic quest. George Lucas was actually inspired to create *Star Wars* from this very book.

I first discovered Joseph Campbell when I saw him interviewed by Bill Moyers in 1988 in what is now known as the groundbreaking and timeless conversation called *The Power of Myth*. In a six-hour conversation Campbell and Moyers explored the classic and enduring hero patterns that exist in literature, religion, movies, and real life. It remains one of the most popular TV series in the history of public television.

In this interview, Campbell encouraged us to view our life as a heroic journey and to discover what really makes us come alive and feel engaged. You can find samples of the program on BillMoyers.com or buy the complete DVD interview online. For a condensed overview of Joseph Campbell and his theory, I highly recommend Patrick Takaya Solomon's *Finding Joe*, available at FindingJoeTheMovie.com.

These three acts mark the stages of a hero's journey:

- Act I: Separation/Departure: The Call to Adventure
- Act IIA: Descent: The Road of Trials and Temptations
- IIB: Initiation: Achieving the Gift or Boon
- Act III: Return: The Road Back

Act I: The **Separation/Departure** is when we hear the call and either say no or go forth; sometimes, it is something we have heard for years, that we have not wanted to admit even to ourselves that we feel called to do, and sometimes, it's something we wish we could refuse but seem unable to.

Act IIA: The **Descent** is where we find ourselves facing dragons; our fears will really be potent here. This part of the journey tests our mettle. We will find temptation here as well; usually, the ultimate descent is a death of some sort, sometimes literally, sometimes to a belief or a way of living. It's where we find ourselves being separated from something we thought we could never release.

Act IIB: The **Initiation** is where we have our own sort of resurrection. We find ourselves reborn after our "death," and we find we have a different relationship with all things. This is the boon or gift. While it's tempting to stay in this paradise, we know we have the responsibility to bring this gift and our wisdom back to the people. Sometimes, we resist bringing our gift to the world because we know it might not be appreciated. But back we know we must go regardless.

Act III: The **Return** happens when we return to our tribe or home and bring the wisdom to those who have yet to begin their journeys.

Some classic examples of this journey that Campbell and other scholars cite are the stories of Osiris, Prometheus, the Buddha, Moses, Muhammad, and the Christ. Not to mention modern day interpretations such as: Harry Potter, Superman, Luke Skywalker, King Arthur, Batman, or Thomas Anderson aka Neo.

The most critical insight that Campbell wants us to absorb and awake to is that *each of us* is the Hero of our own life. Now you may say, "No way, not me!" But I assure you it's true. You are the Hero of your own story. I realize you may not feel like one, but underneath your Clark Kent or Diana Prince exterior lies your own Superman or Wonder Woman just waiting to be birthed, just waiting to be called forth. We tend to focus so much on the pivotal moment of a Heroic journey because it is the exciting part, yet we need to realize that there are many moments that precede that one key action.

I doubt that on December 1st, 1955 at 6 p.m., after a long day of work, Rosa Parks, who was forty-four years old at the time, felt much like a hero when she was arrested after refusing to move on that downtown Montgomery bus. Yet every day prior that she lived and endured segregation brought her to that one pivotal moment where she stood up for herself.

No matter what is happening in your life in this moment—you have a choice to stick with the status quo or be brave enough to be afraid and follow your own heart.

The chrysalis is where the caterpillar turns into the butterfly, and it's often forgotten as soon as the butterfly comes out, but it's in there, in that darkness, where all the work is done. Realize even though it may appear to be quiet within you, there may be much happening below the surface. I would argue that even your choice to read this book could be an indication that your own Hero may very well be ready and raring to come forth. You might be ready for your own transformation. Campbell says, "We must be willing to let go of the life we planned so as to have the life that is waiting for us. The old skin has to be shed before the new one can come." Is it time for you to leave your chrysalis behind?

Anything is one of a million paths. Therefore, you must always keep in mind that a path is only a path; if you feel you should not follow it, you must not stay with it under any conditions. To have such clarity you must lead a disciplined life. Only then will you know that any path is only a path, and there is no affront to oneself or to others in dropping it if that is what your heart tells you to do. But your decision to keep on the path or to leave it must be free of fear or ambition. I warn you. Look at every path closely and deliberately. Try it as many times as you think necessary.

This question is one that only a very old man asks: Does this path have a heart? All paths are the same: they lead nowhere. They are paths going through the bush, or into the bush. In my own life, I could say I have traversed long, long paths, but I am not anywhere. Does this path have a heart? If it does, the path is good; if it doesn't, it is of no use. Both paths lead nowhere; but one has a heart, the other doesn't. One makes for a joyful journey; as long as you follow it, you are one with it. The other will make you curse your life. One makes you strong; the other weakens you.

Before you embark on any path, ask the question: Does this path have a heart? If the answer is no, you will know it, and then you must choose another path. The trouble is nobody asks the question, and when a man finally realizes that he has taken a path without a heart, the path is ready to kill him. At that point, very few men can stop to deliberate, and leave the path. A path without a heart is never enjoyable. You have to work hard even to take it. On the other hand, a path with heart is easy; it does not make you work at liking it."

—Carlos Castaneda, *The Teachings of Don Juan:*
A Yaqui Way of Knowledge

Opposite is a map that depicts in more detail the various stages of the hero's journey. I often find myself looking at this map to determine where I am so that I may better navigate the terrain. Ask yourself, where are you on this journey right now?

This internal or external journey is what anyone who is seeking more consciousness will have to endure. If we want to transform, then we will indeed need to embark on our own eventually.

Now we will hear *The Teachers of Consciousness* define or articulate what the **Internal or External Journey** means to them. Then stories from *The Wall Street 50* will provide an example of what **Internal or External Journey** looks like in practice.

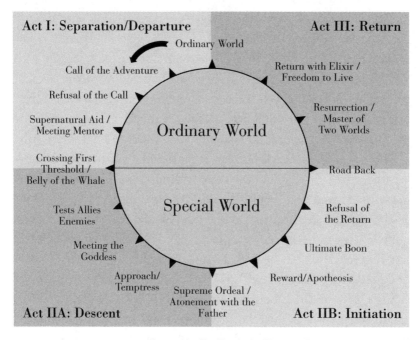

Inspired by *The Hero with a Thousand Faces* by Joseph Campbell
Designed by © Alina Wilczynski of www.moonkissedmedia.com

CONSCIOUSNESS TEACHER

Alan Cohen *Practice Four: The Internal and External Journey*

HERO'S JOURNEY

Alan Cohen, MA, is an author, speaker, and leader in the personal growth movement encouraging outer change through inner awakening, and is a featured presenter in the documentary *Finding Joe,* which celebrates the teachings of visionary mythologist Joseph Campbell.

KIM: Speak about Campbell's Hero's Journey Model—how do you view that map?

ALAN: Well, it's a great map. I'll boil it down to six elements. Most people can identify with the fact that their current life has been shaken up and that they're reaching for more, and that they have allies and/or have enemies, people who are trying to squash them. They do have to confront their inner dragons and something does have to die in order to live and they will have a break soon. There is a moment where you're going into the cave and you have to face Darth Vader and you get out your light saber and you go for it. And then, of course, if you emerge, you come back higher, better, and clearer, and you do have a gift to bring back to the community. This is the basic model. Most people can understand where they are on it. Usually by the time they begin coaching, they've started the journey or they've at least had the irritation and the sense of limitation that the old life is not working and they want more. So people on the journey are hungry because they've been catapulted into an adventure that they don't quite understand. This model, people like it, because they don't feel like they're weird or something's wrong with them or they're doomed or cursed. They feel, "Okay. This is a natural part of the journey. I'm facing Darth Vader, but okay, it's part of the game. I'll play it."

In college, I was a psychology student and I didn't . . . frankly, I didn't learn that much in psychology. I think my professors needed a psychologist more than they were psychologists. I was living a very intellectual life and I had learned to play the academic game. But I can't say I was really happy or had a direction. When I went to graduate school, I was invited to participate in what they called in those days, "A Human Relations Laboratory," where they basically took 100–200 college students away to a camp for a week and then . . . we went off to caverns and had a facilitator and talked about what was really going on in our lives. I realized in that weekend that I was living a very shallow life. I was playing games. I was into image management and my communication and my relationships did not have a lot of substance, which is why I still felt hungry. I realized in that moment, in that weekend, that most people are living in a fairly shallow level existence. And even if they're successful in the outer world, they may be aching, hungry, or weeping in their inner world.

So I shifted my intention from looking cool and being acknowledged to living in a way that would satisfy me inside as well as out. And that has been the story of my life for the past forty years. And it's only going deeper. You know, I only recognized more and more that it's how we're feeling about our life and how we're experiencing pleasure and joy or not that makes a difference in all our world. It's not what it looks like, it's what it is. And so that has been my experience.

CONSCIOUSNESS TEACHER

Rasanath Das   *Practice Four: The Internal and External Journey*

FROM WALL STREET TO MONASTERY

Rasanath Das is a monk and former management consultant and investment banker. His TEDx talk describes his incredible journey—from being what he describes as an "external achievement machine" to one who is rich in spiritual introspection, integrity, and true connectivity.

I had a calling to give myself a life where I could do the inner-work 24/7. I had seen how the monks at the Bhakti Center that live in New York City were living and it was not a reclusive life. It was a life being lived in the midst of action and in the midst of chaos and yet they were living a life of integrity and honesty.

My calling came in April 2006, right about the time I had my internship offer. So, life is very interesting because, usually, when you follow a calling you also have things you voluntarily have to shed. One of the challenges for me was a fourteen-year dream starting to become fulfilled. I wanted to be on Wall Street since I was in ninth grade, since 1992. That was when Rupert Murdoch made his big entry into India with television. That was the first time I saw the movie *Wall Street*, which had an immediate impact. I wanted to be on The Street. I wanted to own a yellow convertible and a blue motorboat. I knew the specific colors. I had ambitions and dreams. Then fast forward to 2006—fourteen years later.

Of course, a lot of things happened in between in terms of my really understanding life and then experiencing a spiritual calling in 1997–1998, which I then pursued. At eighteen, my focus of the world was existential in nature. First of all college. I went to IIT Mumbai. It's like MIT in the USA. It has a 1 percent acceptance rate. So, getting in there, well, life was good at that point, but something deep inside told me I was going to lose all of this at some point and that it would be taken away—everything that I loved and had worked for. So, the question in my mind was "What's the purpose then? Why am I doing what I am doing if everything is going to be taken away?" That question started an inner-spiritual journey, which I pursued. What is interesting is that your ambitions live with your spiritual pursuits, and it is only at a certain time do the two really start to converge. If you want to spot the point of convergence, you have to cross a point where they are actually diverging. So, I usually tell people that when you face a paradox that means your paradigm is not big enough to accommodate those mutually contradictory things because, if both are true, then the only way they will live together is if your paradigm expands to accommodate them. That's a way to create harmony.

So, for me, that was a very crucial point. I found this calling and the calling was very honest, sincere, and I would say also it was not just idealistic, it was actually a calling. It was not just dramatic, it was deep. It was something I didn't really share with too many people, but it was there.

At the same time, I was really attached to this dream of being on Wall Street, and I couldn't just really shut that side of me down and say this is garbage. It was real. It was not just about making money because that was there, but I actually loved making a difference to companies. I also had a head for strategy; I did consulting for four-and-a-half years before that at Deloitte. I loved strategy, and I had it in me to identify issues and come out with practical solutions, but I wanted to do it on Wall Street through the medium of finance. So, that was real.

For me, how to bring the two together was a very big challenge and what I had to encounter was what else came along with it—which was image, power, money, prestige. And those were big too. I had to see them very clearly and imagine my life without these. In my dreams, I started playing out things, and with my family—which was a big thing. So, to actually come to a monastery and live as a full-time monk, well, what would my family members think? My mother, whom I really adore, the amazing childhood that she gave us, both my parents did, but I am specifically attached to my mother, her dreams would be shattered. Actually, I saw the dreams of my mother dying and all these fears actually played out. So what I decided to do was live in a monastery so I could get the inside experience of what it was like. Making the transition, I wasn't even sure whether I would be able to transition, but what I had really wanted to do was be sincere about the fact that I wanted this life, and I am going to go as close as possible to it, even with the conditionings that I have.

Earlier in my life when I was in India pursuing my spiritual calling, I frequently used to visit a monastery, practically every week. I lived in the monastery after my exams. I used to spend four or five days there just spending time with the monks, just studying with them, but I thought this would be more intense.

KIM: Did your family know at the time?

RASANATH: No. [laughter] I should tell you, it was so funny, I had made a resolve in my life that whatever I would do, I would actually tell my parents everything; even if it meant that we'd disagree, they'd know exactly what I was doing. It was my way of actually showing respect for what they had given me. I would never do anything hidden but, then, it is amazing how life gets you. I had to come to spiritual life in order actually to hide things. One thing I knew was if I told them I was going to a monastery, they would make me feel guilty about doing it. But I really wanted to pursue it. I wanted to see it for what it was. It was one of those things where . . . one of those many gray areas in life where I finally said, "For a higher cause, I think I have to keep this from them and do this."

When I graduated from school, I finally told them. By that time, this inner world had watered down that concern in my life so I could speak the truth then. And they were seeing the changes in me. So when I came to the U.S., right after professional school, I had a job offer to work for Delloite Consulting in New York City. As I was coming here, the monks there said it would be nice for me to connect with a monastery here, so I could still come to a monastery and stay on this plane. When I used to come back to New York over the weekends, I spent some time in the monastery doing simple things: washing pots, cleaning the floor, along with my meditation. Also, gradually, contributing financially to the monastery. When I lived here I paid all the rent. In many ways, the *Bhagavad Gita*, which is the text I really pursue, talks about karma yoga, which means you work, you have an intrigue, you have an aptitude, but then how do you engage that aptitude in a way that gradually uncovers the evil structure? That's the nature of karma yoga, so money, position, whatever comes, use it for a good cause. I once asked my teacher, "How much should we give?" and he told me, "Give 'til it hurts a little." So it was fascinating, and I only understood that when I was working in the banking world, because you have to give the money you earn, and then, you go to a point where it's like, "What's the right amount to give?" That is when you are starting to get attached. These are things I learned when I was living here and working on Wall Street.

KIM: How long did that go on for?

RASANATH: Two years.

KIM: That's a long time. Did your colleagues at work know?

RASANATH: Yes, I made it very open. I moved in here . . . it was April 2007. I was with Bank of America at that time. When I did my internship with Bank of America, it was 2006. I went to business school after Delloite, so this was coming out of business school. Summer of 2006 was when I interned with Bank of America. Then I came out with a full-time offer. In 2007, I joined them full-time. So, in 2006, I lived here during my internship and worked at banking so that was ten weeks. That gave me the confidence that it could be done. When I joined full-time, I said I am just moving in here.

KIM: How did your colleagues, in the beginning, respond?

RASANATH: People don't know what to say. [laughter] I just told them that this is what I am doing. If people didn't know, I would say, "Well, I live in a monastery." I said that I lived in a monastery and they would ask, "What does that mean?" I would say, "Simple things, two hours of meditation every day." That was shocking because in the banking world you work . . . I did work weekends when I was there for two years. You know, I used to average about ninety hours a week, eighty to ninety-five. So, it was a commitment I made never to give up my meditation practices no matter what, even if it meant I'd survive with less sleep—and I don't drink coffee; I don't drink tea; no Red Bull; complete vegetarian. So it was shocking . . . different responses when you are sitting at a party you get made fun of. "Oh, we are sitting here with a Buddhist monk in a steakhouse." People laugh at you sitting at a bar. I used to order cranberry juice or something like that so it looked like a cocktail. People make fun of you. I asked once, "What would you say about a gymnast when she is four-years-old and she stops eating ice creams and chocolates because she wants to medal in the Olympics?" So, they said, it is difficult, but it is definitely praiseworthy. So I said, "Well, because you realize that a gold medal in the Olympics is such a big thing, it is praiseworthy, but because pursuing a goal that is fully going to get you in touch with your essence is not so praiseworthy, you think my life is . . . just nonsense." They got it. I didn't really feel threatened by their questions because, deep inside, I knew I was doing the right thing. I think because of that, the way I was explicitly able to explain my life came from a place where I didn't want to fight them; I just wanted them to understand.

KIM: Did you find, once people knew that this was your life choice, that the way they interacted with you, in dialogue or just in business matters, was more genuine or authentic?

RASANATH: It was different for different people, actually, and what is interesting is that in the banking world there is such an alignment and an inertia in the way it works that people get caught up in it. What I had to do was carry this energy with me every day to work, which means the way I interacted with them, the way I dealt with them, the way I dealt with my work, the way I dealt with difficult situations at work was all a way for them to come into that space too. So different people approached it differently. Some of my analysts at the end of 2007 started coming to the Bhakti Center, even having lunch with the monks, so that is one extreme. They really appreciated what I was doing. We became close friends. I even would take them out for meditation every day to Central Park, spend a half-an-hour toward the evening with just two or three people sitting down, meditating for a few minutes, then coming back into work. They really appreciated it, and it became a regular practice. We didn't really tell this to anyone. But with some other people, you just cannot penetrate them. I did get to a point . . . late in the nights when working . . . where I had some very personal conversations with people and, based on my level of vulnerability, they began to start becoming vulnerable with me because they knew they could trust me. For me, there was nothing to hide. I could speak about my struggles very openly because this was who I was. I didn't want to live with an image.

KIM: Anything unusual to deal with in regards to your supervisors or bosses? Was that at all a challenge for them?

RASANATH: One thing I told myself was that I really wanted to do what I did very well. So, six rounds of layoffs happened when I was there and I was still there at the end of the year. There are unofficial ratings that go around. I was the number one associate in technology. As far as work was concerned, it's not that I didn't make mistakes; I made mistakes. Success I feel is not just how well you work, but also how you embrace your mistakes. And I think just living at the monastery, being more in touch with myself, there was a way that if I made mistakes, I could say, "Yeah, it was a mistake. I can correct it and give it back." At the same time, also addressing somebody else's mistakes, you are coming from a place of dignity and always keeping in mind that human potential is just incredible. I could see that I could either crush someone's potential or develop it in the way I dealt with them.

KIM: When did you come to the decision not to continue?

RASANATH: My last big project was for Playboy. [laughter] I had been living in the banking world for almost two years. When I was in that world, it was during the crisis, and it really started to show its true colors. And I started seeing the futility and the shallowness of the whole model and the way it worked. And how very image-centered the model was. Very unconsciously, people are pulled away from authenticity and lack of authenticity doesn't necessarily mean you don't do good work, but it was not good work. *Good work to me meant something extraordinary—something that was real.*

In a conversation with one of my vice presidents, again late in the night, I asked him something I had felt in business school, but I never really asked because in business school you weren't supposed to ever ask the "wrong" questions. If you do ask them, then you don't get a job, even in the classroom, because your professors recommend you to potential employers. So one of our professors was a head of global trading at Morgan Stanley. Here he was in a class of 120 students, talking about structured products, CDOs. Students were asking all kinds of questions, and I was sitting there telling myself that I didn't understand a thing about it. I really didn't. It made me feel really foolish because I felt everyone else understood more than I did. But the biggest thing I didn't understand was, "How does this credit default work?"

There are no checks and balances to this entire thing. So, what if somebody were to come out and say, "Well, I want all my money back at one time." Then this whole product would fail, so it was the "emperor's new clothes question." But I didn't dare ask that. And slowly, in retrospect, I realized I didn't dare ask that because I was attached to an image. I was part of the whole show. That is what innocence is all about, right? A child says, "The emperor is not wearing any clothes," because what does the child know with an innocent heart? So I didn't have the innocence. It was not about knowledge. It was not about information. It was not about being intelligent. It was about having an innocent heart.

So this time when I was sitting with my vice president, once the relationship and trust were established, I finally dared to ask the question. I said, "Tell me honestly, does this really work?" And he looked at me and he said, "Well, you have to know it is a game of musical chairs. When the music stops, everything comes tumbling down." That was one of those conversations that was real and honest. So after having lived in that world . . . this was in December 2007, I decided I was quitting. One really wonderful person, one of the best people I worked with in banking, told me, "I am really happy for you that you are quitting and making a decision for your life."

Some people who work on Wall Street, I've come to realize, have a deep desire inside to be cheered—to be loved, to be appreciated. But when it plays out, it can become very distorted. So if you can touch the core, you will see there are those on Wall Street who are suffering. This is a very different feeling than you might have otherwise thought. Knowing that people are really after that, you can be more compassionate. You can actually come from a place of compassion instead of hating them.

For me, the main reason why I took to monastic life is I felt that getting in touch with my own true heart I would be able to give so much more to people.

The way we have the monastery set up is, none of us take the vow of staying a monk for the rest of our life. Part of the reason for that is that when you start tapping into some of the darker sides year after year, then sometimes you need a space. You need an emotional partner. You need a partner who can be with you and be with you emotionally to work through those things. There might be emotional needs you need met. But, then, the important thing is family life actually becomes a venue for you to pursue your spiritual life in a deeper way and you can find a partner who can actually help you. So it's based on that principle. When the monks come out of this training, their spiritual practices are very deeply consolidated in this place and, based on their needs, they carry that with them even though they go outside. Then, for a few people, this becomes their life. This is what they do. That's the way we have the monastery set up. It requires tremendous emotional courage, actually, to go into this monastic life. You are living with nine or ten other people. No door to close behind you, no privacy. Everything that we carry is out there. You don't even have your own room. You carry your own shortcomings, your own failures, and other people see that, and everyone else is in different stages of his own spiritual evolution, too, so not everyone sees your faults or even kindness the same way. What is interesting is it amplifies your own inner critic. Really, truly to hold all of that in kindness and compassion requires a lot of emotional strength.

CONSCIOUSNESS TEACHER	*Practice Four:*
Neale Donald Walsch	*The Internal and External Journey*

ASKING GOD

Neale Donald Walsch is a modern day spiritual messenger and the author of *Conversations with God: An Uncommon Dialogue.*

Well, as anyone who knows my story can tell you, I was living a perfectly wonderful life. I had everything going my own way more or less. I had a series of really fine jobs, never really a terribly bad job, one good job after the next. Some lasting for ten or twelve years. Some lasting a shorter period of time, but a wonderful occupation that allowed me to express various aspects of myself—in broadcasting, in journalism as a professional journalist, as a member of the working press, as a managing editor of a newspaper, as a program director of a radio station, as a nationally syndicated radio talk show host, as the director of public information for one of the nation's largest public school systems, and on and on.

I had a wonderful time, and then I had an automobile accident and broke my neck. A man turned right in front of me in a car, and I had a serious injury. It required me to stop working for two plus years—two-and-a-half years of rehabilitation. Soon my unemployment benefits ran out. My social safety net ran out. All was pulled out from under me. I ran out of benefits, simple as that. I thought it wasn't going to be a problem, and it would be for a couple of week or months. I thought I'd find something. But it is difficult to find work when you are walking around Philadelphia with a stabilizing device that doesn't allow you to lift more than three pounds. I wasn't allowed to lift so much as a half-gallon of milk. And nobody wanted to hire me. At the time of the accident, I was self-employed, but I couldn't go back to that work. I ended up living on the street. And, by the way, not for a month or two, or a couple of weeks, but for an entire year.

One might think it's not that big of a deal to live outside for a year, but just try it for a weekend. Go outside on Friday night and don't come back inside until Monday morning. But when you go out there, don't wash your hair or your body and wear the oldest clothes you can possibly find, so you smell and look exactly like a person would look if he had been out there for a long time. And take no money with you. Leave the house without a dime. Then multiply that times fifty-two weekends and all the days in between. There is no college that can teach you what you have learned on the street in fifty-two weeks of being outside, dumpster diving and grabbing solo cans and beer bottles just to turn in the five-cent deposit so you can just buy a bag of French fries. And then imagine walking down the streets of the city asking people, "Do you have any extra change at all, a quarter? Truly, a nickel would help. If I had a nickel for everybody who passed me today, I could eat tonight."

At the end of that experience, I finally found a way to get a little weekend part-time job. I filled in as a radio announcer at a tiny little radio station in Southern Oregon. It brought me a little bit of cash in my pocket—fifty dollars a day, a 100 dollars a week, 400 dollars a month. When you are on the street, and have been there for a year, you need to understand that 400 dollars a month is a fortune. So I actually managed to buy a little car. And just as this was all happening, the car I had just gotten was stolen. So I looked up to God and fell to the ground on the sidewalk right in front of where the car had been parked. I crashed to my knees and I said, "God, what do you want from me? How much more do I have to let go or not have? What is this all about? What's happening?" So this wasn't a spear in the chest experience. This was just a breaking open to my entire being. And I wasn't twenty-five or thirty-five or even forty-five. I was fifty years old! Had I been young and resilient, I would have had some sense of, "Oh, I can always bounce back." Eventually, I got a little dinky job in a little radio station. It was a weekend job, and I got myself back on my feet. I was good at broadcasting, having done broadcasting before. Ultimately, I ended up being the program director of another radio station in the same small market. They needed somebody with experience. I had twenty-six years of experience in the media at all levels. Radio, television, newspaper, etc., and they hired me. I was making money and I was back in the game.

And that's when I realized the utter shallowness and meaninglessness of the game itself. Go and work eight, twelve, in some cases, fourteen hours a day. Come home paying the few bills I could pay. Scratch through and stay alive for what? What was this all about? What is the point of it? What am I doing here?

So I woke up one night at 4:15 in the morning and I asked these questions of the God of my understanding. I wasn't a terribly religious person. I didn't belong to any faith or tradition. I wasn't a churchgoer. But I did have some sense there must be something larger than me here, some broad understanding. There must be something bigger than just little old humanity. So one morning I woke up and I called to that particular aspect of what I saw was real. What does it take to make life work? What have I done to deserve a life that is such a continuing struggle? Tell me the rules, God, and I swear to you, I swear to all that is holy, I will obey these rules—just give me the damn rule book. And she did. She gave me a series of books called *Conversations with God*, which went on to sell sixteen million copies in thirty-seven languages.

EXAMPLES FROM THE WALL STREET 50

WALL STREET 50	*Practice Four:*
Brad Katsuyama	*The Internal and External Journey*

CHOOSING INTEGRITY OVER MONEY

Brad Katsuyama is the President, CEO, and Co-Founder of IEX Group. Katsuyama and his team are also the focus of *Flash Boys*, a book by Michael Lewis about high frequency trading (HFT) in financial markets. After Katsuyama discovered HFT's unfair trading practices, he decided to challenge fundamentally the business of the stock market, leaving RBC in 2012 to start a fair and transparent stock exchange. He also has created www.IamAnInvestor.org, which educates and informs us on how each of us is an investor and how to reclaim our rights as one.

I think the biggest example would be when we figured out, how High Speed Trading was really working. When we were first building the test case and realized that you could take advantage of the geographical separation of exchanges and that there was an actual way to get in front of trades, the light bulb went off and there were two obvious choices of what to do with that information. I could bring it forth and try to internalize strategy and make money for myself, or I could try to help others save money. I think the most direct benefit for my bank account would've been to try to trade this myself. But it was just . . . this wasn't necessarily that hard of a decision, but the decision was there. And I'll be the first to admit that we weren't the first to discover what we discovered. I just think we were the first ones to do something different with that information.

WALL STREET 50	
Josh Brown	*Practice Four: The Internal and External Journey*

BEING HERO ENOUGH TO LISTEN WHEN THE
NAGGING VOICES BECOME TOO LOUD

Joshua Morgan Brown, is one of the top financial bloggers in the world.

Known as The Reformed Broker and author of *Backstage Wall Street*, the inspiring and eye-opening story of his leaving retail brokerage. He is the CEO of Ritholtz Wealth Management where he works with individuals, corporations, retirement plans, and charitable foundations.

I think I have always had nagging suspicions and regrets that I had to kind of tamp down in order to be effective at what my job used to be and, at a certain point, they started to be too loud and they couldn't be stifled anymore.

When you are young and ambitious and you don't really know anything, you get offered an opportunity. My dad says, "Hey, you should meet my friend, he is super successful." When you are young, you equate success with happiness and you figure anyone that has got a lot of money, a nice car, and a nice house is probably happy with himself, so you end up taking jobs with people, being shown the ropes. You don't really question anything you see because you figure these are adults and I am only twenty-two. I am sure whatever they are doing, it is what they are supposed to be doing and I can't wait to learn it. And it is not until you get to know people better and you see that a lot of it is a mirage, they are miserable, they have made compromises that they can't come back from, they themselves are trapped, they themselves are hiring and indoctrinating younger guys like me so they can continue to live their lifestyle and then you realize you are being used and lied to. You are working with people who have lost any sense of morality if they ever had any to begin with.

But that process doesn't happen in thirty days. That process happens in months, in years in my case. The problem is once you have gone down that path, all of a sudden other avenues are closed to you, other opportunities, because you have spent so much time in a specific business, you have built enough that you have something to lose by walking away. And then you have the argument within yourself where you say, "Well, these guys are bad, but I can do this, and I can be good; I can figure out a new way to do this the right way." Then at a certain point, after a few years, you come to realize that it really doesn't matter what I do because this is inherently hurtful to the people who are supposed to be clients—this is inherently a conflicted business model, and my morality and my scruples will never allow me to be happy doing this. It is only going to get worse and there is nothing within my power to make it better, other than to stop doing it. Once you get to that point, then the fear sets in. You realize, "How do I escape?" Now I am married. Now I have kids of my own. Now I have a mortgage. Now I have bills. It's not so easy to walk away when you are thirty-two as if you were twenty-two. That's my journey. And all those realizations that happened along the way, they got louder, and at a certain point, they become impossible to ignore.

Even worse than that, you get to the point where you realize the characters you work with are remarkably similar to let's say the guy who runs the orphanage in a Dickens' novel where he is basically raising kids to be pickpockets and prostitutes. You get to the point where they start handing over more responsibility to you. They continue to bring in young guys and they put them under your wing to mentor them. And then they offered me a position of being in charge of the trainees, so now I am passing on all of these things I have learned to younger generations. You can't have any doubt when you are in that position because you are getting paid to be a supervisor and a mentor. You can't publicly express doubt. "Hey, maybe we should be doing this?" The entire edifice is built on confidence, so any of those nagging doubts about, "Hey, what am I doing?" all have to stay internalized, which makes it really painful and probably delays the process of speaking out loud about it or bouncing it off of other people; it probably prolonged the realization.

KIM: You didn't even share these doubts with your wife?

JOSH: No. The thing about not sharing with your wife in particular is because your wife has friends and they have husbands and they are also people who are successful, etc. And the last thing you want to do is bring any doubt home with you and have that be something that affects the relationship. But towards the end it is unavoidable. Toward the end, when you just say, "Now I am going to coast. I can't do this stuff anymore. I am just going to do the bare minimum until I figure out a way out." Then the money stops coming in and you get to the point where you just go to the movies instead of going to work because you can't bear another day of it. At that point, the conversations at home start where the wife says, "What are you doing with yourself? What's wrong with you? Why are you so miserable?" so at a certain point you can't hide it.

KIM: In your book *Backstage Wall Street*, you talk about that conversation with your wife. Was there more of a response from her than what we read there?

JOSH: No. I think what I said out loud was what she had been thinking for years. I think there was a little bit of relief, an "Okay, finally, he knows he needs to make a change." I'm fortunate. My wife is my high school sweetheart. She knows me from when I was doing really stupid things in high school, so she believed in me before I ever accomplished anything. I don't know if a marriage, a relationship that was only a few years old, would have survived my last few years in the brokerage business.

KIM: How long did that gnawing go on for?

JOSH: Forever, like ten years.

KIM: And then how long 'til you came to the place of, "I really can't do this anymore."

JOSH: That's probably a year and a half. The first thing I did was tell my bosses, "Take all responsibility from me. I am done. I am not managing. I am not supervising. I don't want to be listed anywhere as a supervisor. I don't want anything to do with your business. I'm just going to be here and make money for myself." Once you do that, then the weight on your shoulders is, "Well, now I have to look at these people every day." That can't last forever, so maybe that goes on a year and a half.

KIM: How scared were you?

JOSH: I didn't allow myself to be scared often because I kind of was drinking. Anything to escape for a little while, but I also started writing, and writing was something that . . . I am not good at a lot of things, but all my life, I was really able to communicate well in writing.

KIM: Were you writing in any way before that?

JOSH: I started the blog just as my mental state was starting to break down. It was a great outlet because the whole world was breaking down at that time. It wasn't just that I was going through this; Bear Stearns and Lehman's were collapsing, and Bernie Madoff was revealed to be a fifty billion dollar fraud. This is late 2008. I started writing in November of 2008, two months after Lehman went bankrupt and about a month before Bernie Madoff's announcement came out. And it seemed like the perfect time just to go for it and start putting my thoughts somewhere. And so that was my first outlet. And as you start to write, you start to realize that people are reading, and you say, "Well, I can't be a fraud. I can't be a bullshit artist and be writing one thing and then doing something else in my actual professional career." You have a choice to make. Either I am not going to write honestly anymore and I am just going to go on doing what I am doing, or I am going to remove myself from all the things I know to be wrong, distasteful, and unethical, and off the edge, and I am going to keep writing. That's what I ended up choosing [the latter] to my own financial detriment, in the short-run.

KIM: There was detriment in the short-run?

JOSH: Yes, when you stop doing certain kinds of business completely, where you were making a lot of money. I knew it was a bad business and I just didn't want to do it anymore. By the way, by bad business, I don't mean illegal—just that it is really not in the client's best interest, so I chose to not do it anymore. And I didn't care how much it costs me. Any business where you are selling financial products to people, there are going to be inherent conflicts, but, unfortunately, the way the industry is set up, the worse shit you sell to people, the more it pays you. I talk about that in my book, *The Reformed Broker*, I call it "Brown's Law of Financial Product Compensation"—the more the broker gets paid to sell something, the worse it is for the client. It is a fact. The things that pay the highest fees to brokers are the ones with the least shot of being a good investment. That's why they have to pay the highest fees. They tend to be the most opaque. They tend to be the most complex and convoluted and, you know, that's why they carry the high fee. If I sell you a C-share mutual fund, it is probably a pretty good deal for you because it is only paying me 1 percent as a broker. If I sell you a private placement, the firm is giving me 10 percent of what I raise, so if I put a hundred thousand dollars of your money into C-share mutual funds, I make a thousand dollars gross commission. If I take that same hundred thousand dollars and I put it into a private placement which doesn't trade publicly—doesn't have publicly available filings or financials, so no one knows anything about it, nobody to contact—I get paid ten thousand. So it is in my best financial interest in the short-term to buy you the private placement. But long-term, that sucks for me as a broker, because I will probably lose you as a client. Most brokers are living hand-to-mouth. They have obscenely high expenses. They all drive fancy cars, have big watches, have houses in the Hamptons. Most of them are divorced, pay child support. They are probably, as a group, the most miserable people I have ever met. They are good people who just got trapped. And then there are people that just don't know better or don't know anything else to do. Then there are some really bad people and the really bad people tend to rise to the top and run these firms because they don't get tripped up by the conflicts and morality. To those few, it's completely irrelevant; they are like sharks swimming toward their prey.

KIM: Was there any point where you thought to yourself, "There is another place within this industry of finance other than brokerage." A sense of, "I can't do this, but I can do that."

JOSH: That is what I am doing now. I knew the way to run this business, all along. I got licensed to be an advisor in 2002. It was ten years ago. The firm I was with was not licensed as a firm to do that kind of business. The way they kept stringing me along was, "Look, pay your dues, help us run the brokerage business, and eventually, we will get licensed as a firm to become advisors, also. We will be dually registered, and that way, Josh, you don't have to leave. You don't have to take your clients. You can transition within the firm and you can build this out for us." And they kept stringing me along. It seemed like each time they would apply for a license, there would be a reason why it didn't happen.

WALL STREET 50
Eric Carangelo   *Practice Four: The Internal and External Journey*
LOSING YOUR EGO

Eric Carangelo is a Vice President at State Street and has worked in finance for over twenty years. He specializes in large portfolio trades as well as interim asset management for institutions such as pensions, endowments, and foundations, and is active in several charities.

As you grow older, you become less egocentric, right? You realize, "It ain't all about me." When I was three, I thought the world revolved around me. I was wrong. As you get older, you start to realize it doesn't.

Now, I honestly don't think I came to be less egocentric until I got to New York and my brains got beaten. I had it relatively easy up until I got to New York and graduated from college. And in essence, you know, New York just heats you up if you can't compete, so you just have to cut your teeth and compete and realize there's more to it than you sort of bullshitting your way through it and charming people. So yeah, I got my comeuppance in New York, and it went hand-in-hand with being conscious that other people mattered in the world besides me.

KIM: Was there a moment—a particular incident—when you realized that?

ERIC: It wasn't like I had an epiphany where one day I woke up and I said, "Hey, it isn't all about me." Although that certainly happened when I had kids. A big part of that was having kids, but even well before that, I would say when I was twenty-five-years-old, coming to New York City, I think of it almost like negative reinforcement because people don't give a shit about you in New York, by and large. You're one of eight million faces, and if other people don't care about you, you begin to realize, "You know what, I'm not so special and the world doesn't revolve around me." You sort of realize you're not so wonderful and special like your parents think you are, and you are just another one of eight million stories in the naked city or whatever the hell that phrase is. So I guess that's when I started to realize I ought to pay attention to what people are saying and thinking. And if I wanted to be recognized, I ought to give as much as I get.

It was definitely a shock to my system. I was used to having things go my way. And it was pretty clear to me that if you wanted things to go your way in New York, you really, really have to earn it. And you know, I think I did in the end, but there was a lot of pain along the way.

WALL STREET 50	*Practice Four:*
Jason Apollo Voss	*The Internal and External Journey*

THE DARK NIGHT OF THE SOUL

Jason Apollo Voss is Content Director at CFA Institute and author of *The Intuitive Investor*. He previously retired at age thirty-five after being co-Portfolio Manager of the Davis Appreciation & Income Fund, where he bested the NASDAQ, S&P 500, and DJIA by staggering percentages. He has studied the ancient martial art of ninjutsu and Eastern healing techniques. Voss also teaches meditation.

About ten years ago, I went through a divorce, which was a really, really difficult thing for me. Probably the hardest thing I've ever had to do in my life. Ironically enough, I had been saying since I was in my early teen years that the measure of success of a life was not your bank balance; it was how happy you were. And here I was. I wasn't happy at all, even though I was doing well professionally. And what I wasn't happy about was the most important thing to me, being a good husband. I had a person whom I really loved tremendously, who was voting against that version of reality. "You're not a good husband. And in fact, you're so terrible, I don't want to be with you anymore." Okay. So that caused a long, dark night of the soul. And I really had to . . . it is one thing to blame other people for the outcome of something, but there's also a kernel of truth of, well, I was a co-creator of what happened here.

I'd always been a big believer in responsibility. So I started looking at the things I could affect, I had to look at the choices I had made and the way I thought about the world. And frankly, that made me vulnerable . . . in a good way. Vulnerable to new ways of thinking about the world. And what I had realized was up until that moment, I had digested quite a number of very rigid ways of viewing and interpreting the world. Up until I was twenty-nine, I was a dyed-in-the-wool atheist and had been raised that way by my mom, who's probably a deep skeptic, not an atheist. But she was awaiting some sort of verification for a proof of a different way of thinking. Anyway, when I started having experiences around that vulnerability that were positive and they got better and better, then my professional career got better and better. I became a much better money manager by being open to possibility and being open to new ways of viewing the world. And I started, then, looking backward at my childhood and thinking, "Well, where did I go wrong and what happened?" And who were the influences on my life? Whose opinions did I trust, and why did I trust those opinions, and why did I buy them, lock, stock, and barrel? It's all very insidious, very subtle. It took probably a good three or four years of internal work to get to the point where I felt like I was assessing things for what they were, as opposed to what I wanted them to be.

PRACTICE FIVE: Self-Awareness/Mindfulness

Self-responsibility, as opposed to self-blame, assists us on our journey to self-awareness. Feeling angry, disappointed, or ashamed of yourself—or something you've done or even felt—might sound like self-awareness. While it may be the beginning of it (see Practice Three, Emotional Non-Resistance), ultimately, self-awareness is about the ability to observe one's self, feelings, and behaviors in any circumstance with curiosity and neutrality. And mindfulness is about being present to the moment at hand, not in the future nor in the past. These two go hand in hand.

Dropping internal blame while allowing yourself to feel your feelings along with a willingness to own responsibility for your response is how one begins to become self-aware. If you are beating the hell out of yourself with blame, you won't be willing or able to be introspective long-term.

True self-awareness looks within with curiosity; you notice yourself, your feelings, and what is going on for you when you are either stimulated or triggered. It also connects us to be able to notice the affect we and our actions (or inactions) have on others in a multitude of areas, including ourselves and our experiences. Michael Martin speaks about his awareness from a financial perspective in his book *The Inner Voice of Trading* and so does Jason Apollo Voss in *The Intuitive Investor*.

Many practices facilitate developing more self-awareness. Meditation is one of the more profound ways to go. What exactly is meditation? It is the practice of letting go of anything other than this one moment. Ram Dass, the spiritual teacher, has a book titled, *Be Here Now*. Meditation is simply a life-long practice of learning how to *be here now*.

Many styles of meditation exist, so I recommend sampling as many as necessary to find the style that suits your temperament.

I myself have practiced Raphael Cushnir's Present Moment Awareness and Emotional Connection techniques for over eight years.

I participate in Kirtan chanting, a form of mediation done through chanting/singing Sanskrit phrases. I also practice Samuel Sagan's Clarevision's School of Meditation style and am an advocate of His Holiness Sri Sri Ravi Shankar's Art of Living meditation style. All have been effective for me.

Another practice I highly recommend is that you engage in coaching. I personally and professionally do and I can't say enough about how profound and impactful it continues to be for me. The reason I say coaching and not therapy is because coaching is really about you, your goals, your wants/needs, and your motivation. Coaching asks an immense array of questions that will really assist you in getting to know yourself as you attempt to answer them. When I begin coaching people, I send them a "Discovery Packet," which contains roughly twenty-six open-ended questions that require serious self-reflection. Clients have told me that answering the questions is challenging, but in the end, the process reveals for them what they genuinely need to know about themselves so they can begin to move forward toward fulfillment. They have described it as an eye-opening experience.

When you achieve self-awareness, you can begin living the life you truly want. As Seth Godin says, "Instead of wondering when your next vacation is, maybe *you* should set up a *life you don't need to escape from*." To begin to have a life you don't need to escape from, you must be willing to look at the one you currently have with eyes wide open.

Now we will hear *The Teachers of Consciousness* define or articulate what **Self-Awareness/Mindfulness** means to them. Then stories from *The Wall Street 50* will provide an example of what **Self-Awareness/Mindfulness** looks like in practice.

CONSCIOUSNESS TEACHER

Dr. Dan Siegel   *Practice Five: Self-Awareness/Mindfulness*

DISCOVERING SELF-AWARENESS THROUGH
WHAT IS MEANINGFUL TO YOU

Dr. Dan Siegel is a mindfulness expert, clinical professor of psychiatry at the UCLA School of Medicine, Executive Director of the Mindsight Institute, a neuropsychiatrist, and an interpersonal neurobiologist.

When people talk to me in the privacy of therapy, they talk about how meaningless the life of just perusing material acquisition is, but that they feel stuck in it. And I say to them, "Let's see what would have meaning for you." As they begin to do this integrated work, they find there is a deep meaning in giving back to the world, in feeling connected to the world, and they realize there are a lot of things to be done in this world that we may never in our own individual body live to see the result of. There is so much to do, it can be overwhelming, but knowing you participated in trying to make a difference, whether it's cleaning up pollution in the bay here in Santa Monica where I am, or trying to help climate change issues, or working to end poverty, or trying to feed people, or ending violence, brings deeper meaning to life because you're participating in something larger than yourself. Giving back with gratitude and generosity and feeling a sense of belonging as a result has been clearly shown by research to give us a sense of happiness, well-being, and even wisdom.

Meaning is created from this larger sense of belonging. So what I say to people who work on Wall Street or other places is, "You have a choice to live your life and go on the journey." I can't tell them what is meaningful. The research shows that feeling like you are a part of a larger whole, and not just making money, but using the skill set you have to make a company work to make a profit, and then turning those profits into ways that benefit human beings and other living beings on the planet, creates a sense of meaning—that's where it comes from. Where meaning comes from is not a mystery. Find a practice that will make you more mindful and see whether you can get in touch with whether or not your life is meaningful. And if it is, great. If it is not, let's help you walk a path that finds more meaning in your life. That journey alone, research suggests, would bring you to a place of connection to a much larger whole, as well as an experience of more gratitude and generosity.

CONSCIOUSNESS TEACHER

Patricia Aburdene   *Practice Five: Self-Awareness/Mindfulness*

SELF-AWARENESS AND THE ECONOMY

OF CONSCIOUSNESS

Patricia Aburdene is a world leading social forecaster, the author of *Conscious Money and Megatrends 2010: The Rise of Conscious Capitalism*, and one of the earliest members of the Conscious Capitalism community. Some say she was the first to coin the term "conscious capitalism." Aburdene believes, "We the people have the power to transform capitalism as investors, consumers, and managers and capitalism has the power to change the world."

KIM: How does one become more self-aware?

PATRICIA: Begin with self-observation. Awareness, when it is directed at one's self, at one's start, at one's emotions, that's huge, just to become aware of the thoughts and emotions that are going on with you. I mean, heck, that's like a high spiritual undertaking. So I'd start by just observing yourself. What are the kinds of thoughts that are running around in your head during the day? What kinds of feelings do you have? I'm a person who is a huge journaling fanatic, so I would say if you are interested in being more conscious, more aware, one of the best things you can do for yourself, one of the simplest things you can do for yourself, is to observe yourself and then take a few notes. You know you don't have to do it for hours a day, although I've done that in my life. But I also like the suggestions around journaling in Julia Cameron's book, *The Artist's Way.* So just a little bit of self-observation, writing a little bit with some regularity, will increase the person's consciousness and awareness in a very easy way and quite quickly.

KIM: You speak in your book, *Conscious Money*, about the Economy of Consciousness. Can you speak to that a little bit?

PATRICIA: When I was writing the *Megatrends* book with John Nesbitt, we talked about the shift from an industrial society to an information society. Before that humanity had been living in an agricultural society, so it kind of went agricultural, then industrial. We were among the first thinkers who said, "Our economy isn't really based on industry anymore. It's increasingly based on information. And that followed the birth of the first computers. That was the beginning of it, the seed of the information economy. By 1975 we were creating—the U.S. economy was creating—more wealth and more jobs through information than through industries. So we talked about the shift. I was so glad to be there—this was in 1982 when *Megatrends* was published and people almost threw rotten tomatoes at us. This is 1982, only thirty years ago. People thought that was the craziest idea they ever heard! So the world's changing very rapidly, but it's my argument that the information era is definitely drawing to a close. Other people have different words for it, but I call the new era that's replacing the information era: the New Economy of Consciousness, because look at the innovations that come out of Apple, look at the innovations that come out of Google; they don't really come out of information, they don't come out of data that you feed through a computer, they come out of one place and that is the genius of human consciousness. So today, technology is obsolete the minute you create it because technology is nothing more than consciousness externalized with the help of some electrons sorting about and a little hardware and that sort of thing, but really technology comes directly out of human consciousness. So we now create new jobs and new wealth through the genius of human consciousness. So lots of sectors in today's economy are already in what I call the new Economy of Consciousness.

KIM: As a coach, when I hear you talk about this Economy of Consciousness, I'm curious what skill sets need to be increased?

PATRICIA: In his book *The Power of Now*, spiritual teacher Eckhart Tolle talked about the power of being in the present moment. And yet what I'm talking about is taking that ability and using it not in some form of spiritual contemplation but actually applying that as a skill in your work. Being totally 100 percent present to the client, that's being in the "now." That's what I mean by the new Economy of Consciousness. That we use a skill set that is based on our ability to access human consciousness and creativity. Imagine an engineer at Google or Apple grappling with a technological issue. That person would have to be extraordinarily present in his work. Same with the artist. Same with the any kind of scientists. The thing about the new Economy of Consciousness is that the shamans of the world, the artist, the scientists, etc., live in this now. They have this skill set of being totally present. Today in every walk of life, if we want to do well in our careers and our professions, we have to master this ability to be present.

I think there's a passage we're going through. The old, archaic systems of finance institutional system bonds, and I don't mean bonds that you trade, I mean the kind of bonds that bring people together, are shifting. And so we have been used to a money world, a financial world that was the epitome of the mundane grind of reality and we separated ourselves from our spiritual-selves, our inner-lives, our values from that, as though the "money world" were the "real world." As though money were completely separate. I think that as humanity has evolved over time, that kind of separation is intolerable to us, and yet that kind of separation permeates our financial institutions because that's culturally how they were set up. That business is about making money, and then church is on Sunday or temple is on Friday night, and then back to business on Monday morning. There is this notion of separation between those two, and because that awareness has been frozen into much of our financial institutions, they have become truly unconscious, and that's why they're failing. That's why they're failing all around us—because there is such a profound lack of awareness, self-awareness, and to a certain extent, goodwill. I am all for self-interest. I believe self-interest is the midpoint of balance between complete greed and complete altruism. Self-interest, concern for one's self, concern for one's family, is perfectly 100 percent valuable. Where it gets into trouble is when it's sort of self-interest run amok. When self-interest proceeds so excessively that it starts to violate and betray the ideals that we're all born with, it's not a good thing for us, nor for our money, because we're moving into a territory that is unbalanced and distorted. Our values exemplify our hearts and when our hearts and heads are in balance and on the same page, we have a clear sense of direction, we know what we want to do. But when one of those isn't working, if we're just going with our heart and who cares what the head is telling us, or we're just going with our head and who cares what the heart is telling us, then we are truly unbalanced, and it sets up an inner dynamic within us that really distorts things.

That kind of unconsciousness has been frozen into our financial institutions. The recent stuff with banks and the recent stuff with the subprime interest issue—remember this wasn't the first financial crisis in the decade; we have had one after another—and when systems start to repeatedly crash, that's telling you that there's a bug in the system, or probably quite a few. I'm afraid to say I think that's where we are to a very large extent. Old financial thoughts and ideas and institutions are crashing, but the good news is that an alternative system has been growing stronger as these begin to deteriorate. That new operating system is conscious capitalism, and it's ready to take over.

CONSCIOUSNESS TEACHER
Shaman Charles Lawrence

Practice Five:
Self-Awareness/Mindfulness

SELF-AWARENESS AND THE FALSE SELF

Charles Lawrence is a cross-cultural Shamanic teacher who is a former psychologist and businessman. His life took a new course after he was struck by lightning. He was adopted and baptized by the Hopi Indians over twenty years ago and considers himself a Walker of Medicine Ways.

Lawrence has traveled over many years with the Elders of the Hopi, Coast Salish, Lakota, Seneca, Mohawk, and Shoshone, as well as traditional practitioners of Peru, Finland, South Africa, Tuva, and other First Nations peoples.

KIM: What do you feel Wall Street needs to do to move forward into the future?

CHARLES: To slow down and listen. To be aware of the false self. This takes us back to the early levels of consciousness. Recognizing the false self and becoming free of it. There is the real self and the false self. The real self is the conscious self; the real self is the greater self which many of us are wanting. When I experience more and more of that, I also experience a synchronicity, a deeper ease of being; it's not as stressful; there's a flow there. I learned from native elders that if something is not going effortlessly, look for the resistance or what is called kingpin, the log pin. In a logjam, it's that one pin or log that's jamming it all up, and when you pull that out, you have to back out fast. You only have just so much time to get out of the way. Step back far enough and you can see the unraveling process.

I think it's awakening to the truth that this lifetime is limited and you go way out on this limb, develop all this, and then suddenly, you're out in what Joe [Campbell] would call, "You climb the ladder of success, and when you get to the top, you find it's leaning against the wrong wall."

KIM: Could you speak a little bit to some of the anger I've encountered? I was invited to do a TEDx talk and then disinvited because the organizer was so angry at Wall Street that he couldn't hear my motive was one of transformation.

CHARLES: It's so shallow. Well, this goes back to false self. Religions have not exactly been useful on this because they shun "this one" and shun "that one" and say that "theirs" is the only religion that has access to God. So we have generations and generations—thousands of years of that—domestications and what I call "spiritual trafficking." They have trafficked people's sense of spirit and have taught that only "we" have the answers. Look at righteous wars. There's a huge inflationary aspect there, and it takes only a few of us to begin to "otherize." What is the contrast of "otherizing"? It's incorporating and integrating that we are all connected. Back to Joe [Campbell], if one becomes the "lecturer" or the pointer . . . those who point the way and say, "This is it," the truth is that most of those people never go that way themselves. So I'd rather be as Gandhi is—become the change, so the more I am in the state of inclusion. Be careful never ever to judge anybody, "otherize," because who knows, I might be a part of that person's realigning, being realigned, or feeling included.

KIM: If you had a magic wand to wave over Wall Street, what would your magic wand do?

CHARLES: The first wave of thought would be to dissolve the wave of separateness, dissolve the wall. It's false; it's part of the false self. For example, in Catholicism and Judaism, the false self is an embodiment of distrust, of fear. These beliefs of separation. The false self exists right through culture today, especially hierarchical culture; it believes somebody is better than you are, there are different class cultures. It's all false. We're all human. And going back to your earlier question, Rudi [Albert Rudolf] said in one of his lectures that all it takes is one person in any situation to wake up, and the mere awakening of awareness causes the greater awareness in that individual to shift and to stop believing in this invisible wall of separateness; then I'm no longer invested in that wall of separation and know that we are all one. When one suffers, and I use that early definition of suffering which means to undergo a passage, to go under, we can come to this realization.

KIM: So then thinking of suffering in the way you define it, as a passage through, I'm wondering then if what we are currently going through with our economy—perhaps it's because a passage needs to be made?

CHARLES: Yes. It's our soul commanding that we transform. I prefer the words upgrading and enhancing because just our sitting here together—well, there's energy moving between us, and I will find out later, after you've gone on your merry way and I sit and reflect about our conversation, how I influenced you by our conversation. And you too will be affected by my being with you. Parables speak to when you are going down to the river either to wash your clothes or to catch the fish for dinner, and you meet someone crossing the other trail. They're going over the hills to empty their bowls or go hunting or go visit or something, but you stop and engage in a few words. You better stop after you left that person because if you think that you're the same as you were before you engaged, then you were not there for what happened, and that's part of consciousness to me. Each of us as we encounter the other, we are both being changed in some way.

CONSCIOUSNESS TEACHER   *Practice Five:*
Neale Donald Walsch   *Self-Awareness/Mindfulness*

THE SOUL'S AGENDA

Neale Donald Walsch is a modern day spiritual messenger and the author of *Conversations with God: An Uncommon Dialogue.*

KIM: How does one become more self-aware, more conscious?

NEALE: I would encourage people seeking self-awareness and increased consciousness to make a firm decision first of all about who they really are. This is the fundamental decision I will invite every person who wants the answer to your question to consider. Who in fact am I? Am I a soul that has a body or am I the body itself—a conglomeration of biological elements, a combination of chemicals if you will, the result of biological incidents that occurred between my parents? Who am I? If the conclusion is I am the biological outcome of a biological incident that occurred between my parents, one's point of view about life and the purpose of life and what to do in life, will be remarkably different from one's point of view if one imagines that one is a spirit, simply having a body and using it as a tool with which to advance the agenda of the spirit itself. But then we would have to ask the question, "What is that agenda?" A question very few people ask. Therefore, the next thing I would invite people on Wall Street before they undertake any activity whatsoever—go to the office, do a deal, pick up the phones, sign a contract, have lunch with a business partner, or have any interaction with life whatsoever—is to ask themselves just in advance of that next event, "What does this have to do with the agenda of my soul?"

I would dare people literally to put their money where their mouth is. That is, if they think they are a spiritual being seeking to advance their spiritual experience, I would invite them to address that question and lay it against the activities of their daily life as a measure of how far they are advancing spiritually. What does this have to do with the agenda of my soul? For that matter, what is the agenda of my soul?

CONSCIOUSNESS TEACHER
Peter Block   *Practice Five: Self-Awareness/Mindfulness*

GIVING VOICE TO PEOPLE'S HUMANITY

Peter Block is an author, consultant, and citizen of Cincinnati, Ohio. His work is about stewardship and the restoration of community. Here he speaks about our need to create more awareness of the abundance that's already all around us.

PETER: So your question was: What does consciousness mean? Well, it means to choose or live in the context of abundance. That I am enough. There is enough. The world is enough. And to me, that's a simple way of getting at it, the complicated way is to spend your life trying to answer that question.

KIM: So you're saying consciousness is a place, a perspective one lives from, a place one lives in of "There is enough."

PETER: Exactly. That to me is the ground level application of what it means to be conscious. I think what you are posing regarding consciousness in your context is: Is there a place or a way for people . . . who work on Wall Street, let's say, to reclaim, rediscover, and give voice to their humanity, their care for the common good, their care for the wellbeing of all. We have declared as a culture to let poverty exist, and we've made people on Wall Street the current scapegoat, as if *they* are responsible for our greed, our obesity, our hunger. People are hungry and poor and they think the rich are responsible for poverty. And as individuals, they're not. As a culture, we all are. There is enough. There is no reason in this culture for poverty to exist or at least for people to live with the absence of food, shelter, resources, and health. So, it's a distortion of capitalism. All capitalism means is that some people have money, some people run businesses, and the people with money let the people running businesses use it. Capitalism has nothing to do with the need for competition, the notion that markets solve everything. And so, nobody is complaining about capitalism. People are complaining about a culture of empire, a culture of greed, a culture where no matter how much I have, it's not enough.

KIM: So you feel that is really what has everyone disturbed. They're not identifying how or what that disturbance is, so instead they've found a scapegoat, instead of looking at the deeper disturbance.

PETER: I think that's right. The deeper disturbance is that there is a *scarcity world* we've chosen to construct. We've constructed a race to the top. We've constructed high stakes testing. We've decided that, "I'll never have enough shoes." And so, we've allowed ourselves to be industrialized in our soul. That's where the wasteland resides and we've authorized Wal-Mart and Home Depot and McDonalds to define our future for us.

KIM: David Whyte's book *The Heart Aroused: Preservation of Poetry & Soul in Corporate America*, heavily influenced me in the writing of this book, and he represents this idea as the reauthorization of whom we listen to. So how does one reauthorize themselves? How does someone who's never engaged in that begin?

PETER: No one has ever *not* engaged in it. Everybody has toured at the edge of the ocean or knows that somebody died beside a mountain so I don't believe that anybody has not ever engaged in it. Now, they may not talk about it at work but they do have lives and wives and ex-wives so the notion that they haven't even begun to think about isn't true. For people who live their lives only through the business perspective and seem to have no compassion I always think, "Well, their hearts haven't been broken yet." And so, always looking for a sign, a glimmer, a whisper, a tear, an opening of humanity and once you find that, all it needs is attention. All it needs is to be named and you can ask people, "Tell me about your life." And they'll tell you about their lives and then you say, "How is it going?" And for most people, that's a difficult question. People tell me their need for control, their need for capitalism, their need to be more conscious, their need for more compensation. Social activists tell me their need to get rid of the police state . . . they'll say, "Don't let the police wear guns." And I say, "That's a great point. How is it going?" And the reality is most people know it's not going well. This is where the recession is. It's all a bubble burst. It's God's way of telling us, "This isn't going well." And in my mind, to be conscious is to witness the death, the sickness of the story of what's wrong, and the public conversation is a simple story. The simplistic story, that's what you're trying to do, Kim, with your book and your work and your life is to awaken people into understanding what's going on here and to deepen their thought process, to get them to think and realize that their humanity doesn't have to be sacrificed just because they're living within the business perspective.

KIM: If they want to journey into this world of consciousness, how do they begin?

PETER: If they go through a new age bookstore, find the bulletin board that advertises fifty-five places to go, and pick one. You know what I mean? That's how complicated it is.

KIM: So put the foot in the pool?

PETER: Exactly. I'm not worried about people being overwhelmed. Consciousness does not overwhelm. It's too slow. And nobody is more hungry for consciousness than people talking about consciousness. The one thing I would say is you have got to be careful in your work, in my work, in our writing, and speaking that we don't have something in mind for other people. So cast a net. Make an offer. The purpose of a talk is to give people a cheap sample of a possibility. What you're doing is prophetic work. You are saying, "Here's an alternative." You're also expressing your love for people on Wall Street and that's your own mission. You must like to go in unpopulated places, which is high consciousness. But I don't think you want to show up to people, caring whether they become conscious or not. You're great that way, you're curious. You're being that way with me, so you're interested. Just be sure you don't ever substitute that with colonialism, which is knowing what's best for others, and be sure you don't make a distinction between your consciousness and theirs. You're paid to be a friend to people who have trouble finding friends elsewhere. Honestly, you're bringing friendship, enabling it to occur in the institutional environment.

EXAMPLES FROM THE WALL STREET 50

WALL STREET 50
Andy Pritchard   *Practice Five: Self-Awareness/Mindfulness*

THE DIFFERENCE THIRTY MILES MAKES

Andrew Hamilton Pritchard is a financial professional for institutional clients focused on IB and Sales, and has held an industry securities registration for twenty-eight years.

AT some point, I had another reason why I wanted out of New York City. I was trading at Prudential at the time, which was at South Street Seaport, so I'd get up at five o'clock in my condo—I was in Norwalk, Connecticut, and I would blow through different red lights since it was early in the morning. You could see anyone coming, and I'd be rushing to get to the train—All of a sudden, out of nowhere, comes an ambulance. Lights on inside, right by me. I'm like, "Holy shit!" And I see they're working on a guy in the back and they are clearly hitting his chest and I think, "Oh, my God, I hope that guy is all right. Oh, my God, I hope they get him to the hospital in time."

So then I get to New York City and I come in Grand Central where you basically put on your New York City armor. And I get off the subway at Gold Street, and somebody comes flying by in an ambulance just as I'm crossing the street, and it cuts me off because they got a guy in the back, and it flies right past me into the driveway there. And I hear myself say to myself, "Screw that guy. Dammit!" As I walk a little further, I think, "Whoa. What is wrong with me?" And I had to ask myself, "What's the difference? Literally, here I am, thirty miles away, and I'm a different person."

WALL STREET 50
Eric Greschner   *Practice Five: Self-Awareness/Mindfulness*
EXPERIENCING LITERATURE, RELIGION, AND PHILOSOPHY

Eric Greschner is a fee-only financial planner and portfolio manager at Regatta Research & Money Management, LLC, an SEC Registered Investment Adviser. He is also a financial educator and has chaired investment conferences, acted as a speaker and/or panelist, and provided training for organizations around the world. Finally, Eric is also an author, a former attorney, and has worked on Wall Street as an institutional research analyst and market strategist for a leading firm.

KIM: If someone wanted to become more awake, more conscious, how would you advise that person go about it?

ERIC: I'm not a guru, but I will share what I did and what worked for me. My initial introduction to all this was through literature and poetry. It's reflection. It's getting into other people's shoes. It's thinking about things from a different perspective, right? And then I started getting into Transcendentalist poetry, and then there was the Romantic Period and the Victorians, and then Modernism. I started getting into literature and poetry—not pop, but more classics, right? Which, I think, is in certain respects, in certain situations, a form of spirituality. I didn't realize that at the time, but I think that's the case. And then I started reading a lot of references in the literature and the poetry and thought, "Wow, this is fascinating. I want to learn more about the different religions out there, the different philosophies. Tell me about Transcendentalism; tell me about Buddhism, etc." And then I started getting into it. I said, "Wow, this is really interesting to me and has a lot to recommend."

I also went to India. I went to Thailand. I went to Vietnam. And we're taking my nephew to Nepal and Tibet this summer and these aren't just trips. We're there to go enjoy the culture. We'll go to the temples. We'll participate in some of the ceremonies over there. We'll go do volunteer work, etc. I will go ahead and promote just an introduction to poetry and literature, a study of the different philosophies that are available out there. And then I also found that really getting into the meditation and the yoga was really very powerful for me.

WALL STREET 50
Jim Rogers   *Practice Five: Self-Awareness/Mindfulness*

ASK WHAT'S REALLY GOING ON

James Beeland "Jim" Rogers, Jr. is an investor, media commentator, adventurer, and author. He is the Chairman of Beeland Interests, Inc. He was the co-founder of the Quantum Fund and creator of the Rogers International Commodities Index (RICI). Although Rogers' career spans over forty-six years, during the last thirty-four years he has been semi-retired and travels extensively around the world. He was an occasional Visiting Professor at Columbia University. One of his books, *Investment Biker* recounts his riding a motorcycle around the globe during 1990–1992 and what he learned along the way about the world's developing countries and investment markets by seeing them from the ground up. It led to one of his three entries in the *Guinness Book of World Records.*

I grew up in a very small town in the backwoods of Alabama and I seemed to be somewhat different from the rest of the people there. Then, as I progressed through life, even before Wall Street, I realized that life was different from what we were told. So I made a conscious effort to figure out what was really going on. I guess that must have started when I was in my early twenties. I was in the army at the end of the Vietnamese War, so my consciousness certainly grew there. But as I said before, even when I was a teenager in Alabama, and as I think about it, I certainly was more conscious of some things, and understood certain aspects about the world better than many of my contemporaries in that little town and in my school. In the army I was opposed to the Vietnam War, so that certainly helped raise my consciousness. I was most vocal with other soldiers and people in other offices about what a mess it was. And I asked questions when most people in the army didn't.

WALL STREET 50

Deepak Parekh   *Practice Five: Self-Awareness/Mindfulness*

LIVING WITH A CLEAN HEART

Deepak S. Parekh is the Chairman of Housing Development Finance Corporation in Mumbai. HDFC is India's leading housing finance company. The Reserve Bank of India appointed him Chairman of the Advisory Group for Securities Market Regulation and he was made Chairman of the Expert Committee to look into the reform efforts in the power sector. In addition to being known for his vociferous views seeking standardization and transparency in the real estate sector, Parekh is known as the unofficial crisis consultant of the Government. His philosophy on Corporate Social Responsibility is "if a company earns, it must also return to the society" and that companies owe a responsibility not just to shareholders but to all stakeholders.

KIM: When you hear me say something like living consciously, what does that mean for you?

DEEPAK: Well it means living with a clean heart. You don't cheat people. You don't fool people. You don't bluff people. You are transparent and you are open.

KIM: Would you say you have always lived that way?

DEEPAK: I have always lived that way. I have not cheated anyone in my life. I have never fooled anyone. I have not taken anyone on the garden path and then dropped them, or if you are in the lending business say, "Yes, yes, we will give you whatever you need," and then turn it down afterwards. You have to give the impression early on that you know it's difficult to do if it is. It's better to let people know upfront where they stand rather than just to pull them along.

KIM: What do you attribute being like this to?

DEEPAK: Maybe upbringing. What I noticed while I was growing up. My family were all bankers—my father, my grandfather, my uncle, they are all bankers. And they had good reputations, good credibility. Reputation and credibility is the sort of thing that if you do a little something, it's very difficult to mend it. The crack is always there. If a plate is broken, crockery is broken, you can mend it, but the crack will always be there. So you have to protect your reputation steadfastly, whatever happens. Integrity and reputation are more important to me than anything else.

WALL STREET 50
Barry Ritholtz   *Practice Five: Self-Awareness/Mindfulness*

REALIZING YOUR EMOTIONS ARE DRIVING YOU

Barry Ritholtz is an author, columnist, guest commentator on Bloomberg TV, blogger, and equities analyst. He is the Founder and CIO of Ritholtz Wealth Management a financial planning and asset management firm with $130 million in assets. He was named one of the "15 Most Important Economic Journalists" in the U.S. in 2010 and one of the few strategists who saw the housing implosion and derivative mess far in advance.

If you are not enlightened enough to know that emotions are driving you, well . . . One of the ways you can deal with your emotions is to sign a prenuptial with every stock. Sign a prenup agreement for when you buy something, and say to yourself, "Here is my exit," and then have the discipline to stick with it. I am fond of saying, "I am over fifty and have no gray hair because I don't stress about the exits." I know the exits before I marry that stock. I don't have to react emotionally when it's "caught with the pool boy." I know if this happens, it gets jettisoned, because it's in the prenup, and so that's another factor in knowing yourself—having some self-enlightenment so you can take steps to prevent your own worst behavior.

KIM: What would you say to someone who doesn't have much self-awareness?

BARRY: I'd tell them to stay the hell out of the market. If you don't have a degree of self-awareness, this is an expensive place to learn. I give a presentation called, "This is your brain; this is your brain on stocks." The slide from my presentation is "Monkeys love narratives." Think about human history for millennia. The way we passed information along had to be something that was memorable and able to be shared. A narrative fulfills that with memorable characters and a story and a conclusion and a lesson. My pet theory on where most of the Bible came from and Joseph Campbell and all the various societal myths and how similar they are from culture to culture is that they developed so you could pass the information along, whether it was how to farm, or how to gather or stay away from the leaf with the purple berry. . . .

So, we are pretty much hard-wired to like a story, but stories don't help you pick stocks. Stories help people sell stocks. In fact, that we are even talking about stocks instead of broad passive indexing is because stocks all have stories in them, and saying, "Just go buy an ETF" has no story. Every time I give a speech to an audience that is mom-and-pop-oriented, I invariably say, "I am going to give you the single greatest advice that anyone is ever going to give you and I can guarantee you that you are all going to ignore it." I start my speeches with this so years later nobody can say I didn't tell them. I tell them to get two or three broad indexes, a big cap of technology and emerging market, and dollar cost average into that, and don't even look at it. When prices are high, you're buying less cause you're buying the same dollar amount. When prices are lower, you're buying more, and over the course of fifty years, you should do well.

You do that and you'll best 99 percent of your friends and relatives' investments. You will pay less. You will lower your taxes, blah blah blah. Now all of you are going to ignore that. Let's talk about what you are here to talk about. But I feel obligated to say that because that's the best advice you can give anybody, unless someone has a big portfolio and tax concerns, generational wealth transfer issues. The funny thing about the democratization of finance is that everybody starts to fancy himself a portfolio manager, and there is nothing wrong with passive indexing. In fact, for the vast majority of people, it's cheaper, more efficient, more productive, and most likely to outperform than what most people do.

WALL STREET 50

Frank Casey   *Practice Five: Self-Awareness/Mindfulness*

HAVING A MORAL COMPASS

Frank Casey is a member of The Fox Hounds, Harry Markopolos' team that worked nearly nine years to blow the whistle on Bernard Madoff's Ponzi scheme.

Living consciously means you must have some moral compass. And whatever that compass is let it be a seeker of the truth in yourself and the market. As a financial professional, it could be a moral compass of trying to do what's right or make money competitively within the boundaries of the rules of a fair game . . . but living consciously, to me, means being aware of your responsibilities and working within the environment of your endeavor always to be truthful, honest, and transparent. I think I've always been working consciously because I believe that while I'm extremely competitive, I've never undertaken a position or taken a position where it would be to the detriment of my partners or my clients because I was perpetrating some fraud or trading with some misgivings.

This sounds trite, but I believe that to be a great leader, as an army officer for instance, you have to be honest with your people, and you'll have to make honest assessments of the situation in order to save lives. I am not combat tested. I was trained at an extremely high level for combat. I'm an airborne ranger. I was an infantry captain. Never served in combat, but I was trained for the highest . . . the best training one could get back in those days in the military. It was the most elite of training. Navy seals are comparable. I believe you have to have honesty among a band of brothers in order to deal with the adversity of accomplishing your mission. And that band of brothers in my career—now thirty-eight years—has been the financial community. I cannot, nor will I, tolerate working with people who basically move against my moral compass.

There was a guy about five years ago up in Canada. He was a very bright guy. He made a lot of money, and he said to me over a martini,

"Frank, if you have to sum up your whole philosophy of business in one or two sentences, what would you say?" I looked at him for a moment and said, "Gary, I have a sign over my head, 'No Frauds Allowed!'" He laughed and said, "That is the greatest idea." I said, "This is the way I look at life. I don't have time. I don't have time for people who are fraudulent. I don't have time for people who are wise guys. I don't have time. Life is too short."

The collapse of Wall Street happened because there is a lack of confidence by clients who were perpetrated against by the predatory relationships in the financial community. In other words, when you build a structured financial product and are hedging your risk and betting against the damn thing but selling it to your client, there's something wrong with that. That's why I argue with this whole thing of due diligence. Transparency, internal controls, the pedigree of the guy you'd be looking at, and then last, the strategy, and then three quarters qualitative analysis and one quarter quantitative analysis. You have to understand whom you're dealing with. And no contract is thick enough, no placement memorandum is detailed enough to protect you from fraud. You have to understand who you're dealing with. It's a people business.

A Summary of the Five Practices

- **Self-Responsibility** is Practice One and it means owning what shows up in your life, not to make yourself wrong, but as an empowered place to stand. In the examples from the Wall Street 50, Joseph Perella spoke about his father's advice to spend his time with those smarter and more successful than him because they would call him forth to aim even higher. Wall Street 50's Alex Green said envy and jealousy can distract us from what's ours to do. Wall Street 50's Cynthia DiBartolo's moving story of her own health crisis exemplifies turning a challenge into a transformation by choosing to build a financial firm that would be sensitive to the challenges those with disabilities face.

- **Self/Other Empathy** is Practice Two and discusses the lack of empathy we usually have for ourselves and how that impacts our not having nearly enough of it for others. Wall Street 50's Andrew Scheffer discussed how his meditation practice developed his being more in tune to himself and in turn his clients and Wall Street 50's Carla Harris discussed how the more she contributes to the empowerment of others, the more empowered she becomes. Wall Street 50 Mayra Hernandez discussed how her grandfather's fundamental concern for the environment and his company's employees co-created a much more successful banking firm.

- **Emotional Non-Resistance** is Practice Three. It is the practice of "being with" unpleasant emotions and feelings and even pleasant ones. Staying with whatever shows up, not trying to fix it or change it, but noticing the *now* and being present to it. Wall Street 50's Jason Apollo Voss tells us how much his audience struggled with his suggestion to "tune into the temperature of the room." Wall Street 50's Arnaud

Poissonnier's experience of how those in great poverty were still able to find joy in their day to day lives inspired him to change his career. And Wall Street 50's Brad Katsuyama discussed how his interview process with Michael Lewis encouraged a deeper introspection for himself and his motives, as well as how his entire firm's ability to "be with" their very low odds of succeeding surprisingly moved them on—knowing none of them were going in blind.

- **The Internal and External Journey** is Practice Four and it speaks to how each of us is on his or her own Hero's Journey. At some point in life, we each will be called to do or survive something that seems larger than life itself, and it will seem impossible to imagine victory at the time, but our journey through it will bring us to our bliss. Wall Street 50's Josh Brown's story of how he became the "Reformed Broker" captures powerfully how a typical journey begins with nagging doubts and feeling unfulfilled. He is honest about the messiness and challenge he endured at the beginning, yet it all brought him to the great success he has now.

- **Emotional Self-Awareness/Mindfulness** is Practice Five. Being able to be self-aware is much more than a cursory overview of what you feel; it's burrowing underneath what you feel to see what's informing it. It's the ability to "notice" yourself in a moment and neutrally observe how you show up. Wall Street 50's Andy Pritchard displayed deep self-awareness when he noticed that his reaction to a NYC ambulance was significantly different than the rural one. It's a powerful example of being mindful and present to one's own reaction. Wall Street 50's Barry Ritholtz spoke about how important it is to know that all of us are emotional beings, so if you don't know yourself enough to put in place protocols or exits to prevent your own worst behavior, then you should stay out of the markets completely.

Each of these **Five Practices** supports the others, but they can also each be practiced individually. My suggestion would be not to take them all on at once. Find the one that you resonate with the most and begin there. Choose the one you want to focus on and then add it to your daily calendar so you spend a few minutes each day ruminating on it, writing about it, or speaking with someone else about it. At the back of this book in the Appendices is a list of resources. Look under that practice to find books, movies, websites, retreats, and courses that will support you diving deeper into each.

How to Balance Being a Capitalist While Living Consciously

I believe one can live capitalistically while living consciously. In fact, I believe that the more conscious, self-aware, and connected you are to how you tick and how others tick—the more you can experience empathy—the more successful you can actually be in business. Have you watched *Shark Tank* or *The Profit* on television? *Shark Tank* is where entrepreneurs pitch their businesses in front of a group of very successful potential investors. These investors are entrepreneurs themselves, usually more than one time over, and each pitch is usually followed by a battery of questions. *The Profit* is a show where you have one successful investor and entrepreneur alone. What you see on both of these shows are all different kinds of entrepreneurs, men and women, young and old, being asked questions that seem to the viewer so simple and common sense-like, yet they look blankly at the advisor when asked these questions, because it's clear that they've never even thought of it. What to you and me might seem the obvious concern or alternative course of action—just in case—simply didn't occur to them because they have been walking around with blinders on, missing what you and I would think is obvious.

Plenty of folktales and stories have been handed down to us, warning us of great wealth and how easy it is to lose one's values and moral judgment. And I believe it is an important warning, but it's not only applicable to money; it's applicable to every arena. If we are not living consciously, we might lose the relationships with our children. If we are not living consciously, we might lose the relationship with our life or business partner. Or our business itself. Paying attention and being honest with ourselves—not being perfect, but being aware of where our weaknesses are—is the first step.

I believe it is possible to live a consciously lived life while living as a capitalist, but there seem to be many who don't think it is achievable. There are those who think that one has to be sacrificed at the expense of the other; therefore, I asked these *Teachers of Consciousness* and *The*

Wall Street 50 whether they thought it was possible to balance both and, if so, describe how they themselves manage it, and how we could be more successful at it in our own practice.

TEACHERS OF CONSCIOUSNESS

CONSCIOUSNESS TEACHER

Rasanath Das   *Balancing Consciousness and Capitalism*

CREATE AN ENVIRONMENT OF INITIATIVE AND CHARACTER

Rasanath Das is a monk and former management consultant and investment banker. His TEDx talk describes his incredible journey—from being what he describes as an "external achievement machine" to one who is rich in spiritual introspection, integrity, and true connectivity.

KIM: Can we live consciously and capitalistically?

RASANATH: Yes. Living consciously for me means being completely in touch with our motivations. Working from a place in the heart.

KIM: Is it possible to live in that place, from the heart, being pure with your motives and working in the world of finance?

RASANATH: I think it is possible. The question is, does the environment really allow such a person to maintain that? Is it really encouraged? Because at a certain point, at least from my experience, you have to "climb the ladder" and that can encourage one going away from things that are at your core, or it might ask you to do something that your heart tells you not to. That does not mean that you, even if you are truly in touch with your heart, can't do excellent work, but at the same time, we need an environment to support you living that way.

KIM: Was doing this in your role, in particular, as an investment banker challenging, let's say, more so than in other roles?

RASANATH: Yeah, definitely. Absolutely, because we are giving financial advice to companies. Especially at the time when I was working there. I was working in structured products so it directly affected me. I tried my best to stay clear of them. I kept myself working on straightforward equity and bond product deals.

KIM: Tell us a little more about structured products.

RASANATH: There were specific segments in structured products that were really toxic that brought the markets down, brought the economy down in many ways. I had to work with some of them when I was in the banking world. I kept it to a minimum. As soon as an opportunity came, I stepped away from structured products to get myself into things that were more real. More honest. There are ways you can deal with something that has greater integrity. I think the fundamentals of capitalism are maximizing human potential. Now in a restricted market—and that is not just in capitalistic countries; it could be anywhere, any institution or any organization—as soon as the rules of the organization shut down the true element of the human being, then that organization actually stifles its own growth. For me the fundamental of capitalism is that human production has to be maximized. So if you look at deregulating markets, I think the purpose of deregulation is to bring to fruition whatever human potential is available. The creativity, the ideas. Making things easy. Deregulating so that things get done quicker, so people who are really motivated by creativity don't feel stifled. So if you work on that principle, then it is fantastic. What capitalism also does is it places the initiative on the individual. If capitalism is a modern way to succeed, then somewhere along the line we have to make sure the people who are taking initiative have enough deliberate character and grounding in character that when freedom of the initiative is given to them, they won't misuse it.

CONSCIOUSNESS TEACHER
Cindy Wigglesworth   *Balancing Consciousness and Capitalism*

PRACTICE CONSCIOUS PURCHASING

Cindy Wigglesworth is the Founder of Deep Change, Inc. and the creator of the SQ21™, a Spiritual Intelligence self-assessment, the first competency-based spiritual intelligence assessment instrument.

KIM: How does one balance capitalism and living consciously?

CINDY: Life is challenging all the time. And you have to decide how hard you are going to work on each aspect. So I will give you an example: conscious purchasing. I am—or at least I am working on being—an emotionally and spiritually intelligent person. So how does being emotionally and spiritually intelligent affect my purchasing choices? Well, there is a whole range of ways people could answer that. Some people might say, "I am going completely minimalist." You have probably seen some of these houses that are 300 square feet. You own two pairs of jeans and three T-shirts, whatever. That's one approach. Some people go completely vegan because they say anything else is not responsible.

The question is how do you reach that? I can't spend all my time thinking about every single thing I purchase. So I outsource some of my decision-making. I buy as much as I can from Whole Foods Market because it keeps updating its information. I keep shopping there and I learn from them—for example the humane meat standards. And I know some of the people who are managing that organization and I like their approach. So I really appreciate that they are trying to support the organic food industry and they are trying to support humane farming and sustainable fishing methods. So I will buy from them whenever possible. And when I am there, they may have a choice between an organic apple and a conventional apple, so I will buy the organic apple.

Think through: How can I settle a bunch of decisions in a clump? This big clump related to food decisions means that I am going to buy from Whole Foods. And within Whole Foods Market, I am going to shop for organic first; I am going to shop for the highest humane rating because they have that wonderful rating on their food. In the beef products, I'll get the grass-fed beef whenever I can. That kind of thing. So, that's one way I manage it.

In making decisions about investments, you could make yourself insane trying to research every stock that might be in your index fund. So how do you handle that? You know I have a mix of stuff in my portfolio. I have some socially responsible index funds, and I have some Fortune 500 index funds, and I own some stock outright, mostly ExxonMobil, because I spent most of my career there. Some people might say, "Well, that's an inherently immoral choice." I happen not to think so because I know that company pretty well. But each of us has to reach these decisions for ourselves, without letting them take over our lives to the point where we become ineffective in our own lives.

If your family is dependent upon you, you need that paycheck. Find the noblest paycheck you can today. And if it is not sufficiently noble for you, then keep looking and find the next best improvement on that paycheck as soon as you can. And then find an improvement on that paycheck as soon as you can. I think the long-term evolutionary pressure is going to help companies where employees feel good working there. And so over time, the employers who are able to get the best employees will be the employers who offer a conscious work environment. That's going to take some time to happen, and there are all these shades of conscious work. There are very few industries that are out and out evil. There are some—if you are working in some form of a child factory worker industry, that's out and out evil. But most of our choices involve: "I am working for a company I don't really respect; the owners are jerks; they don't treat their customers well. Should I quit?" My general advice would be, "Get a job while you have a job. And get a job with the most conscious company you can find."

CONSCIOUSNESS TEACHER

Alan Cohen *Balancing Consciousness and Capitalism*

BE A SPIRITUAL CAPITALIST

Alan Cohen, MA, is an author, speaker, and leader in the personal growth movement encouraging outer change through inner awakening, and is a featured presenter in the documentary *Finding Joe,* which celebrates the teachings of visionary mythologist Joseph Campbell.

Do I consider myself a capitalist? Well, in a way, you might call me a metaphysical or spiritual capitalist because I seek to capitalize in all my experiences and learn from them and grow from them and profit from them and become better off because of them. I do make a profit on programs and books I sell. But I also have a mortgage to pay and kids to feed and a wife to support. I think there's a difference between capitalism and exploitation because I do charge a fee, I do make a profit, but I try to charge a fee that is reasonable and that most people can pay. And if someone cannot pay, I'll either give them a scholarship or work something out with them. So I'm happy to make money, but my primary intention is to serve people. I've worked under the model all my life that service comes first and money comes second. Money is a byproduct of service. I've never found that to fail. The more I take care of people, the more the universe takes care of me.

ANSWERS FROM THE WALL STREET 50

WALL STREET 50

Jack Schwager *Balancing Consciousness and Capitalism*

UNDERSTAND INCENTIVES

Jack Schwager is an industry expert in futures and hedge funds and the author of a number of acclaimed financial books, including the best-selling Market Wizard series and the Schwager on Futures series. Schwager is one of the founders of FundSeeder.com, a platform designed to find undiscovered trading talent worldwide and connect unknown successful traders with sources of investment capital. His prior experience includes a decade as a partner in a hedge fund advisory firm and twenty-two years as Director of Futures Research for some of Wall Street's leading firms, most recently Prudential Securities.

KIM: Do you see any conflict in living as a capitalist and living consciously, ethically?

JACK: No, not at all. If you know economics, socialism as a system just doesn't work because it fights human nature. I tell people sometimes that I can teach you 95 percent of economics in one sentence, a very short sentence. "It's all about incentives." If you can understand the incentives, you can understand and predict everything. You can understand how people will react. I mean sometimes there aren't any consequences, but basically everything is driven by incentives. Any problems you look at are because incentives are misdirected.

WALL STREET 50

Fred Wilson   *Balancing Consciousness and Capitalism*

BE A FORCE FOR GOOD

Fred Wilson is a popular blogger and the co-founder of Union Square Ventures, a venture capital firm based in New York City that manages $1B across six funds. Known for having investments in Web 2.0 companies such as Twitter, Tumblr, Foursquare, Zynga, Kickstarter, and 10gen., Wilson is an active philanthropist and community advocate and board member of DonorsChoose.org

KIM: How do you balance being a capitalist and living consciously? Do you find it a challenge?

FRED: Well, it can be a challenge, so I'd say I have a number of approaches I bring to it. One is that my wife and I like to be very philanthropic. We want to share our good fortune. Another thing is I like to invest in businesses I believe provide some redeeming value to society. We're not a double bottom line kind of investor. We don't have a social mission per se, but when we invest in a company like Etsy that has close to a million people who are making either a living or supplementing their income by being able to make artistic products and sell them on the Internet, I see that the existence of that actually can make their lives better. Or when we invest in something like Kickstarter which allows people to start a project, make a movie, or do something where they couldn't get the money before to do, but now because Kickstarter exists, opportunities are available for people to go do things they want to do to pursue their passions and they've got a vehicle to go do those things. There is a benefit to that and I like that. It makes me feel good that we're using capitalism to make something happen in the world that is actually going to be good for lots of people, not just for us.

And not every one of our investments will fit that criteria. But when capitalism can be a force for good in the world, and there are many instances of where it is the force for good, that is something that we'd like to do, when we can.

WALL STREET 50

Andrew Kuper   *Balancing Consciousness and Capitalism*

STRIVE FOR SOCIAL CAPITALISM

Dr. Andrew Kuper is an investor and entrepreneur in emerging markets, and the CEO of LeapFrog Investments. He founded LeapFrog in 2007, now the largest dedicated investor worldwide in insurance and related financial services to emerging consumers. LeapFrog's companies now serve 19.5 million people in Africa and Asia, 15 million are low-income or underserved, often providing them with financial safety nets and springboards for the first time. President Clinton hailed LeapFrog as "opening up new frontiers for alternative investment." Dr. Kuper is a former Managing Director of Ashoka, the organization that pioneered social entrepreneurship and has backed over 3,000 entrepreneurs across over seventy countries. For his work as a pioneer of profit-with-purpose business, Dr. Kuper won the Ernst & Young National Entrepreneur of the Year award in 2012 and was recognized as a Young Global Leader by the World Economic Forum in Davos in 2013. He holds a Ph.D. from Cambridge and is the author of two books on globalization and governance.

KIM: Do you have a challenge around balancing being a capitalist and living consciously?

ANDREW: Beyond my family and friends, my life is devoted to businesses that both make strong profits and transform millions of lives, and to bringing those two things together. No one should think this is easy or that there are not particular challenges along the way that have to be confronted consciously. But fundamentally, I think the whole promise of LeapFrog Investments, of impact investing, and of social business more broadly is that those two things can be brought together. I think if we can create, pioneer, generate, and scale a form of social capitalism, that really channels the capital markets to incredibly productive and meaningful purposes, then there is no contradiction between profit and purpose. That seems to me to be a valuable endeavor in life and work. If you look at LeapFrog's portfolio companies, as of March 2014, they serve 21.2 million people in thirteen countries. Sixteen million of those individuals are low-income or emerging consumers. The vast majority have had limited or no previous access to financial services such as insurance, savings, and pensions—but they now have essential tools to help secure their families' future and their businesses' sustainability. Our companies also support over 52,000 jobs. Obviously, we have this kind of impact through our portfolios companies, and we are investing in and supporting their ideas and teams. But, fundamentally, the opportunity for our companies and investors, and those millions of affected people, is created when you bring those two things together—and it is really profound. I don't think we should have to choose between profit and purpose.

My family, friends, and colleagues are inspired by this evolution of a better kind of capitalism. We have to get beyond the world where the two options are choosing between Mother Teresa and Donald

Trump. We can't live in a world that doesn't have significant financing of major businesses that deliver incredibly important social services and goods and employ millions of people. Nor can we live in a world where the kind of financing of those businesses operates without any attention to the actual people affected and employed, because then we are fetishizing the vehicles of capital rather than keeping our eye on the ultimate goal of business as building wealth while contributing profoundly to society. We have got to get beyond that radical choice. I think when people are saying we need a "more meaningful form of capitalism," what they are really pointing toward is not some objection to effective business but to keeping your eye on that end goal.

LeapFrog's perspective is that one should be vehicle agnostic, in the sense that whatever vehicles help you to get quality, affordable, relevant products and services out to the people who need them, whatever vehicles help you to get quality and sustainable employment to millions of people, these are the things we should consider investing in. And whatever infrastructure at intermediary and financing levels really works to serve that scale and sustainability and innovation, we should support and enable it. When that infrastructure is radically out of kilter and starts being highly destructive, of course, it is appropriate to regulate; of course, it is appropriate to influence. But part of what we want to do is to do that with the carrot rather than the stick. I see the stick being relevant sometimes, and I think it should come down hard on certain people who behave extremely badly. But the carrot can be more powerful, enabling an allocation within those trillions of dollars of institutional investor portfolios to impact investing, just like there is an allocation now to alternatives that didn't exist decades ago. And when that happens, money automatically flows from the capital markets into purposive businesses, just as it flowed into alternatives.

If we can open the gates of the capital markets, through intermediaries that invest in profit with purpose businesses, we create a radically different world. I think if we can encourage people through our leadership and through demonstrating a different kind of approach to generating returns, then there will be a lot more hope, because people will see it isn't a choice. We will create a word in which Richard

Branson or Muhammad Yunus are role models rather than Donald Trump. Hopefully, that leads to a new landscape, filled with inspiring people, creating profit with purpose businesses and investment houses in some ways following LeapFrog's lead but in other ways achieving things that we can't even imagine yet.

WALL STREET 50
Barry Ritholtz   *Balancing Consciousness and Capitalism*

PRACTICE INTEGRITY

Barry Ritholtz is an author, columnist, guest commentator on Bloomberg TV, blogger, and equities analyst. He is the Founder and CIO of Ritholtz Wealth Management a financial planning and asset management firm with $130 million in assets. He was named one of the "15 Most Important Economic Journalists" in the U.S. in 2010 and one of the few strategists who saw the housing implosion and derivative mess far in advance.

KIM: Do you think there is any conflict with being capitalistic and living consciously? Can one be both?

BARRY: Of course. There is no reason not to.

KIM: You don't find that challenging for yourself at all?

BARRY: It comes back to integrity. If you have integrity, it doesn't matter what you do for a living. As long as you are not a jewel thief; it's hard to do that and have integrity. I just watched *To Catch a Thief,* so that's on my mind. That's a perfect example of a guy who gets out of his business because of his integrity. There should be no conflicts with living capitalistically and consciously . . . now there are certain parts of capitalism that are unseemly. I am not a big fan of leverage buy outs. I think when a management team takes a company, loads it up with debts, extracts a lot of fees and charges, then they are not creating anything, they are just rent-seeking. That's financial engineering. I don't know if you can do that sort of crap with a lot of integrity. You are not creating anything. You are not producing. You are not servicing anybody except your own fees and whoever gives you money, and they say, "Go on; rape and pillage." I am not a fan of that. On the other hand, there are vulture investors whose job it is to pick up the bones from the dead companies and try and find what is left over . . . people think that's unseemly, but you know what? Carrion birds are necessary. They're absolutely required. They help things move along.

WALL STREET 50
John Allison   *Balancing Consciousness and Capitalism*

CREATE A SENSE OF PURPOSE

John Allison is the CEO and President of the Cato Institute and was the longest serving CEO of a major bank in the U.S. when he was CEO of BB&T Bank. Allison is a major contributor to the Ayn Rand Institute and has said that *"Atlas Shrugged* was the best defense of capitalism ever written."

KIM: What does capitalism mean to you, and how do you balance it with living consciously?

JOHN: Capitalism is the system that promotes human flourishing because it is the only system where individuals are free. The fundamental goal of life is to stay alive, and ultimately, to be happy in the Aristotelian sense of that word. A hard-earned, paid for with a little blood, sweat, and tears kind of happiness. If you feel good about your book when you get through writing it, you will have worked hard at writing it, but there will be a deep happiness from this kind of achievement. That is what life is about and, to achieve that, first, you've got to have a context where you are free to act in your rational self-interest. This requires that you ask yourself what kind of world you would like to live in and what you would enjoy doing to help create that kind of world. What you are really trying to do with your book is to help create a world that is consistent with your beliefs, a capitalist world. You are writing a book that you enjoy writing even though it may be work to do it because you believe it will contribute to making the world that you value a reality. We may or may not win the fight, but that's not the point.

I think some people drop the context and think of pursuing their happiness by taking advantage of other people, which is not going to make you happy and not going to make you successful. And, secondly—you hear people described as selfish who have tunnel vision because they are totally self-focused, which is irrational. They are narcissists. They drop the context of the kind of world that would make them happy. Pursuing happiness requires that you have a sense of purpose—a purpose to make the world a better place to live, doing something you want to do for you. You will choose to take care of your body and your mind and try to create successful relationships with people who share your values. Those human relationships are important to us in terms of satisfaction.

Capitalism is the system that allows you to pursue your chosen purpose. Somebody who is running a business, pursuing his own happiness, has to hold the context above making a better world consistent with his personal goals. Some people on Wall Street who made a lot of money and got out before the crisis are still very unhappy people because they got confused that money was the end of the game. At some level, they know they misled people, and they took advantage of people. Now, they drink a lot, and they are not very happy people. If you are conscious about your own life, you know as a capitalist you want a business you can be proud of. Yes, it has got to make money and money is a good thing, but not at the expense of deeper kinds of values.

For example, you don't want to make money by taking advantage of your clients even if you can get away with it. Of course, I would argue you will never get away with it in the long-term. But even if you were to get away with it, this is not meaningful work, and at some level, you will know that. You can't be responsible for your clients, but you want to be sure you do the best you can to help your clients be successful. Not just for them. In fact, it is not primarily for them. It's for you. It's your meaningful work. When I started out in the banking business, I knew that if I wasn't giving people excellent financial advice and helping them be successful, not only would they be less successful, but mostly, I would be less happy. Sometimes my advice included saying, "I am not going to make you a loan because this loan won't help you financially. It will just help you get in trouble." They may not like the decision, but it is the best decision. I am sure when you are counseling people, you have to give some of that kind of advice, the hard truth. But that is meaningful work. Unfortunately, a lot of businessmen don't think about their work in that context, and they don't really understand what being selfish is in the deepest sense of the word. And they are unhappy.

WALL STREET 50
Dara Albright   *Balancing Consciousness and Capitalism*

WORK WITH PRIDE

Dara Albright founded the NowStreet blog in 2011 and is the preeminent resource for education and insight into the burgeoning industry of market structure, private secondary transactions, and crowdfinance. One of the earliest voices covering the JOBS Act and advocating for greater democracy in the equity and credit markets, Albright produced the first major crowdfunding conference in 2012 and co-founded LendIt, the largest and most recognized global P2P and online lending conference organization.

KIM: How do you balance being a capitalist and living a conscious life?

DARA: I think that capitalism benefits society. Capitalism advances the society. If it weren't for capitalism, we would never have had some of the products and companies that went on to change the world. Capitalism made that all possible. I don't associate capitalism with greed. I think that they are two very distinct concepts. I don't even think they belong together. But I think we've got to a point where Wall Street has kind of made it look like they're one and the same, but they are two. They are very, very different. With respect to capitalism, just making money is very noble. Look at what capitalism has brought about. There'd be no telephone without capitalism. We'd all be sitting on our own farm. So I think capitalism makes people want to work hard. I think that's a really important thing. I think hard work is great. It gives you a sense of pride and ownership. Capitalism makes that possible. If we didn't have capitalism, if we moved toward a more socialistic kind of society, that would fall apart very fast. Because the less you have to work for something, the less you are going to work for something.

WALL STREET 50
Marlee-Jo Jacobson   *Balancing Consciousness and Capitalism*

SURRENDER TO THE UNIVERSE

Marlee-Jo Jacobson is the Founder of SafeMoneyMetrics® a managed futures risk management and research service. Analysis provided is a direct approach to identifying, evaluating, and monitoring investment cost, trading talent, and capital at risk relative to realized return using her proprietary algorithms. Jacobson says her obsession is "consciousness as a risk management strategy." She is also the founder of ConsciousKids. org, which provides a journey of empowerment to orphans, inner city, and foster care children.

KIM: What would you recommend to someone in the finance world if they want to begin increasing their own consciousness?

MARLEE-JO: I would start with a book called *The Science of Mind* by Ernest Holmes. The reason I would start with that book is it's a practical guide to universal laws brought into everyday experience. It teaches us exactly what we are, how to use these laws, and how to reshape our thinking. You can't take any steps 'til you know where you're stepping. You can't walk until you see a path. That book gives you a path where you could see it, touch it, and do it. Most people don't like doing anything unless they know there's a benefit there. And they have to know in ten seconds, especially in this day and age, because everybody is so freaking impatient. That book is the most direct path to the benefits of living consciously that I could ever recommend to anybody and they could get it in the shortest amount of time. And once they start seeing the rewards and make their internal changes, the universe will pick them up so they don't have anything to worry about. They just have to be smart enough to listen. Make the space and listen. Once they make the space and listen to what they're being told, they'll find their way. We all have a spirit in us that takes us where we need to go. Our ego is supposed to serve our spirit. Once we stop fighting the spirit, we'll be taken. We're carried. Just like the bird flies, we're carried. Just get out of the way. We're always in the way. We are always in the way.

WALL STREET 50

R. Paul Herman — *Balancing Consciousness and Capitalism*

CREATE A MORE THOUGHTFUL APPLICATION OF CAPITALISM

R. Paul Herman is the founder and CEO of HIP Investor Inc., and President of HIP Investor Ratings LLC. An internationally recognized expert in impact investing, Herman invented "HIP = Human Impact + Profit" in 2004 to show that the strongest portfolios and leading companies source much of their competitive advantage and shareholder value from improvements in quantifiable human, social, and environmental capital and their associated impacts on profit.

KIM: How do you balance having capitalist tendencies and living consciously? And do you find there to be a challenge in living both of those ways?

PAUL: Well, the thing is they're not inherently inconsistent. So they are presumed to be inconsistent today. Just like Republicanism has now become something very different than thirty years ago. So thirty years ago, Republicans were about deficit reduction and it took higher taxes to reduce deficits and Republicans did that in a way that wasn't as contentious as it is now. So in 1986, there was tax reform under President Reagan and it was implemented. Today, we can't have a constructive conversation because Republicanism has become something else. Same thing with capitalism. It has become bastardized by this extreme focus on making that next penny and taking it out of somebody's pocket . . . putting it in and concentrating it out of something that is of lower societal value. That's not necessarily in everybody's best interest. If we ask ourselves, "What are we trying to do? What am I trying to do?" then we can create something that intersects self-interest and group interest. And in something like microfinance, which I do think supports capitalism and the capitalistic mindset, you're making loans to somebody who's going to pay you back and you're charging him interest, that's a capitalist process. And that is a process by which everybody makes money when it works. And that is not inconsistent with capitalism. That's a lot of what Adam Smith talked about in the *Wealth of Nations* and Peter Drucker talked about in his thirty books. It's consistent, but what it has become is an excuse to be selfish because of a lack of forward thinking and a philosophy of, "Money in my hands is better than in your hands." And it's not to be a socialist or a communist about it, but to be thoughtful about it. We need a more thoughtful application of capitalism. Because doing good and making money are not inconsistent. They're actually synergistic with each other.

WALL STREET 50

Michael Stuart   *Balancing Consciousness and Capitalism*

MAKE MONEY AND CREATE OPPORTUNITY

Michael Henry Stuart is the co-founder of Clark & Stuart, an investment firm in Portland, Maine, serving as the principal research analyst and portfolio manager since its inception. He earned the Chartered Financial Analyst designation in 1991. Stuart earned a B.S. in Economics-Finance from Bentley College and a Master's in Urban Affairs from Virginia Tech, starting his investment career in 1981 as a securities analyst with The Old Colony Trust Department of The First National Bank of Boston. Mr. Stuart has served on the finance and investment committees at schools and churches attended by his family.

KIM: Do you consider yourself a capitalist?

MICHAEL: Yes and you know, there's a book I want to write. The title is *Profits Are Good*. It would be a book for fifth graders. When my oldest, Katie, got to fifth grade, I was invited to come in and talk to her math class. They always called the unit the Stock Market Game. And I didn't like that. I would say, "I don't want to be teaching kids that it's a game." I would talk in the context of companies, in owning companies and businesses, and what companies were all about. That companies are a collection of people trying to make a product or a service that other people want. And in order to grow and provide more opportunity for other people, you need profits. And as the owners, you get to share in the profits by providing value. Taking the emphasis off the "stock market." Because I do think, in this country, we're infected with most adults thinking that the stock market is a game. We talk about running money or playing with money. We don't run money or anything like that. We don't play the market. But I think that starts early.

These things go in cycles and I'll live long enough to see a different cycle, but for the time being, corporations are bad guys again. It's not just in finance and in investments. It's the corporate world is the bad guys again. The reality is that the bad guys of the last twenty years are not worse than the bad guys twenty years before that or eighty years before that. And there's probably just as many good guys now and have been over the last twenty years as there were before. But people are busy, and a lot of people didn't take economics when they went to school. They don't naturally understand how the system works, and they're busy with their own lives, their jobs, their families, and they just get little pieces of understanding. And so, if they're being bombarded with negative news about the corporate world, they tend to develop a negative view of corporations. And then they start to look at corporations as something other than people.

KIM: Is it a challenge for you to live consciously and be a capitalist?

MICHAEL: No, I believe in making money, and I'm okay with making a lot of money. I don't need too much, and there are, unfortunately, a lot of people who are making too much. They're making way more than necessary. But not just in the financial business. I try not to be too judgmental about that because you never know what people are doing with their money. Everybody knows now what Warren Buffett is doing with his money, but most people, you don't know. I do think as a society we way overpay short stops and point guards, pro golfers, financiers, and movie stars. I think we just way overpay for those things because I think most of the time we don't pay enough for the people who teach our children to read. Or the people who sweep the street, operate the elevators, clean the hotel rooms. I'm okay with making money. I think it's okay to make a lot of money. The problem is, you can't let money become your guide. Money is not the root of all evil. It's the love of money that's the root of all evil. Money makes possible opportunity and the greatest gift that you can give to anyone is opportunity.

WALL STREET 50

Bill Ackman   *Balancing Consciousness and Capitalism*

FIND THE FOR-PROFIT OVER THE NOT-FOR-PROFIT SOLUTION

William A. "Bill" Ackman is the founder and CEO of hedge fund Pershing Square Capital Management LP. In 2002, Ackman engaged in a six-year campaign warning that the $2.5 trillion bond insurance business was a house of cards. He continued on in spite of being branded a fraud by the *Wall Street Journal* and *New York Times*, as well as enduring an investigation by Eliot Spitzer and the SEC. Later, he made his investors more than $1 billion when bond insurers kicked off the collapse of the credit markets. Ackman's testimony is available online via Christine Richard's book's website: *Confidence Game: How a Hedge Fund Manager Called Wall Street's Bluff*. Ackman is a signatory of The Giving Pledge, committing to give away at least 50 percent of his wealth to charitable causes, and in 2011, he was named one of the most generous donors on "Philanthropy 50" a list put out by *The Chronicle of Philanthropy*.

KIM: Do you find it challenging to be both conscious and capitalistic?

BILL: I think they're totally consistent. What's interesting is that our Pershing Square Foundation has given over $200 million in the last five or six years. And the more time I spend doing the not-for-profit stuff, the more I feel like what we've accomplished in the for-profit world vastly overwhelms what we've been able to accomplish in the not-for-profit world. I think I've had a bias that if you're doing something that's for profit, there's a little bit of a little taint associated with it, which is ridiculous. Part of this is perhaps the media, or . . . I don't know why I would have that bias as a Harvard Business School educated capitalist. But you always think that a not-for-profit charitable thing is inherently good . . . and a business, well, it's a business. They're trying to make money, and that somehow taints it. For example, think of the founders of Home Depot—what they did for the world by building Home Depot. They've employed hundreds of thousands of people, millions probably. They've enabled people to live better, build out a nicer kitchen at much lower costs for homes and families and reconstruct towns after storms. And people who've bought the stock made a fortune and the pension funds that own it, they've done really well, right? So if you think about all of the positive things that came out of that . . . Arthur Blank and Ken Langone the founders, these guys have made an enormous contribution to the world before anything that they've done philanthropically. So my view is that, if there's a problem, you should always look for the for-profit solution to the problem, before you look for a not-for-profit solution to the problem. I think for profit solutions are better than not-for-profit solutions.

WALL STREET 50
Alex Green   *Balancing Consciousness and Capitalism*

HAVE WHAT YOU WANT BY GIVING OTHERS WHAT THEY WANT

Alexander Green is an author and the Chief Investment Strategist of The Oxford Club and Chief Investment Strategist for Investment U. A Wall

Street veteran, he has over twenty-five years' experience as a research analyst, investment advisor, financial writer, and portfolio manager.

KIM: Do you consider yourself to be a capitalist?

ALEX: Absolutely. I would call myself an unrepentant capitalist. It's funny; I was walking down this street one day and this women came walking toward me in this tight black top with sequins on it that said, "Unrepentant Capitalist." I laughed as she went by. I know she meant it as she likes to shop and she is not shy about it, but I also consider myself an unrepentant capitalist for another reason: capitalism is an economical liberty. Without economical liberty, you can't pursue your other liberties, including political. What use is your vote if you can't spend your life doing what you want to do, or earning the money you need to do the things you want to do. I think in today's society, capitalism has a terrible image problem that is wholly undeserved. I mean two hundred years ago, 85 percent of the world population lived on less than a dollar a day; now today, less than 17 percent do. And the ones who live in that kind of over-grinding poverty, overwhelmingly live in non-capitalistic societies. The reason for that is capitalism, more than any other factor, pulls people out of the kind of grinding poverty where people don't have an opportunity to exercise their skills, live a fulfilling life. Why does capitalism have this image problem? Because, and especially on one particular side of the political aisle, capitalism is mis-viewed as greed and selfishness and exploitation.

In most cases, capitalism is nothing more than a voluntary exchange for mutual benefit. I probably should begin by saying that even if you are the greediest person in the world, you're not going to earn one dollar until someone decided that you've provided a dollar's worth of value, either in products or services. Anything else is theft not greed.

People say we have an economic system based on selfishness, but I prefer to think of it as rational self-interest. Adam Smith really hit the nail on the head in 1776 in *The Wealth of Nations* when he said it's not from the benevolence of the baker or the brewer or the butcher that we expect our dinner, but from their regard for their own self-interest. It's when you give people what they want that it furthers your own self-interest. In fact, the beautiful part of capitalism is it basically says you can have whatever you want if you give enough to other people of what they want. Where is the immorality in that system? That's how you get ahead, not by cheating people. Cheating people is not capitalism; that is a crime. All those things we need, your food, your clothing, your shelter, your health care, they are not provided by the government. They're provided by individuals who are paid to provide those services. When you go down the street, the reason there is a tire store on this side of the street and the bank on the other side and the dry cleaner on the other side is not because someone planned it but because someone said, "Hey, there is not a tire store within ten miles; it's probably a good place to set up a tire store, barbershop, or dry cleaner, or a medical center. And it's individuals pursuing their own self-interest that provides all of us with what we need.

KIM: How do you balance being a capitalist and living consciously and do you find it challenging in any way?

ALEX: I don't think there is any contradiction between being a capitalist and being conscious, or being a conscientious capitalist, because, again, when I was on Wall Street, I tried to help people achieve financial independence. I charged a fee for it. In every case, people came to me voluntarily, turned their investments over to me to manage voluntarily, and only stayed with me voluntarily if I did a good job. Now I'm a financial writer and trying to do much the same thing. I'm not selling financial services. I'm selling newsletter subscriptions, and to a lesser extent, the books I write, but again, we are offering it only if you should desire that we should help you. I don't see anything unconscious or immoral about anything we were doing.

And listen, everybody has been cheated in business one time or another. All businesses are run by fallible human beings. Sometimes they're going to make mistakes. Sometimes they're going to breach contracts. Sometimes they're going to injure individuals or the environment. When they do, the transgressors should be punished, but that doesn't make capitalism wrong, any more than democracy is wrong when a congressman has been found with stacks of hundred dollar bills in his refrigerator. I mean we're all imperfect, fallible human beings, and mistakes are going to be made.

WALL STREET 50

Cynthia DiBartolo   *Balancing Consciousness and Capitalism*

FINANCIALLY BACK SOCIAL CHANGE

Cynthia DiBartolo, ESQ. is the Founder and Chief Executive Officer of Tigress Financial Partners. She has thirty years of corporate and securities experience with Merrill Lynch, Smith Barney, Citigroup, and Bear Stearns. In 2009, in the prime of her career, she was diagnosed with Head and Neck Cancer. The extensive surgery left her with a reconstructed tongue, tracheostomy, and significant limitations in speaking. So she took leave and spent the next two years learning how to talk again. Her disability also sidelined her career on Wall Street; as a result, she decided to found Tigress Financial Partners, a woman owned and operated investment bank and broker dealer sensitive to people with disabilities and dedicated to the principles of diversity and inclusion.

KIM: Is it hard for you to live consciously yet capitalistically?

CYNTHIA: No and honestly, I don't know why it would be for anyone. I look at myself as somebody that has an education, has lots of experience, my business has so far been blessed, so being a capitalist is a way for me to achieve certain things—to choose where I can bring change to the world. Social changes require financial backing. I mean, it's that simple. So many wouldn't be able to achieve their goals without that. I'll tell you, when I started this business, I didn't think of it as mine; I thought of it as "ours."

Being Morally Tested

Did you see the movie *Margin Call*? I think it is one of the more powerful films out there regarding Wall Street. The story takes place over a thirty-six-hour period at a large Wall Street investment bank and highlights the initial stages of the financial crisis of 2007–08. It's a horror to watch because you know only too well what awaits us all on the other side. Watching it could make almost anyone want to join the Occupy movement afterward. But one of the things this director did that I've not seen done quite so well was to allow you to relate to some of the characters, especially Sam Rogers played by Kevin Spacey. Roger's "crisis of conscience" is so deep you can't help but empathize with him, at least initially. He is completely outraged and yet you can see him twist and turn while being caught between a rock and a hard place. We watch him slowly but surely not stand his ground and, ultimately, become and contribute to the very darkness he abhors. Roger Ebert wrote in response to the film: "I think the movie is about how its characters are concerned only with the welfare of their corporations. There is no larger sense of the public good. Corporations are amoral, and exist to survive and succeed, at whatever human cost. This is what the Occupy Wall Street protesters are angry about: They are not against capitalism, but about Wall Street dishonesty and greed."

While I agree with Ebert that corporations have not been concerned with the impact their actions have beyond their spreadsheets, I think the important point here is to look at the heart of this story, and it transcends Wall Street—this film is about the moral dilemmas each of us will face at some point in our lives whether or not we work on Wall Street. This question has been asked of mankind since the beginning of time. When faced with a moral challenge, will we face the challenge and not succumb to the temptations? Each of us is like a character in our own Shakespearean play. This movie and our lives are as much a survival story as anything. This film's story asks us: How does one survive in this world when faced with temptations and keep his or her integrity intact? How does one stay true to oneself when there is a gun to one's head, financial or otherwise? I wanted to know how these financiers were able to find the courage of their convictions when so much was at stake. And so I asked them how they did it and what it cost them.

ANSWERS FROM THE WALL STREET 50

WALL STREET 50
Eric Carangelo   *Morally Tested*

BE ABLE TO LOOK IN THE MIRROR

Eric Carangelo is a Vice President at State Street and has worked in finance for over twenty years. He specializes in large portfolio trades as well as interim asset management for institutions such as pensions, endowments, and foundations, and is active in several charities.

KIM: Have you been morally tested?

ERIC: Early in my career, I worked on a sales team where the territory someone covered was a huge factor in the person's success. When one of our team members left for a better opportunity, Adam, our boss, had a knee-jerk reaction to hire another salesperson but we, the team, lobbied to divide the vacated territory among us; it worked, sort of.

In a scene reminiscent of Chicago back-room politics, every one of us lobbied for the big money states, chief among them, California. Our boss' office was a revolving door of whiny salesmen. I had some strong ammunition in this fight; I covered California at one point in my career, I was the longest tenured veteran of the team, and often, my boss mentioned that I was the most knowledgeable.

One day, the boss called me into his office and said, "I'm thinking of giving you California; let's call Steve and let him know what states he is getting: Kansas, Nebraska, and Missouri." My retort was, "Great, but shouldn't John (our third team member) be part of this conversation? He is on a train back to our headquarters and should be here later this afternoon."

Well, that was the wrong response for me to make because even though I desperately wanted California again, my boss didn't hear that; he heard only weakness, and he interpreted it as me having no desire to travel. I tried to explain that was not the case; I just wanted to be fair to the others. I figured that my argument was strongest anyway, and if we all had a forum, the right decision would be made. It was fairly obvious that whoever had California would make significantly more money, but there was no way I could say, "Yes," knowing that my colleagues would feel shafted by the haphazard process.

So I walked out and called John. "Hey, where are you?" I said. "Get in here as soon as you can; the territory is being broken up." I headed to lunch and John hurried to the office.

When I came back from lunch, my boss gave me the news. "John is getting California; you'll get the Pacific Northwest, Montana, Idaho, the Dakotas, and all of those other states up there." Instead of John staying there until I returned, he grabbed what he could and left me the scraps.

Would I do it again? Yep, albeit without leaving for lunch. After all, I'm the one who has to look at myself in the mirror—nobody else.

WALL STREET 50
Rob Davis   *Morally Tested*

QUESTION YOUR MOTIVATION

Rob Davis is a Managing Director and head of business development at McAlinden Research Partners (MRP), a division of Catalpa Capital Advisors, LLC. Including his time at MRP, Rob has enjoyed a long career in various aspects of the capital markets for firms including Bank of America, Morgan Stanley, Dillon Read, and Oppenheimer. His first job following graduation from SUNY New Paltz was teaching elementary school, where he first witnessed the harmful effects of child abuse. It was an experience that, years later, led him to start Hedge Funds Care,

Help For Children (HFC), a charity dedicated to the prevention and treatment of child abuse. HFC is now an international movement with chapters in fourteen cities and five countries. Following his ten years as Chairman, Davis continues to serve as Chairman Emeritus. Since its founding in 1998, HFC has donated more than $40 million through over 1,000 grants to organizations dedicated to saving children from the trauma of abuse.

KIM: Have you ever been in a situation where money was on the table, but you felt it asked you to compromise your own integrity?

ROB: There is one situation I can think of where I came to the conclusion that I had to leave. I was leading a very large position, a stock position in the company, and I would lose it if I left. I'd also lose a big bonus that was coming and very big potential earnings. Yet I concluded that I had to leave and made an appointment with the guy I worked for to resign the next day. I couldn't work for him anymore because of the things happening that I felt he was responsible for at this company. And that very night, I received a phone call from somebody who I had worked for previously, who offered me a job, to come back and work for them again. It was almost as if the Universe took care of me. I had another situation where I was forced to leave another place where it didn't work out quite that well, but, you know, everything like that drives you on to whatever is next. And I am still in the game all these years later.

KIM: What would be your advice today to somebody who faces his own moral dilemma?

ROB: I definitely think it is really important to look in the mirror and make sure of what you are reacting to—that it is the right thing and not out of your own ego. Are you being a grown-up, or are you being a baby? But if you find yourself in a situation which is untenable, you should find another situation. The issue always is that we attract to ourselves who we are. You always have to be careful about understanding why you are there in the first place. How did you go to work for that person in the first place? How did you get introduced to that? And what is your motivation? Your motivation is a very good place to look when looking at these things.

WALL STREET 50
Fred Wilson   *Morally Tested*

DON'T TAKE ADVANTAGE

Fred Wilson is a popular blogger and the co-founder of Union Square Ventures, a venture capital firm based in New York City that manages $1B across six funds. Known for having investments in Web 2.0 companies such as Twitter, Tumblr, Foursquare, Zynga, Kickstarter, and 10gen., Wilson is an active philanthropist and community advocate and board member of DonorsChoose.org

KIM: Was there a moment when money was on the table but it conflicted with your values so you left it on the table?

FRED: There have been many instances in my career where I could have gotten involved in something where it was pretty clear we would make money, but I didn't like the business. Maybe I felt the business was taking advantage of people in some way, so we just decided we didn't want to be in that business, even though we knew we could make money.

And I don't begrudge the people who made those investments because someone's going to make those investments—but we didn't want to do that. And there's plenty of ways to make money in this world, so you don't have to necessarily go into businesses that are cynical or zero-sum businesses. And you know, someone could probably look at our portfolio and say, "Hey, this company is a cynical business model. It's taking advantage of people." So I don't want to act pure, high and mighty here, right? Nobody is perfect and I don't know that we're perfect either, but there are certainly plenty of instances where we've just said we don't want to make money that way.

WALL STREET 50
Josh Brown   *Morally Tested*
KNOW WHEN YOU'RE DONE

Joshua Morgan Brown is one of the top financial bloggers in the world. He is known as The Reformed Broker and author of *Backstage Wall Street*, the inspiring and eye-opening story of his leaving retail brokerage. He is the CEO of Ritholtz Wealth Management where he works with individuals, corporations, retirement plans, and charitable foundations.

KIM: Was there a moment when there was money on the table but it conflicted with your values so you left it there?

JOSH: Yes. I spent two years doing that basically—managing a branch with thirty-five brokers, watching them beat the shit out of their accounts in 2008 when the market was free falling. I couldn't be responsible for it any longer, so I left. To me it wasn't even a tough choice. I woke up one day and just said, "You know what, that's it. I am done. I am not doing it anymore." And so, yes, I left a lot of money on the table, but only for the short-term. It is hard to think long-term when on one hand you could say, "Yes, I could probably get away with this for another year and do really well for myself," but one has to also factor in what happens if this, that, or the other thing happens, so I guess I learned how to walk away at the right time.

WALL STREET 50
Schuyler "Sky" Lance   *Morally Tested*
RETAIN YOUR HUMANITY

Schuyler (Sky) Lance is a managing partner of SustainVC LLC, which manages the Patient Capital Collaborative series of early-stage impact investment funds. Associated with Investors' Circle, PCC invests on a for-profit basis in companies that provide meaningful social and/or environmental benefits to the world. Previously, Lance was Co-Founder and Managing Principal of private equity firm Windjammer Capital Investors with nearly $2B under management today.

KIM: Can you remember a time in your life when you had to choose being conscious or ethical, over the financial benefit?

SKY: In my history of investing, even before I started SustainVC, I have been faced with situations where, yes, the economics say I should just say, "See you later" to this company and let it crash and burn. But the human side of me said, "There are people working at this company and their families are dependent on their salaries," so just "see you later" doesn't seem a moral thing to do. So I spent more time with companies that the financial model showed I shouldn't have spent time on in order to help them in their transitions and find other revenues for them. Sometimes, their business models didn't work, because not all business models will work. I still worked with some of them for an orderly transition, as compared to just "See you later." And even in my own job, I felt sometimes I was criticized for spending so much time on companies that were troubled even if we had very few in our portfolios, just because of the time allocation. But, if I spend this time, it's going to be better for all of these people who work in that company, so I am going to do that.

And that was part of what I was feeling at my prior company, that private equity firm, that there wasn't much room for the human aspect for what we were doing. It was more spend time where you think you are going to make the most money and minimize your time in areas where you are not going to make money. Right now, and that's why it is so meaningful, what I am doing now, is investing in companies with both social impact and financial returns. We are looking to make a profit, but we are also, even in those cases where things might not have gone according to the plan or might not be as profitable as we were expecting, as long those companies continue and grow, and even if we don't make a great return on our investment, but there are social missions to continue to move forward; that's partial success. And my investors know that, and there is just a wonderful group of people that has been terribly supportive of what I am doing here. They want to have these companies succeed, and they are less concerned about whether they are going to make 18 percent, 12 percent on their money.

WALL STREET 50
Eric Greschner *Morally Tested*

RESPECT YOUR CLIENT

Eric Greschner is a fee-only financial planner and portfolio manager at Regatta Research & Money Management, LLC, an SEC Registered Investment Adviser. He is also a financial educator and has chaired investment conferences, acted as a speaker and/or panelist, and provided training for organizations around the world. Finally, Eric is also an author, a former attorney, and has worked on Wall Street as an institutional research analyst and market strategist for a leading firm.

KIM: Was there ever a time when your values were at stake and money was on the table, but you left the money to be true to your values?

ERIC: Yes. Actually, I did. Right when I first started, I worked for a large brokerage firm, a wire house firm that was promoting commission-based products. In this particular case, it was an annuity. And I had a longtime family friend who was pushing me to go ahead and transfer the annuity over to the brokerage firm. And I went there and did the analysis, and the one the brokerage firm was offering was a 7 percent commission, where they continue to forward a sales charge of 10 percent with a holding period of seven years, limited number fund offerings. And I was pushed by our sales manager to go ahead and promote that product. I just couldn't do it. I found it extremely distasteful because it wasn't what was in the best interest of the client and our paths in the business. It was a large annuity—$800,000—that size annuity generates a gross commission at 7 percent, or $56,000, which was significant to me at twenty-five-years-old—in my first job.

But I couldn't do that to the client and I couldn't do it to myself. So I literally said, "Look, I can't go ahead and do this. It's just not in your best interest." I don't want to be overdramatic, but it was quite literally as simple as that. When you're a beginning broker, you're under pressure at a wire house to go ahead and meet your sales targets, right? They will go ahead and pressure you to sell. They would listen in on your phone calls with the clients, etc. And I felt a lot of pressure from the wire house to go ahead and do it, but I couldn't do it and I didn't do it.

You know it was kind of physical. There's a physical state associated with that. It wasn't just mental. I said, "I can't do this; it's annoying my stomach; I feel pressured. It's not the right thing to go ahead and do," and so, of course, I didn't do it. But that particular situation was actually one of the catalysts for me saying, "I can't operate how this system is set up." And this is back in 1995, you know, before fee-based really started to take off. I couldn't believe the industry was set up like this. It was a very rude awakening to how things were done.

And then they would have conference calls with the registered representatives in the region. They were marketing conference calls, regional sales meetings, and they were set up to incentivize and reward and point out certain registered representatives who were generating a high amount of sales and set them up as examples. And these registered reps would give presentations to everyone about what they did. What came across was those who were lauded were not those who were necessarily doing the right thing for their clients, meaning the best hits with the right product. The discussions were, "This is what I've told them in order to sell this product and I generated x amount of commission, and this product generates a lot more commission than the others. And let me tell you why, and here is the approach. It was so not "This is in the best interest of the client," but instead, "Look what I got away with." It's egregious!

It's a complete lack of fiduciary standard and the thing is I'm an attorney also. I took ethics. These things violated the very basics of fiduciary standard. And I found it distasteful and I didn't want to be involved in that. Sometimes those negative experiences could be a huge positive catalyst. I said, "One day, I want to open up my own firm and we're doing fee-only no matter what." I wanted to go ahead and set up my own firm with that hat of fiduciary standard for our clients and that was fee-only, no commissions. You represent the client as an advocate, right?

We should not be having these types of structural, ethical issues and debates about duty to a client or duty to the firm. These are archaic debates and just about every other profession has resolved in favor of the client a fiduciary standard a hundred years ago, whether it's medicine or law. Why are these issues even still up for debate? Back in 1995, it was very small and I don't have hard statistics in front of me, but it was in the little single digits, 2 or 3 percent, where fiduciary is in fee-based. Now, increasing—I can easily find this fact for you but I would imagine it's about 30 or 35 percent are fee-based and fiduciary, and it's the most rapidly growing portion. And a lot of the wire houses, who aren't really changing their ways, are fighting to maintain the old standard because they make more money that way. They are still the majority, but it's rapidly diminishing, thank goodness.

And, I'll tell you, in the United Kingdom, they just force everyone in the profession to adopt the fiduciary standards. The entire brokerage industry switched to the fiduciary center with one law, with that of a trustee. It's mandatory across the board. We're still fighting that archaic, anachronistic fight here in the United States in the financial service industry. I just don't understand that.

WALL STREET 50
Andrew Kuper   *Morally Tested*

KNOW WHEN TO WALK AWAY

Dr. Andrew Kuper is an investor and entrepreneur in emerging markets, and the CEO of LeapFrog Investments. He founded LeapFrog in 2007, now the largest dedicated investor worldwide in insurance and related financial services to emerging consumers. LeapFrog's companies now serve 19.5 million people in Africa and Asia, 15 million are low-income or underserved, often providing them with financial safety nets and springboards for the first time. President Clinton hailed LeapFrog as "opening up new frontiers for alternative investment." Dr. Kuper is a former Managing Director of Ashoka, the organization that pioneered social entrepreneurship and has backed over 3,000 entrepreneurs across over seventy countries. For his work as a pioneer of profit-with-purpose business, Dr. Kuper won the Ernst & Young National Entrepreneur of the Year award in 2012 and was recognized as a Young Global Leader by the World Economic Forum in Davos in 2013. He holds a Ph.D. from Cambridge and is the author of two books on globalization and governance.

KIM: Was there a moment when you were tested to be conscious or ethical at the cost of a financial benefit?

ANDREW: Absolutely. We have had several seemingly excellent businesses that we could have invested in, in more than one of our markets, which we walked away from because we understood there was corruption or a lack of integrity by the company. I think having a zero-tolerance approach to choosing ethical and non-corrupt partners is better from both a financial and social perspective. So, yes, we have made very clear decisions along the way to walk away from anything that smacked of a lack of integrity or corruption. And I have no regrets about that.

KIM: And in those moments when you made those choices, what would you say was the motivator? What gave you the courage to say, "No"?

ANDREW: I don't think there was an option, given who we are. There are some things that are impossible for me to do. To be in some way implicated in unethical activity just doesn't fit with the identity of me or LeapFrog, so I wouldn't even say it was a choice. I don't think you can rationalize present behavior by thinking that you will be good later on. Life is path-dependent. If you behave badly now, it will only encourage further bad behavior in the future. If you act ethically now, the likely journey is an ethical one. And opportunities for ethical action and for positive social business start to open up tremendously. We have attracted partners who know of this determination on our part and who share it, and perform better as a result, so our determination has had, as I said, a positive long-term effect.

WALL STREET 50
Henry Kaufman   *Morally Tested*

ASK ETHICAL QUESTIONS

Dr. Henry Kaufman is President of Henry Kaufman & Company, Inc. For twenty-six years, he was with Salomon Brothers, where he was Managing Director, Member of the Executive Committee, and in charge of the Firm's four research departments. Kaufman earned the Dr. Doom nickname as a result of his consistent predictions in the 1970s and early '80s that interest rates would rise and bond prices would fall. In 2009 he wrote *The Road to Financial Reformation*.

KIM: I understand because of your ethics you have been called Dr. Doom, as mentioned in Michael Lewis' book *Liar's Poker*. Can you tell us how that came about?

HENRY: On a personal level, no one in the organization directly at the senior level ever said, "You can't do that; you can't say that." Many traders at that time would call me and say you said something and that questions a lot of money we have positions in or we are long or we are short. That didn't bother me that much as long as no one in the executive committee said, "Hey!" However, the pressure was there to adopt the tools and there were decisions made about the direction the firm was going, which I questioned. Very broad issues. We were getting out of the commercial paper business, growing the junk bond business, looking at risk-taking more diligently and so on. The pressure came on me when the senior management structure changed. The office of the chairman was created and I was part of that office of the chairman. As a result, I resigned as the Vice Chairman and as a member of the public board. Then, a year later, I left. My concern was that I would have diminishing influence on the overall policy and the decision-making. It was also my view that the way we were going was not really the best way. So that was going through my conscience. It wasn't so much a sense of righteousness. I felt a fear that things might malfunction and I would have no influence on the process.

KIM: Can you give an example of when you stood your ground in spite of the money at stake?

HENRY: There are a number of instances, perhaps, throughout my career. For example, I usually committed my views to writing. Particularly when I might have been tempted to change a view in the direction of the mob. That, of course, the traders didn't like. I got a number of calls many times from traders that this created problems, and where's the benefit, or blah blah blah. That didn't bother me because I knew I was fair. When we were in partnership, that view was never opposed. That came in toward the end, when we became a co-operation. I was able to withstand the heat.

KIM: What do you think helped you "withstand the heat?"

HENRY: I was eventually in a senior capacity to withstand the heat. I will also say that in the organization, my work in research was represented right in the executive committee since I was a member of the executive committee representing research and other things. In most Wall Street firms, banks, and so on, the head of research is not a member of the senior management. That is a problem. If the head of research is not in the senior management, there is a fair chance of compromise. That's why you say sell-side analyst, because they have to sell something. It's not a good term, but that's what it is.

WALL STREET 50
Michael Martin   *Morally Tested*

DON'T DO ANYTHING THAT WILL CONFLICT YOU

Michael Martin has been a successful trader for twenty-five years. He is the author of, *The Inner Voice of Trading: Eliminate the Noise, and Profit from the Strategies That Are Right for You*. It focuses on how traders can learn about themselves so they can be profitable. He teaches through UCLA and the New York Society of Security Analysts (NYSSA), and is a member of the CFA Institute.

KIM: Was there ever a moment when your values were tested?

MICHAEL: When I started on Wall Street, I worked in a wire house as a financial advisor because that was pretty much the only job I could get at the time. They weren't really interested in my track record, and I didn't have a long enough track record with enough money to warrant handling a discretionary portfolio. It was also a very different time than it is today. You know, in terms of doing that. There was not a lot of what we will refer to as emerging managers and emerging CTAs, or whatever, so as far as that's concerned, it was a very difficult environment. And I just wanted to be in the business of finance and learn more about money. I was very ignorant about what a person's role was in that job. I thought my job was to make my clients money, and the people who hired me knew my job was basically to get on the phone and gather assets and create commissions and fees. I always had a hard time with it, so I kinda knew very early on I was going to raise money, develop a track record, and then as soon as it was financially feasible, leave and go out of my own. I did that.

So, I do think it can definitely be complex when your branch manager is looking at you asking why your commission and fees don't have you in the first quintile. And you know you could very easily take profits, or at least talk your clients into doing more activity in their accounts, which really doesn't benefit them as much as it does the branch or firm at large. You know the firm at large is usually shoot first, figure it out later, and you know at the same time they want you to diversify and buy, so it's a very conflicted place to be if you are a conscious capitalist. So that was more than twenty years ago. These days, no, I don't. If I don't make money, I don't get paid. I share in the winnings and I don't share in anything else, and I don't kick back and I don't have any self-dollars. I don't have any give ups. I don't have anything that would conflict me or put me at odds with the client and what their goals are.

WALL STREET 50
Sol Waksman   *Morally Tested*

ASK HOW'S THAT WORKING OUT FOR YOU?

Sol Waksman is the Founder and President of BarclayHedge, founded in 1985. It serves institutional clients in the field of hedge fund and managed futures performance measurement and portfolio management.

KIM: Have you ever left money on the table because you refused to do something unethical?

SOL: [Yes, and when I refused to do it] I wondered to myself, am I putting myself on some kind of pedestal, you know, saying, "Oh yeah. I could say to myself, I didn't do this and everybody else is doing it." And I didn't really know what my real motivation was in it, but now years have passed. I'm no longer involved in that transaction. And in retrospect, I'm glad I didn't do what on one hand I would've liked to, and on another hand, I was a little afraid to do.

KIM: What would you say it was that kept you from doing it? What do you attribute that to?

SOL: Ego, self-image. You know, I consider myself a certain type of person and venturing into this gray area would not have been consistent with my self-image. And self-image is ego.

KIM: And am I hearing . . . that ego is not necessarily the enemy always?

SOL: No. It's there, you know. We have our view of ourselves and it may not be the way other people see us. You know, we're all trying to present ourselves in a certain way. It's like in that movie *Fight Club*. There is this one line in the movie that is absolutely brilliant and it's when Ed Norton and Brad Pitt first meet each other on a plane. And in this particular scene, Ed Norton is like the busy little executive, very straight, and so on. And Brad Pitt is more of a rebellious, free-wheeling kind of person. And they're sitting next to each other on the plane and they're talking a little bit. Ed Norton is fumbling, stuttering a little bit, trying to be very straight and so on. And Brad Pitt is coming at him with out-of-the-box type questions. And then Norton gives him some kind of a very straight-laced answer. And then Brad Pitt looks at him and goes, "How's that working out for you?"

You know meaning, putting out that image. "How is that working for you? Are you happy with what you're putting out there?" And that was such a great line, you know, because we're all doing that. You know, we're all on the stage presenting ourselves however we want. Most of the time, we don't see it.

WALL STREET 50
Michael Stuart   *Morally Tested*

PUT YOUR FAMILY FIRST

Michael Henry Stuart is the co-founder of Clark & Stuart, an investment firm in Portland, Maine, serving as the principal research analyst and portfolio manager since its inception. He earned the Chartered Financial Analyst designation in 1991. Stuart earned a B.S. in Economics-Finance from Bentley College and a Master's in Urban Affairs from Virginia Tech, starting his investment career in 1981 as a securities analyst with The Old Colony Trust Department of The First National Bank of Boston. Mr. Stuart has served on the finance and investment committees at schools and churches attended by his family.

KIM: Was there a time when you left money on the table to honor your values?

MICHAEL: Once I was interviewing and had an opportunity to come to New York. And we lived near the University of Connecticut. It was a very bucolic setting. We're out in the country. It's very quiet and peaceful. Four miles from the university. I can drive from my house to the university and not hit a stoplight. While we were reluctant to give that up, I had the opportunity to come to New York and it would've been for a lot of money and a really good job. Eventually, I would've made even more money because the company ended up selling itself, and so I would've been a shareholder, and would have done very well with them. But it would've meant uprooting the kids from that life or leaving them there and me having an apartment in NYC going back and forth. Finally, I said, "We're not going to do this." I said to my wife, "Rocky (my business partner now) and I are going to start our own business, but it will mean going two years without a paycheck." So, I not only said no to the New York job with a fair amount of money, I even asked the family to make a sacrifice. There was going to be no income. We would live on what we had saved. I said, "It'll take five years to get back to what we used to make." And she said, "Okay."

I remember I was with the two boys one time, and they were at that age where they define success and money by the type of car one drives. We had gone somewhere and the two of them were asking me, "Well, Dad, if you had gone to New York and taken that job, could we have had a nicer car than this? Could we have had a Volvo?" I said, "Oh, yeah. You know, if we'd gone to New York we could have had a Volvo." "Well, could we have had a suburban?" And I said, "Oh, yeah, we could've had a suburban." And then Alice said, "Dad, could we have had a Porsche?" And I said, "Yeah, yeah, we could've had a Porsche." "Dad, what are you, crazy?" And I said, "Alex, you could've had all of those and you wouldn't have had me." And over time, things were getting better financially and my daughter Katie said, "You know, we used to be rich and we didn't know it." So the real benefit of making that sacrifice wasn't just for me. I think everybody should be poor at some point. Everybody should know what it's like either not to have a dollar bill in your pocket or to be hungry because it makes you appreciate it more. So all my kids are in that camp and I think that was the great gift of saying no to a job that would've been very lucrative, could have done great things for the family but we wouldn't be who we are today. They might have still been really good, but now . . . my kids are incredible.

WALL STREET 50
Bill Ackman

Morally Tested

DON'T SETTLE AND TELL THE TRUTH

William A. "Bill" Ackman is the founder and CEO of hedge fund Pershing Square Capital Management LP. In 2002, Ackman engaged in a six-year campaign warning that the $2.5 trillion bond insurance business was a house of cards. He continued on in spite of being branded a fraud by the *Wall Street Journal* and *New York Times*, as well as enduring an investigation by Eliot Spitzer and the SEC. Later, he made his investors more than $1 billion when bond insurers kicked off the collapse of the credit markets. Ackman's testimony is available online via Christine Richard's book's website: *Confidence Game: How a Hedge Fund Manager Called Wall Street's Bluff*. Ackman is a signatory of The Giving Pledge, committing to give away at least 50 percent of his wealth to charitable causes, and in 2011, he was named one of the most generous donors on "Philanthropy 50" a list put out by *The Chronicle of Philanthropy*.

KIM: Was there ever a time when money was on the table, but your values would have been compromised?

BILL: Oh, yeah. The darkest moment . . . have you read *Confidence Game*? [Written by Christine Richard about the situation Bill describes below.] You have to read the whole story. My business was in wind down. MBIA did not like me and they sicced Eliot Spitzer on me. I was under investigation by Spitzer, under investigation by the SEC. I was in the newspaper every day. The press on my firm had been very favorable for the first nine years, and then it got incredibly grim for the end of my previous firm. And it was at a time where a lot of Wall Street people were going to jail and we were his next target. And the press portrayed things in a way that was very negative. But I believed fundamentally in free speech, kind of basic American tenets of existence. And that the truth will set you free. I'm kind of a big believer in that. And I've always told the truth no matter what the consequences. I mean, for better or for worse. And generally, it served me well, so I'm not going to stop.

KIM: Was there something that you did . . . that anchored you during that time? Was there something you leaned into?

BILL: Yeah. Friends, family, Karen. But I had a very good foundation. When the storm comes, you figure out which buildings were not constructed well, which don't have good foundations. I was constructed well. I had a good foundation. Therefore, I could withstand the storm. But, you know, it was grim. There was never a temptation to do the wrong thing, but they tried to get us to settle. Settle. Pay a fine. Just admit wrongdoing and you can go on with your life. And I wouldn't do it. And they threatened. At the darkest moment, Spitzer's chief lawyer said, "Tell Bill to bring his toothbrush." Meaning they're going to lock me up. That kind of thing. Really threatening. When the government comes after you and you are a target, and if they lead you to the press, everyone thinks you did something illegal. Do you settle, or do you fight for your name? I wanted to be able to be in this business again. And my name is incredibly important to me. I was prepared to go to the end of the earth to prove I was innocent. You can read my testimony on Christine Richard's website (www.confidencegame.net). There's some great stuff in there that never actually made the light of day, but some of this stuff is quoted in Christine's book. There's a lot of material in there, but the transcripts of my interrogation by the government are on the website. She foraged it and got it from the government. I should read it again. It's been a while.

KIM: I imagine that was a crucible moment.

BILL: Yeah, no question.

WALL STREET 50

Oswald Grubel   *Morally Tested*

TAKE FULL RESPONSIBILITY

Oswald Grubel is currently the Chairman of La Zagaleta. During 2002–2007, Grubel was CEO of Credit Suisse, and from 2009–2011, Group CEO at UBS AG. In 2011, a rogue London-based trader committed fraud and Grubel resigned as CEO of UBS taking "full responsibility." When I asked him why during my interview, he said, "I think as a CEO, you have to take responsibility even if you couldn't have prevented it; if it gets big enough, it becomes a reputation issue for the company, and that's why you have to take responsibility—nobody else can take it but you." Mr. Grubel is a board member of the Swiss-American Chamber of Commerce, the Institute of International Finance, the Financial Services Forum, and a member of the International Monetary Conference.

KIM: I was struck by your assuming all responsibility for what happened with the rogue trader in 2011. When you resigned from UBS, you said, "As CEO, I bear full responsibility for what occurred [at UBS]." That, to me, is such a powerful, rare statement to hear today. Where does that come from, to be this type of person who takes full responsibility for what occurs?

OSWALD: I have always wanted to be fully responsible, mainly because I have always wanted to be a CEO. I have always wanted to be the one in charge, even when I was a much younger guy. I didn't want to have anybody above me tell me how to do my job. So, obviously, then, if you want to be running things and be the one who makes the decisions, you have to take full responsibility. This is one thing that goes with the other. As CEO you have full responsibility. It is not even a question for me. And if you have full responsibility for things, even things you cannot influence, you have to take it, depending on the size of what's happening. If you are running a big corporation, which is in fifty countries, has fifty thousand or more employees, every day something happens in some country, and it is impossible to look after. But you have to make sure that the rules, the laws, and the compliance issues are followed up. You are depending on a lot of other people, then to do it, and if someone down the line isn't doing his job and other individuals aren't being the big hero, in relation to the whole profitability of the company, I think, as a CEO, you have to take responsibility, even if you couldn't have prevented it because you didn't know about it.

Why I say you have to take responsibility even if you could not have prevented it is that if it gets big enough, then it becomes a reputation issue for the company, and that's why you then have to take responsibility. Because nobody else can take it. You can have counterarguments to that. Most people bring this counterargument—what I hear in most cases is, "Oh, I couldn't have prevented it, so, yes, I take responsibility, but I don't necessarily resign because there is nobody better to do the job than me." And that often is their defense. Unfortunately, that doesn't improve the credibility of the company because most people will say, "Wait a moment. Is that the best they have?" Then they will not trust that CEO again, or as much as before, or the reputation of the company.

In 2001, when I was with Credit Suisse on the executive board, I didn't agree with the strategy of the chief executive and chairman at the time, and I resigned. I said, "Look, that is one strategy you want to embark on and it will cost the company dearly. And I am convinced by how I understand banking that this will not work." And his answer was, "In that case, then you have to resign." So I did. It was the same chief executive and chairman who called me a year later and said, "Can you please come back?" I am not the kind of person who says, "I told you so." And so, they convinced me I should come back.

KIM: Where do you think that courage comes from?

OSWALD: I think it was that I was convinced I could find a job immediately somewhere else. Mainly because I was convinced I was right. I understand the business, and if I am convinced I am right, nobody can change my mind. What helped, very clearly, is that one has to keep a certain independence for oneself. I tried to achieve that independence from the first day I started in the finance industry, by trying to make as much money as possible, but mainly to simply have independence. First, you have to understand the business. You have to know what you are doing. That is a kind of independence and is the most important probably. But you also need financial independence, because as long as you are financially dependent, it is difficult to say no. Knowing you could lose your job makes it much more difficult. Especially in big companies—as a company can fire you any minute, but you have to be financially independent to make good decisions. Clearly, financially independent means different things to different people. I mean financially independent so you can go on living for a considerable amount of time without working or depending on the government.

KIM: What would your advice be to people at that crossroads of following their conscience and supporting their family? What would your advice be to them?

OSWALD: I think in the end it always has to be to follow your conscience, even if it means you are going to have hard times because if you don't do that, things will get worse and not better. And you are living for a short time in a false world and things will catch up with you. You may even have a direct boss or someone else say, "Look, if you don't say anything, I will promote you. I will pay you more, or whatever. These things happen in real life. But if you do that, you are a bought person. He/she, the buyer, will do whatever he wants with you, and it will get worse.

WALL STREET 50
Janet Hanson   *Morally Tested*

WATCH OUT FOR THE CONFLICT OF INTEREST

Janet Hanson is the Founder and Former CEO of 85 Broads, a global net-work of over 30,000 trailblazing women worldwide who invest in each other's professional and personal success. Hanson joined Goldman Sachs in 1977, became a Vice President in 1983, and became Goldman's first female sales manager in 1986. In 1995, she founded Milestone Capital, the first women-owned institutional money-management fund in the U.S, managing at its peak over $2.5 billion in assets. From 2004 to 2007, Hanson was a Managing Director and Senior Advisor to the President and COO of Lehman Brothers.

KIM: Was there a time when there was money on the table and your values were at stake?

JANET: This is crazy, and might make me sound dated and old, but the answer is no. But that's the old Goldman. Back then, all we thought about was how lucky we were to work for this insanely great franchise. I realized early on that the tough part of being in fixed income is that you have an inherent built-in conflict of interest. Your trading desk wants you to sell its bonds at the highest price. Your clients want you to sell them bonds at the lowest possible price. Talk about having to live in the moment! Somehow you have to figure out how to make both sides of the trade happy. The defining "ethical moment" is determining what is fair. And that takes real guts because you know "the house" always wants to sell bonds at the highest pos-sible price. And your clients—and I had some very powerful clients—want to believe, even though they can't see you, that you really and truly are representing their best interests. Every single day, you have to have the intestinal fortitude to reason with both parties, and if you can't do that, you should choose another career path.

KIM: To what do you attribute your intestinal fortitude?

JANET: *Wanting to make people happy. Always being a pleaser.* If my client was unhappy, I felt terrible. If the trader was unhappy, he or she would look at me with tremendous disappointment. Making both sides of the trade happy was not something I achieved on my first day on the sales desk. *If you can visualize what is the most successful outcome, then your behavior and your actions convey that to both parties.* And over time, both parties have a heck of a lot more respect for you. Diplomatically handling the super-sized egos of your traders and your clients is a delicate balancing act. The key is to convert as many trading opportunities into successful transactions without offending anyone in the process. If you can do that consistently, it's the best job in the world.

KIM: What was your experience?

JANET: Well . . . I think I had the best of both worlds. I was respected by the traders and I was respected by my clients. I had to work very hard to achieve that goal, mainly because having your trader look at you with disappointment was awful. One of the most powerful traders on the desk was Jon Corzine. He was the great and powerful Oz. Letting him down was gut-wrenching. Having said that, if you consistently tried to do your professional best, he respected that. The truly great salespeople at Goldman inherently knew that if you tried to make money at your client's expense, you weren't long for the firm.

WALL STREET 50
John Whitehead   *Morally Tested*
MAKING YOUR COMPANY A BETTER AND SAFER PLACE

John C. Whitehead is an American banker and civil servant, and currently a board member of the World Trade Center Memorial Foundation. Whitehead joined Goldman Sachs in 1947 and became chairman. After more than thirty-eight years at the firm, he retired in 1984 as co-chairman and co-senior partner. He served as U.S. Deputy

Secretary of State from 1985–1989, and was awarded the Presidential Citizen's Medal and is former Chairman of the Board of the Federal Reserve Bank of New York as well as former director of the New York Stock Exchange. Whitehead served in the U.S. Navy during World War II and landed at Normandy. He has been critical of Goldman Sachs since his departure and some of that is captured in his book, *A Life in Leadership.*

JOHN: I always thought I wanted a job at a place where I would be happy every day, where I would enjoy the work I was doing, and if the time came when I didn't enjoy the work I was doing, I would leave the company. That was my daily satisfaction, not necessarily every day, idealistically, or anything, but I wanted a job I enjoyed. I've seen people with jobs they didn't enjoy, and yet they felt bound to them and stuck with them, so when I was picking a job, I wanted to have something I would enjoy doing. And so I came to Goldman Sachs out of business school and was there for thirty-seven years. I enjoyed it really more than I expected to enjoy any business job, and I realized soon that I was going to be there as long as Goldman Sachs would have me. So my object became to make Goldman Sachs a better and safer place for me to be bound to. I saw some of the problems for Goldman Sachs in the future, and I felt that since I was probably going to be staying at Goldman Sachs a long time, I better do something about those problems or Goldman Sachs might not prosper in the future. If I didn't try to make people recognize these problems and handle them better, then we might not stay alive and competitive. So I got myself involved in some difficult changes to be made at Goldman Sachs to keep us going—corrected some weaknesses I saw with the firm for the long-run. I was fortunate I was able to make those changes. I became a partner and had more responsibilities. I was able to keep at those changes, kept myself sort of at the core for making Goldman Sachs a better firm, better organization. I saw it before I was a partner, and since the changes would upset the applecart, I waited until I was a partner before I began to implement the changes.

I had to set up a structure. There was no structure. There was no budget. There was no planning. There was no thought of new activities or old activities. We just sort of went along in a very informal and relatively unorganized way. I don't say disorganized, but an unorganized way. Then there came a time when we were one of five firms. We were among the five leaders in the beginning of my time as a senior partner. These five leading investment banking firms were all about the same size, and there was little difference between us since we pretty much did the same thing and were pretty much good at what we did. More or less, we were the same. So I said, "What is going to distinguish Goldman Sachs from these other firms so we get a majority of the business instead of one fifth of the business?" I saw that not one firm claimed it had high ethical standards.

Everybody was a little suspicious of investment companies—every company's management was a little suspicious of investment bankers. They were seen as a different world and thought of as shrewd and tough, and they were profitable. People felt you had to be very careful when dealing with investment bankers. Really, we had a lack of trust that wasn't, at that time, specific to Goldman Sachs, but in general. So I said I would try to find a way to make Goldman Sachs respected for high standards and as a firm that you can trust, compared with the other firms. That's a difficult thing to do. It was an intangible thing that was my ambition because I thought that would make a difference in the effectiveness of the business, if we could be concerned with having a firm that had high standards.

I looked for things that could indicate whether we had high standards. And it happened at that time there was a practice of corporate raiding where one company would make a surprise raid by making an overnight offer to buy up another company in an unfriendly way. I looked at the examples of what they'd done quite carefully, and I saw that, really, they didn't work well afterwards because the management of the company being acquired was alienated toward the acquirer. And then, usually, left for another job, and left the acquirer stranded where the company would be left with no men, no good management, or a lack of management. So I said, "Is this a good practice for Goldman Sachs to be a part of?" And the idea came to me that we should have a standard that we don't manage unfriendly tender offers. We are not going to do that for our clients because we don't think they work successfully. We lost business right away on two of our old clients, one of which used to be General Electric, one of our biggest clients. It wanted us to do an unfriendly tender offer for it, and it had to use one of the other four investment banks. And when it took the business from us, it was very unpopular with my clients and with my partners. The partners felt we should make an exception for General Electric. But I held my ground and said, "No, absolutely not; this is our policy and we don't believe these things are going to be successful. Therefore, we are not participating." We held very firm and we did lose some business upfront, not anything too serious, but still, attractive projects that we didn't rank as everybody knew we wouldn't do them and we didn't get asked.

But then it began to dawn on companies that if they were ever being raided, that Goldman Sachs would be a pretty good company to come to because they could be sure we would never turn on them the next day and run against them. It was to our and their advantage to deal with us—to defend themselves against an unfriendly raid. And the policy began to attract a large number of clients that hired us to be a standby defense and would meet with us and learn how to defend their companies from an unfriendly offer. That was beginning to bring in far more than we would have gotten if we were tendering those other offers.

And that grew, and grew, and grew. And finally, as the practice continued without any competition, we had almost 100 percent of the defense assignments. We found ourselves getting 100 percent of that business because of this new ethical policy we had imposed on ourselves. And so everybody was now making auditory comments about Goldman Sachs' standards and that this firm has principles—it's willing to give up its own short-term business interests in order to protect the industry and economy against unfair, undesirable practices.

I wanted Goldman Sachs, as a firm, to have high ethical standards, and I didn't think that investment bankers were known as an industry where ethical standards were particularly high. I did want us to have more ethical standards, and I didn't realize they would also make us successful. I thought it would cost us business to be more ethical, and that, maybe, in the long-run, it would benefit us, but I thought initially it was creating damages. Instead, it helped us initially and it helped us in the long-run, too.

KIM: Did you express what you did see happening at Goldman since your departure?

JOHN: Oh, I saw them doing things that I thought were improper.

KIM: Did you express your discontent?

JOHN: Privately, I pointed out to the then current management this was a bad thing to do and they should stop doing it.

KIM: Was there any response to that?

JOHN: They usually agreed that, yes, what they had done was a mistake and they wished they would not have done it. They would change the internal rules or wouldn't do it again. And sometimes they thought what they were doing was okay and that I was being too picky about it. Or that this was an isolated case which didn't happen often and they were going to make a big overhaul of the organization to correct it. So there were mixed responses. Overall, I certainly have not been entirely happy with the responses. I wish they had tried a little harder to stick to their respect for ethics.

Being morally tested shows up in many ways. Sometimes it has nothing to do with money, sometimes it has to do with being true to the still small voice within when all the voices around you are "shouting their bad advice" as they do in Mary Oliver's poem, "The Journey":

> One day you finally knew
> what you had to do, and began,
> though the voices around you
> kept shouting
> their bad advice—
> though the whole house
> began to tremble
> and you felt the old tug
> at your ankles.

How does one stick with the journey when that house trembles and you feel the old tug at your ankles? You must be someone who can trust him- or herself. Do you trust yourself? This is the first question each of us must ask ourselves. If you don't, then it's time to rebuild that trust.

In the above examples, you may or may not agree with how each of these fifty navigated theirs. I remind you that these *Wall Street 50* aren't living perfect lives. They are human, just like you and me, and they wrestle, as we all do with what living in integrity looks like. Yet each are doing their best to do so. Some listened all along; some had wake-up calls come late in life. I share these stories for you to see that the tests come in all sizes and shapes. I believe these tests come for us to see what we are made of. Being morally tested is really more about you and your own relationship to yourself than to another. The reward of self-trust is a peace of mind that goes beyond all understanding, no matter the consequence you may face. It allows you to look at yourself in the mirror and respect what you see.

> But little by little,
> as you left their voices behind,
> the stars began to burn

through the sheets of clouds,
and there was a new voice
which you slowly
recognized as your own,
that kept you company
as you strode deeper and deeper
into the world,
determined to do
the only thing you could do—
determined to save
the only life you could save.

—Mary Oliver, "The Journey"

PART III

THE FUTURE OF CAPITALISM

If I Had a Magic Wand

In coaching, we are taught that the more open-ended the question, the better. That's where this question comes from. It allows the person not to have any limitations on what he might suggest. It allows the person to brainstorm in a much more flexible and powerful way. It invites one to step into complete and total possibility. You know the term "childlike wonder"? We have that term because when we observe children, we witness and experience pure awe and creativity. They have yet to comprehend the concept of "impossible." They live in perpetual curiosity. That's why they are able to create and imagine so vividly.

Ben Zander, the author of *The Art of Possibility* tells this story:

Two salesmen went down to Africa in the 1900s. They were sent down to find if there was any opportunity for selling shoes, and they wrote telegrams back to Manchester. And one of them wrote, "Situation hopeless. Stop. They don't wear shoes." And the other one wrote, "Glorious opportunity. They don't have any shoes yet."

Our perspective influences what and how we see. I thought if these smart women and men were able to create from a place unrestricted by what is considered "possible," then some unusual solutions might bubble up. Looking back over the last few years, never mind centuries ago, much of how we live now would have once seemed impossible.

Throughout the crisis and Occupy Wall Street, I kept wondering why the President of the United States wasn't creating a Special Forces Unit filled with the men and women of integrity from Wall Street to seek their wisdom and counsel. It's my hope that these *Wall Street 50* will have the opportunity to co-create real solutions not only for Wall Street, but for the world's economic future. In this book, we have some brilliant suggestions from these men and women, and there are countless more who have so much to share. I hope this book facilitates a platform that will allow these ideas and solutions to be heard. It is time to hear from those who are experienced, smart, and have a moral conscience so that real change can begin for the benefit of *all* of our nation and world.

ANSWERS FROM THE WALL STREET 50

WALL STREET 50
Josh Brown   *A Magic Wand*
_____
END RETAIL BROKERAGE

Joshua Morgan Brown is one of the top financial bloggers in the world. Known as The Reformed Broker and author of *Backstage Wall Street*, the inspiring and eye-opening story of his leaving retail brokerage. He is the CEO of Ritholtz Wealth Management where he works with individuals, corporations, retirement plans, and charitable foundations.

KIM: If you had a magic wand to wave over Wall Street, the regulators, D.C., what would your wand do?

JOSH: I would end retail brokerage tomorrow. It is beginning in England. It is not so farfetched. The FSA said, "No more commissions for transactions," for everyone in England, if they work for the public. I don't mean end brokerage firm institutions where sophisticated people conduct business. I mean no more people who call themselves "investment consultants" or "wealth managers." No more of those types of people being able to sell products as opposed to selling advice. I think there is a huge difference between an advisor and a broker. Seventy-eight percent of advisors are dual registered as brokers; I would end that as well. No more, "I wear this hat when I do this with you, but then I wear that hat when I do that with you, and then I will pay myself accordingly." I think all of that has to end and it probably will . . . they are going to fight it tooth-and-nail, they are going to lobby against it, but that would be the magic wand I would wave.

I don't come from a standpoint that Wall Street is evil or financial services in general are evil. I would even say it is an important industry because you are dealing with money. And nothing elicits more of an emotional response in people than money. As a matter of fact, surveys say, people are more emotional about money than health. Because money is not just money; money is options, it is opportunity, it is flexibility, it is the ability to make the people you love happy. Those are the things we attach to money. So financial services are key. The problem is, at a certain point, financial services forgot their purpose or willfully cast aside their rightful purpose in society, and decided it was an end in and of itself. We are going to move money for the sake of moving money and we are going to make profits on money as opposed to finance construction and company formation.

All of a sudden, something happened where the financial industry became 12 percent of the workforce. It is not only stock mortgage stuff. It is bonds. It is credit. It is banks. It is real estate. It is insurance. The FIRE economy (finance, insurance, real estate economy) got way too big and started to feed off of itself. And it started essentially to be a situation where the best and the brightest minds in the country literally were off in a corner trading among each other, as opposed to going into engineering and medicine.

My take is that financial services are not inherently evil. They got too big and have to shrink. Historically, it has never been this big before, and it shouldn't be because once it is this big, then bad products start to be created en masse and a lot of dumb decisions get made. And there's too much borrowing and too much speculation. So, thankfully, that process of deleveraging and shrinking and rationalizing is already under way. It is painful, but it was inevitable.

WALL STREET 50
Hazel Henderson   *A Magic Wand*

CREATE A TAX ON POLLUTION AND CORRECT FIAT CURRENCY

Hazel Henderson is the founder of Ethical Markets Media (USA and Brazil) a Certified B Corporation and the creator and co-executive Producer of its TV series. She is a world-renowned futurist, evolutionary economist, a worldwide syndicated columnist, author and consultant on sustainable development. Henderson has been in good part concerned with finding the unexplored areas in standard economics and the "blind spots" of conventional economists. She has delved into the area of the "value" of such unquantifiables as clean air and clean water; this led to the development, with Calvert Group, of the Calvert-Henderson Quality of Life Indicators. In 2004, Henderson started EthicalMarkets.TV to showcase video of people and organizations around the world with socially responsible endeavors.

KIM: If you could wave a magic wand over Wall Street what would you do first?

HAZEL: What we need is pollution taxes. Not just carbon taxes, but taxes on all pollution. Because that forces companies and financial players to internalize those costs and get the prices right. Once you get the prices right, you shift the whole system.

You have to look at, at least, seven levels in the global economy because the first law of ecology is everything is connected to everything else. And so the most important thing is the reintegration of human knowledge and the connecting of all the dots. And that process is happening. You look at that metaphor connecting the dots, everybody's doing it, you know, which is the beginning of what has to happen in terms of the paradigm shift. And then at the international level, we need to downsize bubble finance. You know, the real bubble is in finance. Because the point is that when you change the paradigm, you change the game and you change the scorecards and you change people's attention. And reality is what you pay attention to. And so there's nothing wrong. We have everything we need. We just have to pay attention to different things. So the point is the levels are the global level where we must downsize the bubble of finance and one of the ways of doing that is with a financial transaction tax, so you would only hit the high frequency traders.

The other thing we have to do is to correct all these fiat currencies because these money circuits are all based on fiat currencies, which are being printed by central banks . . . this part Ron Paul had right. He doesn't know what to do about it, but he got the analysis right. If you have all the world's central banks printing money, what happens is you end up corrupting the money circuitry so that it winds up blowing out, which is what it's doing. Create this massive bubble and what you do is completely delink money from what's going on in the real world. And so it's reforming the way money is created. I've done a lot of work on this. I'm working with a British group called the "Green Money Working Group." It is looking at all of the alternative currencies, and we do need an international currency, which should be based on special drawing rights. Then nations do need to keep their own currencies for domestic transactions, but you also need to have municipal currencies. Like in Brazil, 200 Cities have been authorized by the Brazilian Central Bank to have their own city currencies because you can clear your own markets without having to circle it through the Central Bank. Why would you need to do that? And then, of course, what's happening is that all of these electronic currencies and cell phone transactions and crowd-funding and all of this other stuff that our friend, Dara Albright of NowStreet is following—they are doing the job for us. They are bypassing central banks. They are bypassing the old money circuits. They are bypassing Wall Street and the City of London. And that's all going on really at every level.

And then you can have, at the national level, all kinds of useful national level legislation like standards for renewable energy production. You can have standards for efficient appliances. You don't actually have to spend money. You just create all of the standards for much more efficient use of energy and materials. But you also probably should have a carbon tax or pollution tax to hurry along the process.

And then, at the regional and local level, there are all kinds of different ways of shifting the system, whether it's doing away with some of the subsidies to the old form of industrial agriculture and encouraging more farmer's markets, encouraging more local control from energy facilities. So lots of cities are putting up their own wind generators and their own solar panels. The whole system transition means there's no magic bullets. You have to understand the whole system and then figure out policies and economic arrangements that, instead of being focused on killing one bird with one stone, kill five birds with one stone, to use a rather unfortunate analogy.

I coined the name the "Love Economy." What is really true is that the love economy is the unacknowledged support of the official GNP-measured money economy. And the love economy, which is 50 percent of all of the useful work that's being done, is done by women, unpaid. My alternative analysis is that the love economy is the real economy, and it underpins and subsidizes everything in the money-based economy. You actually have to have some sense of what people are ready for. Here's the two things for you: There's more and more understanding of all the social costs that are coming back and hitting us in the face. And at the same time, there's more and more of this planetary awareness. And so it is all coming together to drive the process and I have always felt—and this is actually true biologically—that stress is evolution's tool. And we humans are stressing ourselves. We've created all of this stuff out there based on our limited consciousness, which is now coming back and hitting us in the face. And that is driving the breakdowns in every part of the system. The breakdowns are now driving the breakthroughs, and that's why the breakdown in finance is so important. Because it's an awakening.

WALL STREET 50
Brad Katsuyama   *A Magic Wand*

GET RID OF SELF-SERVING PEOPLE

Brad Katsuyama is the President, CEO, and Co-Founder of IEX Group. Katsuyama and his team are also the focus of *Flash Boys*, a book by

Michael Lewis about high frequency trading (HFT) in financial markets. After Katsuyama discovered HFT's unfair trading practices, he decided to challenge fundamentally the business of the stock market, leaving RBC in 2012 to start-up a fair and transparent stock exchange. He also has created www.IamAnInvestor.org, which educates and informs us on how each of us is an investor and how to reclaim our rights as one.

KIM: If you had a magic wand you could wave over Wall Street, what would you do?

BRAD: I've worked with some really, really fantastic people on Wall Street. I've also encountered some really horrible people. And the unfortunate part is the horrible people, at times, are in positions much higher than the great people. I'd love to see Wall Street rid itself of a bunch of useless managers who have just no place being there in the first place. I think Wall Street's biggest error is that it turned the biggest producers into managers and sometimes the qualities of your largest producer don't necessarily reflect well into being a leader of other people. And I think that it just seems to be a cultural distinction of Wall Street and that might lead to some of the cultural issues that you see out there. I do feel like there's an entire layer of people who only make Wall Street worse. Some of my best friends work on Wall Street, and there are a lot of good people and, unfortunately, everyone gets defined by the bad actors. That's just the sad state of where we are, but I think that can change. So get rid of those who are self-serving. They have become impediments to productive enterprise. The self-serving individuals really are only in their positions because they've taken credit for other people's work. So it's only a matter of time before they get found out anyway. But it would just be good to get rid of all of them in one fell swoop. There'd be some holes in some organizational charts, but those organizations would function much better without these people. The CEO doesn't know of every decision. Part of the whole point of having an organizational structure and a hierarchy is so decision making can be delegated, right? It's just about ensuring that at each point along that line of delegation you have a person of integrity. And when you discover there's a person in there who does not have integrity, you fire him.

WALL STREET 50
Schuyler "Sky" Lance   *A Magic Wand*

INVESTING TO DO MORE GOOD IN THE WORLD

Schuyler (Sky) Lance is a managing partner of SustainVC^{SM} which manages the Patient Capital Collaborative series of early-stage impact investment funds. Associated with Investors' Circle, PCC invests on a for-profit basis in companies that provide meaningful social and/or environmental benefits to the world. Previously, Lance was Co-Founder and Managing Principal of private equity firm Windjammer Capital Investors with nearly $2B under management today.

KIM: With regards to where we are now in the economy, and what has happened in the last few years, what would you like to see done for us to move forward?

SKY: I wish Congress would recognize this for profit impact investment space to the point where they would make more dollars widely available to provide professional funds managers, such as us, capital, so we can do more good in the world. Because the government offers important grant programs and things, but it also runs up the deficit at the same time, which we are not happy about. So to me it just makes sense, as opposed to all that money going into the grant side of the equation, why not allocate a few hundred million dollars and say to each of these established impact investment funds out there, here is a hundred million dollars. Go do what you can with that money toward what you are doing. If we just look at a broader agenda, in essence, we are creating companies, creating jobs, creating employment, and they have been created in the right areas, the sustainable futures of our businesses. And it is not just money being spent, it is money being invested. If we all do a good job, that money then gets returned to the government as a profit and can be recycled. It is not spend, spend, spend a lot of money.

The federal government recognized the impact of investment space to some degree and had set up some programs through the SBA and OPEC. It is very narrowly defined. You've got loops to go though, and as opposed to being a broader space to match these established groups out there . . . you know we've considered, "Do we apply for this SBIC money?" and at the same time, we have to restrict our investing to be in other specific categories they define, but there are other companies we are trying to help as well. So with these companies, do we just say, "We don't do that anymore?" So it is a real change that needs to be made there, to make that process simpler and broader for a dollar to flow into that space. So it would be one of my suggested solutions out there.

KIM: What would you say to those who are frustrated with Wall Street in general?

SKY: All individuals out there, even if they feel powerless, have a fair amount of power. Partly by educating themselves such that they can write a letter to their Congressman for specific change, but then also they can move their money. If you add up everyone who is angry out there, there are a number of socially conscious mutual funds and management firms that can move their money to try to make good as well as profit. We just need to continue to be vocal about the change required. I know people are angry, but it's easy to complain and hard to come up with a solution. The one protest out there that would be very effective is to put money in impact investing. And the people from B Lab, they would be saying, "Well, you should be working to change legislation to allow corporations to focus on . . . and take into account other things than just profit, like changing legislation because in most states, the board of directors responsibility is to the shareholders, and it has been interpreted over years of court cases as trying to make as much money as possible for the shareholders. And the shareholders could take that money and do whatever they want to do with it. How about if it is okay if the corporation might spend a little money here on employees, or to help a supplier move to a less negative environmental impact process, or maybe we can give away 5 percent of profit to the most effective nonprofit organization in our industry, and not get sued by our shareholders for not *having shared money to do these things.*

There are a lot of studies out there. If you do these things, treat your employees well, treat your vendors well, your customers well, and do a lot of community development, let your employees work for five days a year at community development kind of things, it is also good for business. Also a lot of boards of directors are afraid if they let the employees work for Habitat for Humanity, they might get sued. So there is a need for meaningful legislation. If everybody has their own different piece and focuses on it, then together we could fix the problem out there. I'd encourage people who are protesting to go educate themselves on all these different issues, and pick one that matters to them, and go be vocal about it to try and create the change that can help solve the problem. Even for those who are asking, "How can I have an impact as an individual?" those people who have only five thousand dollars to put into something, do some homework, and if those things are chosen by your employer, then be vocal to the employers and tell them, "I want a socially conscious investment alternative." Think about how effective that would be, if IBM and GM had, instead of just the standard small cap, mid cap, large cap, federal funds offer, some social environmental fund options! To make this happen, employees are going to have to say, "We want to put our money in there, so give us that as an option."

WALL STREET 50
Carla Harris   *A Magic Wand*

INCREASE TRANSPARENCY AND EDUCATION

Carla Harris is a Vice Chairman of Global Wealth Management, and Managing Director and Senior Client Advisor at Morgan Stanley. For more than a decade, Ms. Harris was a senior member of the equity syndicate desk and executed such transactions as initial public offerings for UPS, Martha Stewart Living Omnimedia, Ariba, Digitas, and others. Harris is also a speaker, gospel singer, and author. President Obama appointed Harris as the chairperson of the National Women's Business Council.

KIM: How would you change things on Wall Street if you had a magic wand?

CARLA: With a magic wand I would increase what is happening now—greater transparency and more education. I think the more people are educated about what this industry is and what we do—and then increase the transparency, which will help everyone understand it—then people will have a more accurate picture of it and be able to understand what they don't know. Case in point, I went to Harlem this weekend to talk to kids who are in a music program, and I was supposed to talk about them following their passion, but the truth is they wanted to speak about finance, what's going on in the economy, and what's the difference between a public company and a private company. They wanted to know why is one company's stuff more expensive than another company's stuff, and what happens with performance?

WALL STREET 50
Rob Davis *A Magic Wand*

UNDERSTAND THE LAW OF CAUSE AND EFFECT

Rob Davis is a Managing Director and head of business development at McAlinden Research Partners (MRP), a division of Catalpa Capital Advisors, LLC. Including his time at MRP, Rob has enjoyed a long career in various aspects of the capital markets for firms including Bank of America, Morgan Stanley, Dillon Read, and Oppenheimer. His first job following graduation from SUNY New Paltz was teaching elementary school, where he first witnessed the harmful effects of child abuse. It was an experience that, years later, led him to start Hedge Funds Care, Help

For Children (HFC), a charity dedicated to the prevention and treatment of child abuse. HFC is now an international movement with chapters in fourteen cities and five countries. Following his ten years as Chairman, Davis continues to serve as Chairman Emeritus. Since its founding in 1998, HFC has donated more than $40 million through over 1,000 grants to organizations dedicated to saving children from the trauma of abuse.

KIM: If you had a magic wand to wave over Wall Street what would you have it do?

ROB: I think that the country needs, Wall Street needs, anybody who is in a position of responsibility needs, to have its duties. When you had to be in the army, you had to serve, you had to do duties. I think every adult, before they get a driver license at some place, should have to study ethics, and read Emerson essays and things like that. There is, in fact, a Law of Cause and Effect. Just like the Law of Gravity. You don't have to see whether gravity exists, and the Law of Cause and Effect is *the same.* There is no way to get around this. You know, when you perpetrate stuff you are planting in your garden. If you plant a weed in your garden of life, you do not get flowers. When you plant weeds, you get weeds. And that's the way it is, and people do not get that. People do not realize there is a Law of Cause and Effect. The whole mortgage crisis would have never happened if people were thinking that and really knew that was the case; then this stuff would have never happened. This was total selfishness and greed and complete lack of concern or understanding the consequences of actions. And the smart people who were supposed to be watching, supposed to be the caretakers, they all just blew it.

WALL STREET 50
Jack Schwager   *A Magic Wand*
BE UNABLE TO LIE

Jack Schwager is an industry expert in futures and hedge funds and the author of a number of acclaimed financial books, including the best-selling Market Wizard series and the Schwager on Futures series. Schwager is one of the founders of FundSeeder.com, a platform designed to find undiscovered trading talent worldwide and connect unknown successful traders with sources of investment capital. His prior experience includes a decade as a partner in a hedge fund advisory firm and twenty-two years as Director of Futures Research for some of Wall Street's leading firms, most recently Prudential Securities.

KIM: If you had a magic wand to wave over Wall Street, what would you do?

JACK: Well, I'd like everyone to be like Jim Carrey in *Liar, Liar,* where you can't NOT tell the truth. I would be very comfortable with that, because it wouldn't change me much. I would love to have everybody else forced to always tell the truth.

WALL STREET 50
Fred Wilson   *A Magic Wand*

HAVE YOUR OWN SKIN IN THE GAME

Fred Wilson is a popular blogger and the co-founder of Union Square Ventures, a venture capital firm based in New York City that manages $1B across six funds. Known for having investments in Web 2.0 companies such as Twitter, Tumblr, Foursquare, Zynga, Kickstarter, and 10gen., Wilson is an active philanthropist and community advocate and board member of DonorsChoose.org

KIM: If you had a magic wand to wave over Wall Street—what would your magic wand do?

FRED: Well, I think people should have real skin in the game. That when they make investment decisions with other people's money, they should have some of their own money involved, right? And it's hard because young people who come into the business early on, their careers don't have any skin in the game.

I think a lot of the really reckless stuff that goes on in the world of finance happens when people don't have anything to lose personally. They're using other people's money, they're leveraging it up to the hilt. They're making these enormous bets and there's no personal financial consequence to them if the bets go wrong. They write it off. So I like the ideas that reduce the amount of leverage, reduce the ability to be— using basically everyone else's money and not your own and make people have some of their own wealth involved. And you know, when I look at the world of hedge funds and things like that—some of the best run hedge funds that have lasted for ten, twenty years—one of the things you see is that the partners of those funds have all their net worth tied up in those businesses. So they did not make these crazy, reckless decisions because they have as much to lose as anybody. So I like that as a general rule of thumb.

KIM: Anything with regards to Washington, or the regulators?

FRED: I'm not a big believer in regulation because I've seen again and again and again that regulators miss things and auditors miss things. And I also see there can be unintended consequences from a lot of these things, and that just causes people to work through the loopholes and create crazy structures to get around the regulations.

So I would be a fan of reducing regulation, but putting in simple things like the idea that you can't use very much leverage and you need to have skin in the game. Simple rules that make sense. Rules that are common sense. Rules that enforce self-regulation and enforce people to behave rationally because their own interests are involved.

I also feel that way about healthcare. I don't want to go on a tangent, but I think of the problems with healthcare. The exploding cost of healthcare is because people aren't writing these checks themselves. We've basically outsourced the financial decision-making around healthcare expenditures. So when I'm eighty-five-years-old, I could go get a million dollar heart transplant, maybe live another six months. Or if I don't get the million dollar heart transplant, I'm going to die in two months. If I don't have to write that million dollar check,

I'd make that decision, right? But if I had to write that check, I might say, I'd rather have my kids have that million dollars. We need people to take personal responsibility for these decisions. And the more we require people to take personal responsibility for these things, the more they can regulate them themselves; then humans will behave rationally as opposed to expecting some army of accountants and bean counters to enforce the rules.

WALL STREET 50
Amy Domini   *A Magic Wand*

THROW OUT MODERN PORTFOLIO THEORY

Amy Domini is Founder and CEO of Domini Social Investments, a woman-owned and managed SEC-registered investment adviser that specializes exclusively in socially responsible investing, serving individual and institutional investors who wish to create positive social and environmental outcomes while seeking competitive financial returns. Domini manages three mutual funds with a combined $1.3 billion in assets: the Domini Social Equity Fund, the Domini International Social Equity Fund, and the Domini Social Bond Fund. Analysis of the long-term record of the Domini 400 Social Index demonstrated that social and environmental standards have led to strong individual stock selection and potentially higher returns.

I would point to modern portfolio theory and say, "Who ordained that theory to be king?" It was a bunch of ideas that came out of research and seemed to prove that you could avoid a lot of different kinds of risk by diversifying your portfolio, by buying everything that could be bought. Well, it didn't work in 2007. It didn't matter—there was nowhere to hide. The whole system broke down, and your portfolio broke down. So why the hell are we still diversifying into everything that can be diversified into? Because Wall Street's selling it, not because it actually reduces risk.

It didn't reduce the huge number of risks to the structure. What kinds of risks? Well, I'm a pension fan. I better invest in commodities.

I don't want to take delivery on the week. You know, I don't want a ton of copper delivered. I'd rather buy derivatives on commodities, and I'd rather buy indexes of commodities. But all those things—at the end of the day, I'm a buyer. And if I'm a buyer, I'm competing against the farmer or a business, you know, so I am bidding up all those commodities. Even though I'm buying the derivative form and creating, you know, five dollars on the table for every one dollar of real copper.

So, I would throw out this modern portfolio theory. I would introduce a new concept of portfolio management based on economic return. If you base everything on true economic return, you could rewrite portfolio theory in a way that keeps investors and society aligned. That would change the way business runs. Second, I'd rewrite accounting theory so as to disallow a company to show a profit if the way it does business costs, as an example, the health care system of America a billion dollars. The company won't be able to because now its accounting will have to show that billion-dollar loss. So it is going to change the way they do business. It's called full cost accounting. It doesn't allow a company to count the gains it keeps without counting the costs it creates to others. It is true at the company level and at the portfolio level. If you have an economic return either to your national society or the world as a baseline positive, then a whole bunch of things change from there. So I would change financial asset management teaching and change accounting rules so that we emphasize economic value. That's what we invest to gain, and that's what our return calculations need to be based upon.

If I could wave a magic wand in Washington D.C., where there's a budget, I would have 1 percent or something set aside for disclosure to the public of that budget. So if we're going to subsidize food growers, I think when I buy a can of Campbell soup, I should have full disclosure that's made available by Campbell. If it's not on the can of Campbell soup, then it should be in the annual report of Campbell soup, stating what they benefited or cost the public with that bill that assists them in some way. So if I were in Washington, there would be greater disclosure, transparency, built into every bill.

If I were in the administration in the president's role, I'd also go to the Department of Labor and rewrite the laws that govern what fiduciary responsibility is because, currently, they have had a sort of an assault on the best interest of the beneficiary. That phrase, "best interest of beneficiary," has gradually been replaced with "best economic interest of the plan." So now, under current law, you can kill the beneficiary. It's not going to be tested but—while it doesn't say, "Feel free to kill the beneficiary"—the lens the fiduciary is looking through does not include the best interest of the beneficiary. So it only includes the best financial interest of the fund. So, you know, I have a few specifics.

I put a lot of blame on this radicalization of politics. I had never considered Ethical Investing as a political statement. But over the course of, say, twenty-five years—since the first book was written—the world has changed and corporate responsibility has become synonymous with not believing corporations are owned by only their shareholders and owed duty of allegiance to only their shareholders. The whole thing has changed. So we really went through a decade now where the nation has gotten very divided on the issues of anything that seems to restrict corporations from doing anything they want to do. And that has spilled out in investment theory and in lots of other ways. So if you look at that Domini 400 Social Index, it's still alive. It's a subset of the MSCI family of indexes. And if you pull up that index and look at it, it has still outperformed the 500. So over the twenty-one-year history, it's a better index, a better way of investing. That should make it the dominant theory. Get rid of the modern portfolio theory.

WALL STREET 50
Mori Goto   *A Magic Wand*

DEMOCRATIZE

Morihiko Goto is the CEO of Goto Capital Markets, Inc. and has worked on Wall Street for over twenty-eight years. Goto is a Vestry member for St. Bartholomew's Episcopal Church, in New York City and volunteers often at its Crossroads Homeless Shelter, preparing dinner and staying overnight.

KIM: If you had a magic wand to wave over Wall Street, what would you change?

MORI: I've learned that no system is perfect. And our system isn't perfect but could be made better. And how it could be made better? I'm not really sure with this 1 percent, 99 percent thing. You know, I cannot really quantify that 1 percent versus 99 percent. Maybe there's data to it but the one word that keeps coming to my mind is "democratize"—to make Wall Street more democratic. Meaning, everybody gets in. I think in the business of Wall Street and the financial industry in general, and even broader, American business in general, things could be done in a more democratic fashion. There are certain things that we still don't understand how some people are able to get things done while others aren't able to. So I'd like to demystify that and enable more democracy here in finance. That would be my starting point.

WALL STREET 50
Jim B. Rogers   *A Magic Wand*

ACCEPT REALITY

James Beeland "Jim" Rogers, Jr. is an investor, media commentator, adventurer, and author. He is the Chairman of Beeland Interests, Inc. He was the co-founder of the Quantum Fund and creator of the Rogers International Commodities Index (RICI). Although Rogers' career spans over forty-six years, during the last thirty-four years he has been semi-retired and travels extensively around the world. He was an occasional Visiting Professor at Columbia University. One of his books, *Investment Biker,* recounts his riding a motorcycle around the globe during 1990–1992 and what he learned along the way about the world's developing countries and investment markets by seeing them from the ground up. It led to one of his three entries in the *Guinness Book of World Records.*

KIM: If you had a magic wand, and you could wave that wand over Wall Street, what would it do?

JIM: I wouldn't want the magic wand to do anything. I would want for nature to take its course, and the world to evolve as it's supposed to evolve. People who try to change Washington, D.C. and politicians, they're always trying to change reality. I guess if I could do anything, I'd say, "Okay, let's go ahead and have our crap now and get it over with," rather than fleshing it out over the next twenty or thirty years. But the forces of nature are in place. It's like King Lear trying to hold back the tides. I don't want to hold back the tides. I want it to do what it's supposed to. That will be the best thing for Wall Street and the world. I guess I could say, "Okay, let everybody go bankrupt." There are lots of people in the world who are bankrupt right now, like Greece, California, many places. I'd say, "Okay, let's force them to go bankrupt; let's clean out the system and start over." It would be very painful for a while, but the alternative would be to drag this pain out for ten, twenty years. Japan, for instance, is dragging it out. The Japanese have two lost decades now; its stock market is 80 percent below what it was twenty-two years ago. They should have "bit the bullet" back then and it would be much better now. I guess I would wave the wand to accept reality now, accept our mistakes, and start over to clean out the system. Washington and Wall Street are trying frantically to "kick the can down the road." They're trying to put off reality, and it's going to cost us all a lot more because in the end, the deficit will be much higher.

KIM: What about waving that magic wand over Washington D.C. and regulators? Would there be anything there?

JIM: It's got to be waved over a lot of places. In fact, everybody. A lot of the problems afflicting Wall Street now and through the past fifteen years are due to the regulators. If I had to lay the blame for all the world's financial problems on one place, I would lay it at the feet of Alan Greenspan and the Federal Reserve. That's the main cause of our problems. I would certainly make them, and Washington, and the world understand, "Hey, the best solution is to clean out the system and start over, instead of denying reality."

KIM: Do you feel we need the Federal Reserve?

JIM: No. America has had three central banks in its history. The first one disappeared. The second one did too. They mostly destroyed themselves, due to many crazy mistakes. Granted, the world has problems without a central bank, but this one is making the situation worse, not better. The world has gone on without a central bank many times in history. It's not ordinary that in the last twenty or thirty years, everybody knows about a central bank. One hundred years ago people would have rarely known about it. It's only now that we have this cult of the central bank, and this idea that it knows what it's doing.

WALL STREET 50
Deepak Parekh   *A Magic Wand*

SEGREGATE BANKING

Deepak S. Parekh is the Chairman of Housing Development Finance Corporation in Mumbai. HDFC is India's leading housing and finance company. The Reserve Bank of India appointed him Chairman of the Advisory Group for Securities Market Regulation and he was made Chairman of the Expert Committee to look into the reform efforts in the power sector. In addition to being known for his vociferous views seeking standardization and transparency in the real estate sector, Parekh is known as the unofficial crisis consultant of the Government. His philosophy on Corporate Social Responsibility is "if a company earns, it must also return to the society" and that companies owe a responsibility not just to shareholders but to all stakeholders.

KIM: If I gave you a magic wand to wave over Wall Street, what would your magic wand do?

DEEPAK: I think the current financial system can't sustain itself because banks have become too big, too large. They are too big to fail, too big to govern, too big to run. And you have to segregate what you are trying to do. You have to segregate retail banking, wholesale banking, investment banking, and wealth management into separate entities. They have to be manageable. You can't manage a Citibank that has 200 offices all over the world. It is too large. And ultimately banks are playing with public money; they're playing with public deposits. Look at the financial sector in Europe. Look at the greed. People are not willing to put money in Greek and Spanish and Italian banks. The local people have withdrawn money. The prices have been exaggerated and increased rapidly because local people don't have trust in that banking system. Bank means trust. Financial sector means trust. That trust has been totally depreciated in the last five years, whether you look at developing, emerging, developed, foreign countries, failing countries, wherever.

Our bank has no parent company, no industrial group supporting us. One hundred percent of shares are in the market, so there is no family behind it. And after Tata, we have become the second largest group, yet we have only two companies, the mortgage company and the bank.

I guess the regulators also need to sharpen the pencils. Sometimes what you feel in this, when you read all about it, is that the regulators were too lax. The regulators were colluding with some of them. They knew. Like what is coming out in the LIBOR scandal. Some Bank of England people were aware of it. And the justification was that the banks were in a very precarious position financially. So the Bank of England turned a blind eye to let them make some more money because it would strengthen the balance sheet; otherwise, there might be a run on the bank. So there is always a justification. You can fool someone sometimes, but you cannot fool everyone all the time.

WALL STREET 50
Andrew Kuper
A Magic Wand

SUPPORT EMERGING MARKETS

Dr. Andrew Kuper is an investor and entrepreneur in emerging markets, and the CEO of LeapFrog Investments. He founded LeapFrog in 2007, now the largest dedicated investor worldwide in insurance and related financial services to emerging consumers. LeapFrog's companies now serve 19.5 million people in Africa and Asia, 15 million are low-income or underserved, often providing them with financial safety nets and springboards for the first time. President Clinton hailed LeapFrog as "opening up new frontiers for alternative investment." Dr. Kuper is a former Managing Director of Ashoka, the organization that pioneered social entrepreneurship and has backed over 3,000 entrepreneurs across over seventy countries. For his work as a pioneer of profit-with-purpose business, Dr. Kuper won the Ernst & Young National Entrepreneur of the Year award in 2012 and was recognized as a Young Global Leader by the World Economic Forum in Davos in 2013. He holds a Ph.D. from Cambridge and is the author of two books on globalization and governance.

KIM: If you had a magic wand to wave over Wall Street, over the federal regulators, over Washington D.C., what would that magic wand create?

ANDREW: First, facilitate the creation of investment intermediaries, whether funds or companies, that drive innovative and high-impact businesses. This would be a wholesale way to support businesses that provide financial services, housing, education, clean technology, all those meaningful things, to millions of people. In the ideal world, there would be an enabling regulatory environment that builds competitive advantages for those investors who want to focus on helping those businesses. That's one.

Two, from a Wall Street perspective, I would like to see major firms move decisively into financing and supporting strong emerging markets businesses. Where is growth going to come from? Largely not from the emerged markets, which despite stock market ups and downs are likely to experience long periods of constrained growth. Growth is going to come from the emerging markets, and especially from the more than three billion emerging consumers rising out of poverty into the middle class. Look at India, Indonesia, the Philippines, China, or South Africa, Nigeria, Ghana, and Kenya—where hundreds of millions of people have risen to a level of economic security but billions more are striving to do so. And the opportunity there is just a vast, blue ocean. If investors and the financial services industry were to acknowledge and act on this multi-trillion dollar opportunity, they could tap enormous growth, generate top-tier returns, and I think we would have a quite different world. It is a matter of getting them beyond their familiar contexts, to see what we see every day—this enormous opportunity set.

And the third thing is that almost no one sets out in the morning on his first day in the work world to be a piranha. You know, people may become piranhas because the pond in which they feed encourages them to survive and succeed or not be accepted. I think most people set out in the morning wanting to do something that makes them feel good about themselves and be able to tell their families, their friends, and communities about, as well as to accumulate assets. And so I think if we can provide a route for people to do that, so they can be the dolphin, rather than a piranha, I think most people are going to choose it.

Whether people are entering the workplace or are senior executives thinking about the next leap in their career, I think it is important for them to know that impact investing and social business is a continuum in which they might find their place. The continuum goes right from organizations that are a better alternative to philanthropy, i.e., social businesses that generate return on capital, to businesses that generate extremely robust returns and do so on a risk-adjusted basis that outperforms conventional market players. People can place themselves in that continuum within social businesses and within impact investing.

For those already inside the conscious capitalist tent, I would add that it's not useful to stand at one point on the continuum, steeling for a fight, and say, "This is the way and the truth." Hopefully, what we are all doing is creating an ecosystem with a range of different kinds of financing with differing expectations of financial and social returns. This will allow a variety of career choices. It will enable a variety of businesses, and enable them to get appropriate financing from the right kind of investors. So I would really encourage all of us to have this more disaggregated sense of the impact investing and the social business continuum have, and not to go to war about which point on the continuum is right. Let's recognize diverse investors and leaders for the extremely valuable roles they play in creating financing for a different kind of capitalist enterprise.

WALL STREET 50
Henry Kaufman   *A Magic Wand*
BREAK UP LARGE FINANCIAL INSTITUTIONS

Dr. Henry Kaufman is President of Henry Kaufman & Company, Inc. For twenty-six years, he was with Salomon Brothers, where he was Managing Director, Member of the Executive Committee, and in charge of the Firm's four research departments. Kaufman earned the Dr. Doom nickname as a result of his consistent predictions in the 1970s and early '80s that interest rates would rise and bond prices would fall. In 2009 he wrote *The Road to Financial Reformation*.

KIM: If you had a magic wand to makeover Wall Street or Washington D.C., what would you do?

HENRY: I would breakup large financial institutions. If you have very large and dominant financial institutions, you've created financial public utilities. Public utilities are controlled by government rules and regulations. If you have many financial institutions, then the open market plays a bigger role in the allocation of credit.

The financial markets play a very important role in the development and stability of an economy. Financial institutions have a fascinating role; they have an entrepreneurial role to make money. They take other people's money, other people's temporary money, other people's savings, and intermediate it into long investments and so on. That is a very important role in society; you have to balance that obligation as to making money. That was largely forgotten as we moved into the later part of the '80s and '90s, and then the last decade, the balancing of these responsibilities was forgotten.

There will always be a great need for the financial intermediaries, no doubt about it. The more those responsibilities are balanced, the more moderate the gain in profits is going to be. If you unbalance it, then off it goes. This issue is now hazy because the entrepreneurial side of the financial markets is being seriously challenged by supervision, officially and at a higher degree of concentration in our financial system. Now we have relatively fewer private sector institutions that control the good part of the financial system. Twenty or thirty years ago, that was not the case; there was greater freedom. So when you think about people who want this career, they have been funneled into fewer institutions rather than wide-ranging financial institutions.

KIM: Anything specific you would change with the Federal Reserve?

HENRY: This is not an easy subject because I would require the Federal Reserve to understand, as in the past, the implications of structural changes in the financial markets on financial behavior and economic behavior. For example, we secure mortgages, we package mortgages, and as a result, we were able to create many more mortgages and many more borrowers and so on. The Federal Reserve never fully understood what the implications of that securitization was for the behavior of the financial institutions and what it is going to do with the housing market. That's a great failure. The dilemma I think at the Fed and elsewhere is that we fail to apply judgment. We fail to apply more qualitative judgments in the making of decisions. We rely more on quantitative techniques to make decisions. Quantitative techniques are past relationships without assuming anything changes. In the essence of economic life, business life, financial life the essence has changed. We don't stand slow. There are people who crack and say, "The good old days." There were no good old days. We rely heavily on this past to tell us where we were going and you can't do that.

WALL STREET 50
Erika Karp   *A Magic Wand*

LONG-TERM THINKING, COLLABORATION, AND TRANSPARENCY

Erika Karp is the Founder and CEO of Cornerstone Capital Inc., a financial services firm that applies the principles of sustainable finance across the capital markets in order to enhance transparency and collaboration. Cornerstone works with corporations, financial institutions, and individuals to promote new research in the field of ESG (Environmental, Social, and Governance) analysis. Prior to launching Cornerstone, Karp was Managing Director and Head of Global Sector Research at UBS Investment Bank. Karp is a founding board member of the Sustainability Accounting Standards Board.

KIM: What would you do if you had a magic wand to wave over Wall Street?

ERIKA: Incentivize long-term behaviors, incentive structures to promote long-term thinking, that's one. Two, elevate the ability of managers to drive collaboration among colleagues. That's a very difficult managerial skill, encouraging people to collaborate and to break down silos. I wish I could get more managers with the skills to do that. Third is transparency. Transparency is absolutely transformational. We have seen examples of this in a lot of different industries where something structurally changes, and pricing becomes transparent. Think about the financial sector, the insurance and healthcare sectors, the retail sector. The Internet, and the transparency of prices associated with it, make it much easier to know the market-clearing price for something. The whole evolution of social media leads to more transparency . . . which implies a shift in competitive dynamics in various industries. So, I would aspire for management teams to embrace transparency. They might as well . . . because it's coming anyway. This gets to why I am so involved with SASB: the Sustainability Accounting Standards Board. This organization is about facilitating corporate transparency in financial reporting. It will ultimately help restore faith and trust in the capital markets.

I believe very deeply that healthy financial markets are critical to facilitating economic growth and prosperity. Investors need to be conscious of their own values, and then align them with their strategies. If you want to go into a field where there is constant learning, where there is an opportunity to work with wonderfully bright people, where more and more of them are conscious capitalists, then this is the place for you. We are desperate for solutions, for creativity, for innovation, for energy, for growth.

WALL STREET 50
Barry Ritholtz   *A Magic Wand*

REINSTATE THE GLASS-STEAGALL ACT

Barry Ritholtz is an author, columnist, guest commentator on Bloomberg TV, blogger, and equities analyst. He is the Founder and CIO of Ritholtz Wealth Management a financial planning and asset management firm with $130 million in assets. He was named one of the "15 Most Important Economic Journalists" in the U.S. in 2010 and one of the few strategists who saw the housing implosion and derivative mess far in advance.

KIM: If I gave you a magic wand and you could wave it over Wall Street, what would you do?

BARRY: How far can I go back in time?

KIM: You can go back as far as you like.

BARRY: All right. So I go back to 1980 and stop the bail out of Chrysler. I let Chrysler go belly up. And that does three things. First, brings in competition from Germans and Japanese faster. Their bones get picked over by more competitive people, more competitive companies. It scares the hell out of both the UAW and the senior management of GM and Ford. And that entire industry has a radical redesign.

Then we go forward to 1998 and Long Term Capital Management . . . the FED doesn't get involved. Even though it does not cost them any money, you let them go belly up and it hurts a number of banks. Sometimes you got to get burns so as not to catch fire. Sometimes you have to lose a little money to not lose a lot, and so they tighten up the risk management. They tighten up this, and they know they can't rely on the FED.

The next thing that happens is after . . . by the way, this is Wall Street; I can't stop Hitler; or stop 9/11. We are just talking about finance, right, so then I go to the FED in 2001 and say, "Listen, you can't take rates down to ridiculous levels. You are going to start a spiral in housing and oil and all sorts of stuff. And the ramifications are significant." So, I prevent that. Maybe you have to throw a banana peel in front of Alan Greenspan before he becomes FED chief and we are stuck will Paul Volker, who would prevent . . . Actually in *Bailout Nation*, I put an awful lot of blame on Alan Greenspan as a radical deregulator, but also as someone who, despite being a deregulator, manipulated the market with rates and took them to ridiculous levels.

You have to turn back the clock on the silly belief that companies can self-regulate, that markets are efficient, that left to their own design, everything will be okay. You know that didn't work out well with BP in the Gulf of Mexico; it didn't work out. Look throughout history—Ford Pinto, you know, there is a cost benefit analysis. I have a real issue with that. . . .

You just don't do what was done over the past thirty years; I would reinstate the Glass-Steagall Act, separate traditional banking, which should be like a utility. I would cap the size of banks and make them appreciably smaller. The most important thing is I would align the incentives between the insiders and shareholders, meaning you can't make a ton of money, you can't extract all this value from the company the way the upper management of these banks did and then drive the company off a cliff. Stop and think what I would like to do is wave a wand and make these big investment houses go back to being partnerships, not public. When they were partnerships. Here is the beauty of joint and several liability—if you are the head of Lehman brothers and you have paid yourself a billion dollars in stock and you liquidated half a billion and put it in a bank, you lost 500 million, but you still have 500 million, but you are dumb—you destroyed the company. He should not get to keep that 500 million, in a publically traded company; it's the shareholder's money at risk. In a partnership, joint several liabilities mean . . . imagine Lehman brothers were a partnership instead of a public limited company. So the company goes bankrupt, but the creditors, it's not like all the stocks were zero, you have got nothing else. They get to go after the partnership; then they get to go after the individual partners. So, if you're Dick Fuld and your house is in the Hamptons and you have a big apartment in a city worth forty-million dollars, they take your boat, your house, your Rolex—fuck you, they take everything; you should have thought about that, mother fucker, before you lost all that money.

And I am sorry, but that is the reason these guys went public; all the stories we heard, that was all nonsense. But, hold that aside, because I could talk about the bailouts forever. There is a misalignment of compensation. I mentioned Jack Welsh earlier. So Jack Welsh started as CEO of GE in 1981, and he finished in 2001. Happened to start the year before an eighteen-year boom market and ended a year after the boom market ended. Now I want to see how much he paid himself—he paid himself tons and tons of money. What I am curious about is, how has GE done relative to the industrial sector and how has it done relative to the S&P? We don't just want to pay people because the market is going up. I want to pay them because they are helping the company to be better and out-compete.

Capitalism is a crazy idea; capitalism is about competition in the marketplace. So, don't just get a bunch of . . . crony capitalists. They are not real capitalists. They hire these employment consultants. I don't think there is a group more full of shit than these people, other than the housing appraisers who used these overpriced houses. Oh well, that house went for $600,000, so this is worth $601,000. Well, no, that house isn't worth that. You are not telling me the intrinsic value; you are just confirming the upward spiral in prices. That's what the employment compensation consultants did.

And I want someone to say, "Well, here is how the average company in this sector has done in terms of revenue, in terms of profit, in terms of a variety of other factors that manages the long-term health." Anybody can extract wealth, that's easy. Creating wealth is hard, and so that's what I really see taking place. With all the things that are wrong with Wall Street, that are wrong with business, that's the single biggest one.

The problems with Wall Street . . . it's far too reliant on leverage, far too reliant on rent-seeking behavior, far too reliant on financial engineering. Finance has become an end in itself instead of being the service industry to the rest of the country. Finance shouldn't be: How can I extract a dollar? It should be: How can I create wealth today? Whether that means funding a new technology, funding a new IPO. You look at what Vanguard is. It's a good example of a company that's been innovative in creating indexing and doing what it has done with those sorts of things. Barclays, iShares, and a lot of companies have come up with innovative things that are creative, not rent-seeking. If you try and just squeeze every last dime out of your client, then there is no value there. Lots of people create value but it used to be ninety/ten value creators vs. rent seekers, and I think those numbers have gotten skewed in the past few years.

WALL STREET 50
John Bogle   *A Magic Wand*

MOVE BACK TO STEWARDSHIP

John C. Bogle is Founder of The Vanguard Group, Inc., and President of the Bogle Financial Markets Research Center. He created Vanguard in

1974 and served as Chairman and Chief Executive Officer until 1996 and Senior Chairman until 2000. Vanguard is the largest mutual fund organization in the world. Vanguard comprises approximately 170 mutual funds with current assets totaling more than $2 trillion. Vanguard 500 Index Fund, the largest fund in the group, was founded by Bogle in 1975. It was the first index mutual fund. Bogle's best-selling book *The Battle for the Soul of Capitalism* (2005) and *Enough: True Measures of Money, Business, and Life* (2008) influenced me to write this book.

I would create a federal standard of fiduciary duty, meaning the interest of the clients comes ahead of the interest of managers. It affects what the Investment Company Act says, "A mutual fund must place the interest of their shareholders ahead of the interest of their officers and directors and managers and distributors." We moved from stewardship to salesmanship. There was an articles in the *Times* the other day that quoted a Wells Fargo spokesman who was talking about the difficulty Wells Fargo had getting into what we call retirement plans, and he was talking about the competition, primarily Vanguard, and his last sentence, the last sentence in the article, was that no fiduciary ever got in trouble by recommending a Vanguard fund.

WALL STREET 50
Michael Martin   *A Magic Wand*

FOCUS ON YOURSELF

Michael Martin has been a successful trader for twenty-five years. He is the author of, *The Inner Voice of Trading: Eliminate the Noise, and Profit from the Strategies That Are Right for You*. It focuses on how traders can learn about themselves so they can be profitable. He teaches through UCLA and the New York Society of Security Analysts (NYSSA), and is a member of the CFA Institute.

KIM: If you had a magic wand to wave over Wall Street what would you do with it?

MICHAEL: You know it's interesting. I probably would do nothing. The reason is that I don't have that type of omniscience inside that I think I know what's best for you or I know what's best for Wall Street. I only know what's best for me and how I am feeling in the ever-evolving moment of right now. People on Wall Street have the ability to help themselves. Some of these people have much more means than I do. In terms of capital, in terms of time, in terms of connections, and I think people can help themselves.

I don't, and that's not to say I am not benevolent, I just don't fix people; it's like dealing with an alcoholic, right. You can sit and say that your drinking is hurting you and it's also hurting me, but until that person is ready to quit, he is not going to quit. So whether Wall Street may have an ailment right now or a character defect is not really for me to say. I can choose to engage with them in their current state of existence or not. Mostly, I do not. And, you know, if they want help, I am happy to help them, but I think, generally speaking, everybody in the world can do a lot better by spiritually awakening or by increasing their level of emotional intelligence because it helps them better understand themselves as they operate in the world at large. That typically leads to better relationships, more solidified relationships, and maybe even better referrals, but again, people are only going to change if they want to change themselves—doesn't matter who is telling them.

WALL STREET 50
Dara Albright   *A Magic Wand*

ENDING ECONOMIC DISCRIMINATION

Dara Albright founded the NowStreet blog in 2011 and is the preeminent resource for education and insight into the burgeoning industry of market structure, private secondary transactions, and crowdfinance. One of the earliest voices covering the JOBS Act and advocating for greater democracy in the equity and credit markets, Albright produced the first major crowdfunding conference in 2012 and co-founded LendIt, the largest and most recognized global P2P and online lending conference organization.

KIM: If you had a magic wand to wave over Wall Street right now, what would your magic wand do?

DARA: Oh, that's a good question. At first, I would have to really wave it over the SEC and FINRA. I would have them immediately pass and implement the crowd-funding legislation and lift other solicitation bans. Then I would also wave that magic wand over our Congress as well as the White House and have them get up. As a nation, we've really done a great job over the years of getting rid of discrimination based on gender and skin color and religion, but we are not aware yet when it comes to economic status. I mean here we sit and yet we still discriminate against people with respect to their income level or their assets. I think that needs to change. I think everyone needs to be considered equal. They need to stop trying to coddle people and impress investors in the name of protection, they should be allowed to invest their own hard-earned money the way they want to. That will rebuild America.

WALL STREET 50
Frank Casey   *A Magic Wand*

DEFROCK AND FIRE UNWORTHY GOVERNMENT OFFICIALS

Frank Casey is a member of The Fox Hounds, Harry Markopolos' team that worked nearly nine years to blow the whistle on Bernard Madoff's Ponzi scheme.

KIM: If you had a magic wand to wave over Washington, D.C., or the SEC, or any of the regulators or the Fed, what would that wand do?

FRANK: May I just say that nobody has been fired because of the Madoff situation in the government. There were some people at the SEC who have resigned to pursue personal careers or family matters or whatever, but nobody has been fired. One of the major things we lack in government is some form of defrocking. In the military, you do something bad, you're stripped in public of your badges and your rank and your uniform and you're marked a traitor. That's what we need to do more of in our government. Our government, has moved into the area of a privileged class. Congress writes laws and they're exempted from them. They don't live by the same rules you and I live by. Social Security, their medical insurance, and so forth. They have their own special venues. So the first thing I would do if I were a leader in this country would be to stimulate investment and, therefore, get people employed. But try to adjudicate it from on high—let the markets decide that. The second thing I would do is I would beef up Inspector General Departments and not only have them write reports, I would want internal Courts of Law that defrock and punish evildoers or people who fell down on their jobs. When Harry (Markopolos) testified in front of the Congress, he said that the top ⅓ of the SEC should have been fired. When you fail to accomplish your mission and your troops die, and you yourself don't die in the action, and blatant incompetence and laziness and lack of leadership is to blame . . . you should be defrocked. The investigators at the SEC failed in their mission through complacency and incompetence!

Also, we have too many SEC things settled out of court. Five-hundred million is paid and they neither admit guilt or anything else. I mean, come on. Give me a break. It is not about throwing up an extra couple of billion dollars into the coffers of the U.S. government; it's about restoring the faith of the public. The SEC was formed because of the Great Depression to figure out a way to make the public feel comfortable that there was a level playing field and that they would have a chance in the investment world. Do you think anybody out there now believes they have a level playing field and they have a chance? They just don't believe in the government and its ability to self-police. And what good is it if nobody ever gets fired in the government to start with? I don't understand how one can be true to themselves and to their profession and have a CFP or a CFA or FRM, Financial Risk Manager, designation without adhering to some oath or creed. The doctors have such a creed, "Do no harm." And yet, the finance guys have all of these sexy badges and they say, "Okay. I'm one sexy dude on Wall Street. I've got a XYZ after my name." But then they see something wrong and they don't correct it. Their job is not simply to advise their bosses and say, "Yes, I've done some modicum of due diligence and this is wrong, or I believe this to be phony." It is, "Hey, boss, if you continue to march on this thing, I'm going to take you down because this is wrong."

Now, how do you do that? You, at some point, have to balance your social needs with your capitalistic needs. And that is a fine line. I understand people are married and have kids, but I'll tell you what . . . there was this psychologist once who told me how he had interviewed a bunch of people on their deathbeds and there wasn't one person on their deathbed that said, "I wish I had worked longer hours. I wish had told the corporate lie more often." They all said, 'I wish I had done X. I wish I had taken a greater risk. I wish I had been more true to myself." So we all have to deal with some finality, and when you go out, it's not about a heaven or hell or religious structure. It's about lying on your deathbed and saying, "Okay. I've done the best I could."

Now, Harry and I and the team have always argued for a whistle blowing statute that allows people who are CFAs, CFPs, and so forth to blow the whistle if they see wrong being committed and to get rewarded . . . because they'll never work in that industry again. So the SEC has adopted that because of this whole Madoff thing. It wasn't there before. And so now, people have an ability to balance, perhaps, the risk of financial need and social requirement, and moral requirement.

And morality, there again, it's not religion. It's a personal thing. Being remunerated I think is good. But even in the absence of a whistle blowing statute or financial remuneration—if you see something blatantly wrong and people are going to be hurt by it, it's your obligation as a professional to do no harm but also to proactively prevent the harm if you can.

WALL STREET 50
R. Paul Herman   *A Magic Wand*

LIST PEOPLE AS ASSETS INSTEAD OF AS AN EXPENSE

R. Paul Herman is the founder and CEO of HIP Investor Inc., and President of HIP Investor Ratings LLC. An internationally recognized expert in impact investing, Herman invented "HIP = Human Impact + Profit" in 2004 to show that the strongest portfolios and leading companies source much of their competitive advantage and shareholder value from improvements in quantifiable human, social, and environmental capital and their associated impacts on profit.

KIM: What would your magic wand do over Wall Street?

PAUL: It would have people be the magnet. The magic wand would be for people to open their eyes to what is really happening. And what's really happening is that if you did . . . if people really listened to the data and what's actually happening, they would see that, one, whereas many CEOs say, "People are their most valuable asset." The follow up question is, where are people on the financial statements? And the reality is that people are an expense on the income statement, not an asset on the balance sheet. And so if Wall Street or a Fortune 500 company or the Fed viewed them as true assets, a CEO trying to make his next earnings call is not going to cut people because he'd be cutting his asset base. So if I could wave a magic wand, I'd say people who create products, service customers, work together, are valued financially as assets on the balance sheet. It's already happened. Infosys Technology Company has already done that and they've done that every year since 1998 in their annual report. So far there's no U.S. or European company that has done it.

WALL STREET 50
Michael Stuart   *A Magic Wand*

SEEK HUMILITY

Michael Henry Stuart is the co-founder of Clark & Stuart, an investment firm in Portland, Maine, serving as the principal research analyst and portfolio manager since its inception. He earned the Chartered Financial Analyst designation in 1991. Stuart earned a B.S. in Economics-Finance from Bentley College and a Master's in Urban Affairs from Virginia Tech, starting his investment career in 1981 as a securities analyst with The Old Colony Trust Department of The First National Bank of Boston. Mr. Stuart has served on the finance and investment committees at schools and churches attended by his family.

KIM: If you had had a magic wand to wave over Wall Street or Washington D.C., the regulators . . . what would your magic wand do?

MICHAEL: It would endow everyone with humility. I don't have it. I'm working on it, and I've only come to appreciate the value of humility over the last several years. I think it is the secret of success. I think we all know people, some people, whose lives are models of humility. They're genuinely modest about their own accomplishments, which are usually substantial. There are people who try to shed a light on the achievements of others. There are people who just keep their head down, focus on the job at hand, and get the work done. Humility allows you to endure. Whether it's politics or finance or industry, there are cycles everywhere and especially in this business. The wonderful thing about the financial markets is that even when you might be right, the market will find a way to make you humble. It will confound you and it will make you humble. And if it can't make you humble, if you cannot be humbled, if you can't be reminded constantly that you don't know everything, then you should not be managing other people's money. You probably shouldn't hold elected office. Now, unfortunately, you know, the world is littered with money managers and politicians whose lives are far from humility. But humility allows you to endure and to get through all the down cycles.

WALL STREET 50
Makoto Ozawa   *A Magic Wand*

BREAK UP THE BANKS

Makoto Ozawa entered the financial industry as an institutional sales-person with Nomura Securities in 1986. He worked in New York, Tokyo, and Hong Kong for S.G. Warburg and Deutsche Bank in various roles. After leaving the institutional equity business in 2011, he has been trad-ing at Fountainhead Capital and spending more time with his family.

KIM: If I gave you a magic wand to wave over government, over the regulators, what would that magic wand do?

MAKOTO: It would get rid of Alan Greenspan and what's his name? Geithner.

KIM: Would you get rid of the Federal Reserve?

MAKOTO: Yes, no reason for it to exist. The whole thing is, "Oh, well, they make things—you know, they sort of soften the downside of things." That's the biggest pile of baloney on the face of the earth. Cycles happen, crashes happen. The whole purpose of this whole system that the government has created now has become so convoluted that now, you don't know what's going to happen—the markets are reacting that way. You don't know what kind of crazy thing these guys are going to come up with next. Companies go bankrupt, and I'm sure you've seen it in different forms, any number of times. But capitalism without bankruptcy is like Christianity without help, it doesn't work.

Did you see that whole thing that happened at Knight Capital? The press was going back and forth about it, "Oh, Joyce should resign; it was under his watch." I happen to think that is a great company. He went out over a weekend, spent probably seventy-two hours without sleep, got financing for his company. Yes, he diluted the shareholders to some degree, but no one's lost his job. And the company is still up and running and it's like nothing ever happened. Now, did they screw up? Yes, they did, but that happens. It wasn't something that was evil. They made a mistake. What people have got to understand is that there are the banks where people have deposits, and the government has always protected banks because people's money is there and it needs to be insured. That's what government should be involved in and they should do that. But once we're talking about taking risks with money or property, that's a different business and shouldn't be part of the bank. That needs to be separated.

This is my own personal incredible bias, but bankers as business people suck. They suck at it. And there's no way they should be running a high-risk brokerage operation. Brokerage operation involves risk and entails risk. It's going to happen unless you're a 100 percent agency broker, which really never was a profitable business model. Brokerage houses have risks and the managers control the risk. What has happened is you've allowed a whole bunch of clowns and numbers guys who really, truly don't understand that the markets are social—a social animal. It's not an economic thing; it's not a finance thing; it's not hard numbers. It's not a hard science; it's a soft science. And you can't do things that way. It just doesn't work. Or at least we've seen it doesn't work. You need to separate these things and have them broken up. I would break up the banks. And this doesn't come from someone who is just saying banks are evil. They just can't do it. They are two separate things. And they shouldn't be working under the same umbrella.

WALL STREET 50
Bill Ackman   *A Magic Wand*

SIMPLIFY REGULATION

William A. "Bill" Ackman is the founder and CEO of hedge fund Pershing Square Capital Management LP. In 2002, Ackman engaged in a six-year campaign warning that the $2.5 trillion bond insurance business was a house of cards. He continued on in spite of being branded a fraud by the *Wall Street Journal* and *New York Times*, as well as enduring an investigation by Eliot Spitzer and the SEC. Later, he made his investors more than $1 billion when bond insurers kicked off the collapse of the credit markets. Ackman's testimony is available online via Christine Richard's book's website: *Confidence Game: How a Hedge Fund Manager Called Wall Street's Bluff.* Ackman is a signatory of The Giving Pledge, committing to give away at least 50 percent of his wealth to charitable causes, and in 2011, he was named one of the most generous donors on "Philanthropy 50" a list put out by *The Chronicle of Philanthropy.*

KIM: If I give you a magic wand to wave over Wall Street or the regulators or D.C., what would you want your magic wand to do?

BILL: I think regulation is way too complicated. I think something like a third of Dodd-Frank has been implemented. I don't know how long it's been since Dodd-Frank took place, but it's been a few years and they haven't even implemented two-thirds of it yet. It's just not a functional, workable set of rules. The regulations that were introduced after the market crash and the Great Depression—34 Act and 33 Act—were very good; they're just not generally enforced well. Hence, now we create a whole bunch of more rules that are really complicated and they probably won't be enforced because they are so difficult to enforce. They'll generate a lot more paperwork and busy work without accomplishing anything. They should have a principle-based regulation, so people know what's right and what's wrong. Very technical, role-based stuff, I think. First of all, you might end up violating some law you don't even know exists. That's the kind of stuff that's scary to me. We have just hired another lawyer. We're going to have seven lawyers here out of fifty-something people. It's like 15 percent of the workforce. That's a big number. And I do think it's a meaningful friction for the economy. I'm not opposed to regulation. In fact, I look at this Herbalife situation and this pyramid scheme that has been allowed to go on for thirty-two years. That's a regulatory failure. And part of me thinks that the regulators responsible here don't even want to find it to be a pyramid scheme now because it's an admission that they've been wrong for thirty-two years. But we'll see. We'll see.

When I think of principles-based, there should be fundamental bullet points on what's legal and what's not legal as opposed to thousands of pages of rules. Like the Ten Commandments—Ten Fundamental Divisions as opposed to a bunch of highly technical rules. Unfortunately, the economic compensation for being a prosecutor is not particularly good. So people are motivated to get high profile targets. And the people who have gotten high profile targets leveraged that to get great jobs in the private sector and in government. Rudy Giuliani leveraged Wall Street convictions, many of which were overturned, to become mayor. I watched examples of crooked companies continuing to exist without prosecution and, unfortunately, some innocent people who have been prosecuted. The government is very, very powerful and more powerful than most individuals. And people end up having their lives destroyed because people sell what they can for the costs of defending themselves. So that's on the one hand. Look, it's tough. It's not an easy job to be a regulator either.

WALL STREET 50
Alex Green   *A Magic Wand*

TEACH FINANCIAL LITERACY IN SCHOOL

Alexander Green is an author and the Chief Investment Strategist of The Oxford Club and Chief Investment Strategist for Investment U. A Wall Street veteran, he has over twenty-five years' experience as a research analyst, investment advisor, financial writer, and portfolio manager.

KIM: If you had the ability to change Wall Street, to re-sculpt Wall Street right now, what would you do first?

ALEX: It's a good question. I'm of two minds on Wall Street. If you read my first book, *The Gone Fishin' Portfolio*, the first half of it is one long indictment of some of Wall Street's shortcomings. Let me tell you what I think that great shortcoming is. First of all, it's almost too much to ask that these big investment banks, that are down on bended knee to each of these companies wanting to do their secondary stock offering or a bond issue or manage their pension account, can at the same time turn around to retail investors and give objective, unbiased coverage of what these companies' business prospects are. It can't happen. Because if Merrill Lynch has to sell a recommendation on XYZ Corporation, well then people at Morgan Stanley go to XYZ and say, "Why would you have this company do your bond issue? We think you are a strong buy." So, surprise, surprise, 97 percent of the recommendations on Wall Street are buy recommendations.

There is a conflict of interest there that's tough, and also not enough people are aware that, unlike with a doctor or a lawyer, where you have a fiduciary relationship, most stockbrokers by law do not have a fiduciary relationship with the client. They're basically salesmen selling financial products. I think there is a potential for abuse there, too, but what does Wall Street do right? Wall Street is indispensable for companies needing to raise money. They need to raise money to equity offerings, through debt offerings; they need to make markets in individual security, so they're lots of things that Wall Street does that are good. It's essential to the functioning of the free market system, but there's just been some instances where things have just gone off the rail. Maybe part of it is that some of these investment banks have simply gotten too large—the fact that Lehman Brothers was so big that its collapse was almost enough to send us into the abyss is something; it's a risk we shouldn't be taking and yet the biggest investment banks are absolutely as big as they were before the financial crisis.

I think in that sense there is some reform needed, but Wall Street is not simply a bunch of greedy people who are out to cheat people—it's simply not the case. Take one of the best known instances, when Goldman Sachs put together the securities made up of the worst looking mortgage securities they could find so this hedge fund manager, John Paulson, could sell them short and then package them to retail clients as if it was an income security for them. Here is a perfect example of trying to serve two masters. You're trying to serve the hedge fund manager who wants you to put together this package of rotten mortgages he can sell short and make money on by dropping them. Then the very same company turns around and recommends to its retail clients, "If you're looking for income, these rotten mortgages"—of course, they didn't call them that to the retail clients—"would be a place to invest." So I'm not a great defender of Wall Street in some ways because in some ways Wall Street behaves in an unethical manner. But that doesn't mean that Wall Street should be tarred with the brush that everything they do is suspect. There are instances, especially when you are talking about retail investors dealing with Wall Street brokers, where I think a great deal of caution is necessary.

KIM: If I gave you a magic wand to wave not only over Wall Street but Washington D.C. or the Feds or the Regulators, what would you do?

ALEX: Here is the first thing I would do. It's a shame that people graduate from high school and they don't know what compound interest is. They don't know what a 401K is. They don't know what an adjustment rate mortgage is. They don't know why we have a stock market or what a bond is. They really need to teach basic financial literacy in public high schools because no one with a high school degree should go out into the world and learn the hard way. What happens is they go out and somebody sends them a credit card, and they're so excited they run it up, and they realize they're paying 19 percent interest, so they open an account with that nice young man down at Merrill Lynch and they find out they'll earn 5.75 percent on a mutual fund. I mean it is such a shame that people learn the hard way. Yet I graduated from one of the finest liberal arts colleges in the country and was a business major, and I knew nothing about the way the stock market works, or managing my own financial affairs, nothing. And forget high schools. I mean I graduated from high school a blithering idiot in financial matters. I think probably 99 percent of people do today, so it starts with education.

The second thing is, I think there should be a clear, written disclaimer up front when someone opens a brokerage account that they are dealing with a licensed salesman who does not have a fiduciary relationship with them. Having worked on Wall Street for sixteen years myself, I can't think of a single instance where someone was in a totally transaction-based relationship with a financial salesman that ended up being anything someone would recommend long-term to their friends. I mean they can certainly make a lot of money to bull market and pay a lot of fees, but you can't pay a lot of fees in a flat or down market over a long period of time and expect to get ahead. So, as an unrepentant capitalist, I'm not a big fan of regulation, but at the same time, I do think there needs to be education in the public schools that gives people basic financial literacy, and I think there needs to be a clear disclaimer when people open a brokerage account with a full service broker that you are not dealing with the fiduciary. You are dealing with the licensed financial product salesman. That just needs to be clear.

Then you remember Wall Street is Goldman Sachs, but Wall Street is also Charles Schwab and John Bogle's Vanguard. Well, one thing I would actually make part of financial literacy is that people should know Vanguard has a unique structure in the financial services industry and it is Vanguard is owned by the fund shareholders themselves, so there is no incentive there—Vanguard is a not-for-profit corporation. I call it not-for-profit instead of nonprofit because it's not a charitable organization. But it's a not-for-profit corporation, which means they're not trying to make money. Because the fund shareholders own the Vanguard family, there's no incentive to do anything other than give the best service at the lowest possible cost. The average mutual fund company has expenses that are more than six times as high as Vanguard's, so that's a bit of objective information every investor should be aware of.

WALL STREET 50
Peter Leeds *A Magic Wand*

STOP DEVALUING THE AMERICAN DOLLAR

Peter Leeds is the Founder and CEO of www.PeterLeeds.com and a twenty-year veteran and self-taught speculator in penny stocks. He began after he lost all his money in the first two weeks of trading penny stocks when he was fourteen years old. Now he is the senior analyst and editor of the *Peter Leeds Speculative Stock* newsletter and author of books that teach how to invest safely in smaller shares. He invented the *100% Unbiased Guarantee,* which is now used throughout the financial community to keep investors' best interests at heart by avoiding all conflicts of interest and refusing compensation for any of the stocks his firm reviews or profiles. Leeds also created www.PetersPromise.com in gratitude for his own recovery from health issues and to educate others in how his own doctor's treatments can assist successfully with various illnesses, such as MS, ADHD, and cancers.

KIM: Are there any things you'd wish for if you had a magic wand to wave over Wall Street, Washington, D.C., the Fed, or the regulators? What would your magic wand create or do?

PETER: I wouldn't keep putting new money into the system. I wouldn't keep easing the liquidity issues because what that's doing is it's decreasing the value of the American dollar. If you go back to 1960, you could buy $1,000 worth of goods, but to buy that exact same package of goods now costs you $8,000. And that isn't because the goods cost more, technically; it's just because the purchasing power of the dollar is less. It takes more dollars to buy the same thing. You know, if somebody has a $40,000 house and then years later they sell it for $250,000 and then they say, "Oh, my house went up in value," it might be a little bit of that, but a big percentage of that is because it's just taking more dollars to buy the same thing.

WALL STREET 50
Susan Davis   *A Magic Wand*

FIND YOUR LIFE PURPOSE

Susan Davis left Harris Bank's Personal Trust Group after nine years to start Capital Missions Company (CMC) in June of 1990. CMC created an innovation method highly effective in social investing and other niches of sustainability using principles of generosity and trust. From 1965 to 1979, she helped start five social ventures. Davis used these experiences in business and finance to create this unique networking innovation method now proven successful with twenty-six networks created over a thirty-five-year-period. This method, called KINS Innovation Networks, uses nature as a model for innovation. KINS has been used to create a social venture capital industry (Investors' Circle), a socially-responsible business industry (Social Venture Network), and a family office industry (Harris Family Office Management Conference). Her book, *The Trojan Horse of Love*, which teaches how to start a KINS network, is available for free on her website.

KIM: If you had a magic wand you could wave over Wall Street, what would you do?

SUSAN: I would ask people about their life's destiny, their path, and then I would try to help them achieve it. For example, one very, very wealthy industrialist running three companies in China spent a year asking himself why was he alive. And he worked with shaman and different people. He was a friend of mine and told me he figured out that his purpose was to make solar happen for the world. And so I explained to him how we could use him to do it, and we did it. It is called the solar circle. I described it in my book. It's very successful and it's given him a seminal role in helping make solar happen for the world. He's become a band of brothers with some of the most wonderful men and women in the world. So, my gift to others in finance and on Wall Street is to help them go inside and ask themselves why they are here in this lifetime? What is their real life purpose? And it is not just about making more money. If people are on that wavelength, they will make more money, but that's not going to bring them happiness at all. My magic wand would allow me to have that conversations with everyone I meet, whether they are in finance or not.

WALL STREET 50
Janet Hanson   *A Magic Wand*

MAKE INVESTMENT BANKS BE PRIVATELY HELD

Janet Hanson is the Founder and Former CEO of 85 Broads, a global network of over 30,000 trailblazing women worldwide who invest in each other's professional and personal success. Hanson joined Goldman Sachs in 1977, became a Vice President in 1983, and became Goldman's first female sales manager in 1986. In 1995, she founded Milestone Capital, the first women-owned institutional money-management fund in the U.S, managing at its peak over $2.5 billion in assets. From 2004 to 2007, Hanson was a Managing Director and Senior Advisor to the President and COO of Lehman Brothers.

KIM: If you had a magic wand you could wave over Wall Street, what would it do?

JANET: I would wave my magic wand and turn Goldman back into a privately held firm. I think the pressure to make shareholders happy every quarter puts real stress on the firm's culture. After Goldman went public, one of my friends, who was still on the sales desk, said that the page in the Annual Report that listed the firm's business principles was now perforated. He was kidding, but not really.

KIM: What would your magic wand do regarding federal overseers in Washington, D.C.?

JANET: When I was at Goldman, the relationship between the Street and Washington struck me as a cordial one. Now the common denominator is fear on both sides. The question becomes: How do you get both sides to invest in the best possible outcome? Now defensiveness on the part of Wall Street and skepticism on the part of Washington has created a real mess for everybody. I was incredibly lucky to work at Goldman when the firm's business principles were strongly upheld and believed in. Back then, actions and words both spoke loudly.

The Future of Capitalism looks different to each one of these men and women, from simplifying regulation, supporting emerging markets, having greater transparency, or teaching financial literacy in school. Each of these suggestions would have far-reaching impacts if implemented. Find the one that resonates with you the most and do what you can to have it mobilized into action. Maybe it's what you will personally follow and advocate; maybe you will make your firm or your congressman implement it. Take one on and run with it in whatever way you can.

The Wall Street 50's Advice to Those On or Entering Wall Street

Josh Brown, The Reformed Broker, spoke in his interview about being a young man and how his father unknowingly recommended he go work for some Wall Streeters who ultimately turned out to be men without integrity. This situation happens more times than not. When people around us have the trappings of what the world says is success—a big fancy home, a new expensive car, the "right" neighborhood, etc.—we presume that they must know what they are doing and, in fact, are worthy of our emulation. One of the things I always tell young men and women who are about to begin their careers is to be very choosy in whom they admire.

When we begin to follow in someone's footsteps, we draw to ourselves many of the same features and side effects that person has in his life. Now if you only know the side of the person that he tells you about or shows you, then you might miss the entire picture. When I first began as a coach, I was very inspired by a world famous entrepreneur. He was someone I admired, so I wrote to him, asking to be part of his new venture. Amazingly, he agreed. I thought, "How lucky I am now! I will have his mentorship and learn all his secrets of success up close and personal." But instead, I found a greedy man who did not keep his word. What a disappointment. Had I only seen him from the outside—I would have thought that he had it all. This opportunity, although tremendously disappointing and painful, taught me a valuable lesson. I need to be very careful about those I position as my heroes and make sure that their personal and private lives are congruent with what they preach and claim to live publically.

We are crystal clear on who are the bastards—even those outside of Wall Street know their names, but isn't it fascinating that we don't know the names of the good guys? You know Bernie Madoff's name, but not the name of Frank Casey (the guy who helped bring him down). You know Jordan Belfort, but not Eric Greschner, who said, "Hell no," and walked away.

Having role models who are worthy of emulation seems to me long overdue. I think we all need, in our careers and our personal lives, a wise and experienced elder whom we can lean on and glean advice from. Learn how he or she handled the challenges that came his or her way. Most of these Wall Street 50 have worked in the world of finance for a long time. They have seen it from numerous angles. I thought their advice would serve those already in the industry who need guidance, as well as those who might be uncertain about entering it due to its current reputation.

I'm worried that right now a great deal of young people see Wall Street as the last place they want to work because most of the young people I meet these days are so passionate about making the world a better place. I don't want all those dreamers to go work in Silicon Valley alone. I want them to come to Wall Street and be the change that is needed so dearly. I hope this chapter inspires those who are currently working on Wall Street to be gutsier and to stand up and speak out when they need to. To be the change they seek. To enroll those who sit on the fence next to them to jump on in and help recreate it.

You must never be fearful about what you are doing when it is right.
—ROSA PARKS

ANSWERS FROM THE WALL STREET 50

WALL STREET 50
Jim Rogers   *Advice for The Street*

IF YOU LOVE FINANCE, GO FOR IT!

James Beeland "Jim" Rogers, Jr. is an investor, media commentator, adventurer, and author. He is the Chairman of Beeland Interests, Inc. He was the co-founder of the Quantum Fund and creator of the Rogers International Commodities Index (RICI). Although Rogers' career spans over forty-six years, during the last thirty-four years he has been semi-retired and travels extensively around the world. He was an occasional Visiting Professor at Columbia University. One of his books, *Investment Biker* recounts his riding a motorcycle around the globe during 1990–1992 and what he learned along the way about the world's developing countries and investment markets by seeing them from the ground up. It led to one of his three entries in the *Guinness Book of World Records*.

KIM: What would your advice be for someone who is on the brink of working in finance?

JIM: Dishonesty happens as much in the world of finance as it happens in the world of farmers, teachers, priests, etc. If you love finance, and that's what you want to do, go do it. Don't let anybody stop you. However, I will say that finance is not going to be a very attractive place to work in for the next twenty or thirty years. Throughout history we've had periods when the financial types were the masters of our universe, and then we had other periods when the heroes of war were at the top. In other words, it's cyclical.

Right now, finance is finished. In the '30s, the government came down on finance, and for the next thirty or forty years, finance was a terrible place to be. That's going to be the case again. When I was in Oxford during the '60s, I actually remember my professors saying, "Well, we don't know what to do with you because we don't have anybody as cheerful about the market as you. The market is not important. It's not important to the British economy, or the world economy." And indeed, it was the backwash. I mean, nobody went to the city of London or Wall Street in those days. But I was desperate to go; I loved it so much. So off I went.

Now, in the past thirty years, of course, that has changed. Kids at Oxford are starting hedge funds in their dorm rooms. Everyone wants to go to Wall Street. In 1958, America graduated 5,000 MBAs. The rest of the world graduated none. Last year (2011), America graduated something like 200,000 MBAs, and the rest of the world graduated tens of thousands more. So we have massive competition in finance now, at a time when there is a staggering amount of doubt in the financial community. Not just in the U.S., but all over the world. And also at a time when governments are coming down very hard with laws, regulations, and taxes, to punish and get back at financial types. If you look at Barclays, it's just like the '30s. During that time, the president of the New York Stock Exchange, Richard Whitney, went to jail. Afterwards, finance became a horrible place to be. And that's happening again. But once again, if you love it, then by all means do it. I went into finance in the middle of a very bad time, and somehow I made a little bit of money.

WALL STREET 50

Schuyler "Sky" Lance

Advice for The Street

FIND A B CORPORATION

Schuyler (Sky) Lance is a managing partner of SustainVC LLC, which manages the Patient Capital Collaborative series of early-stage impact investment funds. Associated with Investors' Circle, PCC invests on a for-profit basis in companies that provide meaningful social and/or environmental benefits to the world. Previously, Lance was Co-Founder and Managing Principal of private equity firm Windjammer Capital Investors with nearly $2B under management today.

KIM: What advice do you have for those entering the finance industry now?

SKY: Make sure it's a B corp. I think there is a website where you can look it up. The B I believe stands for Beneficial Corporation. And so, what they have done is they have created standards that measure all sorts of aspects of the business. It is beyond if the product is beneficial to the world. How do you treat your employees? How do you treat your suppliers? Do you have recycling programs? Look at all of the stakeholders associated with the business. How are you doing fair trade with your supply chain? They measure the environmental pollution of your company. . . . So all of the different aspects of the company, not strictly environment, or strictly profit. And so at the end of the questionnaire you are given a rating score. You can be certified and be a B corporation. This is proof that somebody has looked at all of the ways you treat all your stakeholders in your business, including all your shareholders, employees, and everyone else. And it comes out with this scorecard. If you are high enough in the score, you are a certified B corporation.

Interestingly, these [press] people calling you, "We think what you are doing is important and different, and we want to talk to you." You know, it is so fascinating that the funds we have in our management are so small compared to what I was doing in my prior job. But the press hardly ever called in my prior job, but now, even though we are only making investments of a hundred to five hundred dollars per company, as opposed to thirty or fifty million that my last company was, you folks called, capital institutes called, *Inc. Magazine* called, Bloomberg called, Wall Street called, and I was like, "This is fascinating. I am having such a tiny impact out there, but it must be special." So, it also energizes me.

WALL STREET 50
Deepak Parekh   *Advice for The Street*
GREED DOESN'T GET YOU ANYWHERE

Deepak S. Parekh is the Chairman of Housing Development Finance Corporation in Mumbai. HDFC is India's leading housing finance company. The Reserve Bank of India appointed him Chairman of the Advisory Group for Securities Market Regulation and he was made Chairman of the Expert Committee to look into the reform efforts in the power sector. In addition to being known for his vociferous views seeking standardization and transparency in the real estate sector, Parekh is known as the unofficial crisis consultant of the Government. His philosophy on Corporate Social Responsibility is "if a company earns, it must also return to the society" and that companies owe a responsibility not just to shareholders but to all stakeholders.

KIM: What would be your advice to young people today who may be wanting to go into the world of finance?

DEEPAK: I think the financial sector got a terrible beating in the last decade, particularly in the last five years. After the Subprime crisis, within every short period you see more and more scandals in the financial sector. Whether it is derivatives, whether it's trading losses, whether it is making money, whether it's insider trading, it's all related to greed. Single point: Greed doesn't get you anywhere. Greed is one of the biggest sins one can have. I have got this; I want two more. When you die you are not going to take any of it with you. And greed is the single factor that brings everyone down. The financial sector has to come out of it. Currently, it has a very bad name. You see all the regulators are after every bank, every stock broker, every investment bank, every insurance company, and every mutual fund across the world. Regulators are fining J.P Morgan right now, and the LIBOR scandal that just broke, it's horrendous. Now LIBOR is a rate that impacts each and every individual who borrows money, so that means everyone is paying a little more. So that means they are squeezing money out of the common man. They are not being transparent simply to increase the profits of their organization.

KIM: So what is your advice to people that are in finance?

DEEPAK: I think first of all, if you feel any discomfort in any organization, even if you have a hunch, that some trading or some methods are not fair, are not equitable, are not kosher, please quit. If you have the degree, you will get a job. Don't become a part of it; it is very easy to get involved in it. It is very, very easy to do because you say, "He is doing it; why can't I do it? I am a trader, he is a trader, and he is getting more benefits because he is showing more profits." We don't know whether the profits are real or they are cooked up. So just because he is doing it doesn't mean you should do it. You have to distinguish yourself. You have to have that individual personality that if you feel something is wrong in your organization, complain.

Why do you have all these scandals coming out? It's not from audits, but from whistle blowing. Because people complain and then there is an investigation. So it is not that auditors have discovered fraud or that the regulators during an inspection discovered something. The genesis is one anonymous letter or one from a dissent group or a straightforward employee who feels something is wrong.

WALL STREET 50

Amy Domini   *Advice for The Street*

ASK, "HOW CAN MY SKILL SET AND TRAINING
MAKE THE WORLD BETTER?"

Amy Domini is Founder and CEO of Domini Social Investments, a woman-owned and managed SEC-registered investment adviser that specializes exclusively in socially responsible investing, serving individual and institutional investors who wish to create positive social and environmental outcomes while seeking competitive financial returns. Domini manages three mutual funds with a combined $1.3 billion in assets: the Domini Social Equity Fund, the Domini International Social Equity Fund, and the Domini Social Bond Fund. Analysis of the long-term record of the Domini 400 Social Index demonstrated that social and environmental standards have led to strong individual stock selection and potentially higher returns.

KIM: What would you say to somebody who works within Wall Street today?

AMY: I think some people on Wall Street want to get off Wall Street, or they want to get into an environment where they can see a more specific result from their actions. So a start would be to consider your own skill set and training and how that skill set and training can help bring about something different in the world. I was talking to someone who said, "I read your book and I changed my career." This person was at JP Morgan on the investment banking side, and he went over to run their social investment side. He said he put out a hundred emails and a statement on their internal board saying he needed a researcher and that they would make 25 percent of their current pay. He said he had 125 applications come in from JP Morgan.

But there are also a lot of people who can't quite make the jump. I think some are waiting to see an opportunity and then will go for it. They can't quite construct it themselves—but if they would think about their own skill set and what they have a head start with, they probably could turn that setting into something a little more useful and powerful. I mean, you are reading every day in the paper today on this Occupy Wall Street, traders, or whatever coming down and saying, "Yeah, great. You know, I love what you're doing." They recognize they're working in a field where they don't get the kind of personal satisfaction of making the world a better place that they'd like to be getting. And there's no reason why Wall Street itself shouldn't be. I mean, I think it should be. That's kind of what my field is all about, but there are traders who don't seem to know it can be.

WALL STREET 50
John Allison *Advice for The Street*

STAY TRUE TO YOUR PRINCIPLES

John Allison is the CEO and President of the Cato Institute and was the longest serving CEO of a major bank in the U.S. when he was CEO of BB&T Bank. Allison is a major contributor to the Ayn Rand Institute and has said that, "*Atlas Shrugged* was the best defense of capitalism ever written."

KIM: Is there any advice you would give to those working on Wall Street?

JOHN: My advice is to stay true to their principles. I was recently talking to a group of MBA students and there was one student who has been with an investment-banking firm and was unhappy with some of the things he had been asked to do. I told him, "Don't work for a company that you don't have shared values with." People on Wall Street need to be asking themselves, "Is what I am doing something I am at peace with?" There is a very important role for finance—Wall

Street is what makes the economy work. But it is about trading value for value. That doesn't mean that you are responsible for someone else's decision. Every time you trade, you think this is better for you and the other guy thinks it is better for him, but you need to be honest. Don't try to mislead anybody. Don't try to oversell. Just tell the facts, and if you are doing that, don't apologize for the nature of your work. Be at peace that you are operating consistently with ethical principles. Don't do anything you believe is wrong.

KIM: What would your advice be to somebody who finds himself in a situation with a company he works for where he feels uncomfortable with what might be being asked of him? What if he said to you, "What do I do? If I stand up against this, I lose my job, maybe I get blacklisted." What would you advise him to do?

JOHN: Students sometimes decide to pursue an MBA when they are in some kind of bad environment. If the company's basic philosophy challenges your fundamental beliefs, you need to think you can change the philosophy within a reasonable period of time, or at least change it in the context of your group or team. If you don't believe you can change the philosophy and it is inconsistent with your values, you should leave because you are giving up your soul for money, and that is a terrible tradeoff.

If you really leave over that type of issue, I am confident you can get a job somewhere. A similar situation happened to me early in my career. I was reporting to the chief credit officer of the bank who reported to the executive committee of the board. It was a small bank. I prepared a past-due loan report, and one day, I brought in the past-due loan report and the chief credit officer asked me to change the report. He claimed that after the date of the report, a big loan was paid and, therefore, we had less past-due. He also claimed no one would know. I refused to change the report because I knew it was dishonest and I would know even if no one else knew. I really thought that was probably the end of my career at this company. Here is the irony—he didn't change the report. Also, it turned out that the big past-due loan had not really been paid. I am sure he was angry with me, but he really couldn't fire me over refusing to falsify the report. I thought he would get me some day over another issue, but he never did. He left the bank after a few years, and he had serious emotional problems later.

If somebody asks you to do something that is unethical, it is not a very hard decision. Refusing to act unethically is an easy decision. Now, you have to be clear that it really is unethical. There are gray areas in life. But if you are clear that, in your value system, *it is* unethical, then you have to say, "No." Period. "I am not doing it." In the extreme, the German guards in Holocaust prison camps cannot justify their actions by saying, "I am just following orders." You are murdering women and children and that is not justified because somebody orders you to do it. It should be a no-brainer to refuse to act in this manner.

I try to tell students they have to use their own value system. You will always know if you cheated, even if you don't get caught, and you always want to be proud of yourself.

WALL STREET 50
John Whitehead   *Advice for The Street*

DO IT AND RESTORE WALL STREET'S ETHICAL REPUTATION

John C. Whitehead is an American banker and civil servant, currently a board member of the World Trade Center Memorial Foundation. Whitehead joined Goldman Sachs in 1947 and became chairman. Over thirty-eight years at the firm, he retired in 1984 as co-chairman and co-senior partner. He served as U.S. Deputy Secretary of State from 1985–1989, and was awarded the Presidential Citizen's Medal and is former Chairman of the Board of the Federal Reserve Bank of New York as well as former director of the New York Stock Exchange. Whitehead served in the U.S. Navy during World War II and landed at Normandy. He has been critical of Goldman Sachs since his departure and some of that is captured in his book, *A Life in Leadership.*

KIM: If a young person came to you questioning whether he or she should work in the world of finance or on Wall Street—considering its current reputation—what advice would you give?

JOHN: I would give them the advice that, yes, they should. It would be a great career and they can help in restoring the ethical reputation Wall Street used to have. There is restoration that needs to be done. I hope they would choose to come into the business and make it more ethical than it is today.

KIM: I am curious about those who may have found themselves challenged with the mandate to do something that went against their own principles—measuring the fact that they might be out of a job if they didn't. What advice would you give to them if they found themselves being asked to do something unethical?

JOHN: I would urge them to report to their boss what was happening that they didn't like and why they didn't like it, or what they thought was improper. If their boss didn't give them a favorable response, I would go over his head and report it to the more senior people in the firm. All the while being ready to leave if you must. If I worked for a firm that would not course correct I could not have stood to work for them, even in the early years when I had no authority. I could not have stayed if I saw the firm doing something I thought was unethical. I couldn't have stood to stay with them unless I felt I could change the conduct quickly.

KIM: Even if you need to feed your family or pay the rent? What if you informed the senior people and yet change did not occur?

JOHN: If it were me, I would be willing to look for another job. I would not continue to work for an unethical company, and not only because of that but also because I wouldn't believe that company would continue to exist with unethical conduct.

WALL STREET 50
Dara Albright   *Advice for The Street*

GO IN AND CHANGE IT

Dara Albright founded the NowStreet blog in 2011 and is the preeminent resource for education and insight into the burgeoning industry
of market structure, private secondary transactions, and crowdfinance.
One of the earliest voices covering the JOBS Act and advocating for
greater democracy in the equity and credit markets, Albright produced
the first major crowdfunding conference in 2012 and co-founded LendIt,
the largest and most recognized global P2P and online lending conference organization.

KIM: If you were speaking to a young person today who wanted to
work on Wall Street but felt hesitant, what would your advice be?

DARA: I would say, you have to go in and change it. Take your
perspective and bring your passion and bring your point of view and
change it. Make it better. Don't fear it. Don't stay away from it. Just
make it better.

WALL STREET 50
Frank Casey   *Advice for The Street*

HAVE A STRONG SENSE OF SOCIAL COMMITMENT

Frank Casey is a member of The Fox Hounds, Harry Markopolos' team
that worked nearly nine years to blow the whistle on Bernard Madoff's
Ponzi scheme.

KIM: What advice would you give to someone today who wanted to
go work on Wall Street?

FRANK: We need people in finance who have a strong sense of social commitment, while they're doing capitalistic endeavors. And by
social commitment, first and foremost, true to themselves and their

compasses. Second of all, true to their profession. Third of all, true to the industry, the broad financial industry, and helping to keep it clean. When Harry and I and Neal Chelo and Michael Ocrant went after Madoff, he was a very powerful guy, right? And so we knew we were going to try to topple one of the most powerful financiers in the brokerage industry. And truly, one of the bigger guys inside, secretly, the hedge fund industry. And that it could be a dangerous operation and dangerous to careers, at the very least, and maybe, dangerous physically if his partners internationally saw us as threatening their income stream. And since we figured that at one point, it was valued at over fifty billion before the spring of 2008, we knew people get killed for a hell of a lot less. So while initially, we went after him to level the playing field so we could compete, but then as you can't compete against a guy who makes up his numbers, we then quickly knew we had to bring him down because he was a crook. And we wondered, why wasn't everybody taking him down? We knew we had to take him down because it was wrong and he was going to destroy the industry; destroy the SEC. The United States makes a tremendous amount of money running other people's money, and investment banking around the world would have its reputation harmed, maybe irrevocably, for a long period of time, so we knew we needed to stop this thing. That's why we were after him. When you stop and think about it a lot of people probably said, "Well, wait a minute. I can't do this!" We felt there was a higher mission at stake and that we could not *not* do it. We felt we had to take it on as our mission.

WALL STREET 50
Marlee-Jo Jacobson *Advice for The Street*

ASK, "WHAT CAN I CONTRIBUTE?"

Marlee-Jo Jacobson is the Founder of SafeMoneyMetrics® a managed futures risk management and research service. Analysis provided is a direct approach to identifying, evaluating, and monitoring investment cost, trading talent, and capital at risk relative to realized return using her proprietary algorithms. Jacobson says her obsession is "consciousness as a risk management strategy." She is also the founder of ConsciousKids. org, which provides a journey of empowerment to orphans, inner city, and foster care children.

KIM: What would be your advice to those who want to work on Wall Street?

MARLEE-JO: I would tell them to look inside to see why they're drawn to it. They should ask what can they contribute. What can they bring to people that is useful? If they're going in just to make a ton of money, it's a very big mistake. I would tell people to look at why they want to go into it. What do they love and what can they give? Once they have that defined, then the decision becomes clear. You don't go into something to make money. You go into something because you love doing it day-to-day and you have a gift or a talent to share within whatever industry you choose. Once you define that within yourself, then you'll be happy. If it's meant to be finance, Wall Street—what aspect of it? Finance is a huge industry. So the question is, "What do you love doing and why are you going into it?"

WALL STREET 50
Jonah S. Ford   *Advice for The Street*
DON'T DO IT FOR THE MONEY

Jonah S. Ford began his career as a proprietary commodity futures trader in the mid-1990s at the age of twenty, soon bringing him to the floor of the Chicago Board of Trade to work with Core Futures Commodity Trading Advisors. He co-founded Ceres Hedge, a specialized consultancy firm providing hedging strategies to commodity producers and brokerage firms. He is also co-founder and CEO of Bitcomdex, the world's first exchange to utilize digital currencies for commodity futures and options trading. He hosts press conferences for the Minneapolis Grain Exchange, providing expert analysis and forecasts to the media, and has appeared frequently in financial press, including Agweb, Barron's, Bloomberg, and Reuters.

KIM: What would you suggest for those wanting to work on Wall Street?

JONAH: I actually had a twenty-something kid in 2008, three months before everything completely imploded, send me an email saying, "I really want to get into the financial district." I sent him a one-line response. "Go be a poet." And I hope he thanks me for that now. I don't know what he did. I never heard from him again, but the writing was already on the wall.

But if you love it, do it. But don't do it for the money. I believe that if you really love markets and if you really love the whole thing, then you have to do it. But yeah, if you want to make money, go do something else for a few more years, at least, because I think it's going to be an uphill struggle to get into it right now. I do think there will be new opportunities eventually and I'm not really sure what those will be. I do think the worst of it is over, as far as the mistrust. I think discourages me from telling people to get into this business is not being able to trust the companies you work for. And I really think we're at the tail-end of that.

WALL STREET 50
Jason Apollo Voss   *Advice for The Street*

LEARN WHO YOU ARE FIRST

Jason Apollo Voss is Content Director at CFA Institute and author of *The Intuitive Investor*. He previously retired at age thirty-five after being co-Portfolio Manager of the Davis Appreciation & Income Fund, where he bested the NASDAQ, S&P 500, and DJIA by staggering percentages. He has studied the ancient martial art of ninjutsu and Eastern healing techniques. Voss also teaches meditation.

KIM: What advice would you give to those who want to work on Wall Street?

JASON: My advice is, not surprisingly, always, always, in the time you're not dedicating toward what your career is going to be, learn who you are first. I've had interns work for me over the years and people I have mentored and my advice is always the same. It's "Know who you are." This is a Joseph Campbell kind of a thing. He would say, "Follow your bliss." My response is somewhat similar. I would say, "Bring into your life harmony." And you do that by knowing who you are and the sound of your bell and the octave of your bell. And as soon as you know the sound of your bell, you go and find the career that is an octave of your bell. So a lot of people who want to go into finance, they're not really looking for their octave. They're not really looking for something that resonates with them. They've got a prejudice of, "Oh, I need to have a lot of money to be happy." They'll say that that's not what they believe in because they know, we all know in our culture, you don't have permission to say, "Yeah. I'm really interested in money." That's a bad thing, right? But nonetheless, at the heart, there's a sense of insecurity. "I don't have a blanket and the weather is cold." The chill is a lack of resources, and my blanket is a successful career that will protect me against that chill.

Well, I had to eat my own cooking around this, by the way. When I retired, I retired on a budget. I had to be very disciplined about what I would spend every month. Well, I ended very well in my last year of business, so I got a very nice, handsome final bonus. And all that money was invested and was free and clear of expenses—utilities or gasoline, and all of these other things—such that my income was going to be above double what it had been. And guess what? When that money and that windfall came in, I was still just as nervous as when I had made the decision in the first place. And so what that taught me was the amount of money wasn't what's making me nervous. What was making me nervous was my own nervousness, my own anxiety, right? So that taught me I've got to look at my own anxiety.

So my advice to people is, figure out who you are and figure out what your handicaps are. Figure out if your choices are being made to compensate for something, a lack. Find your octave. Being an investor demands being a fully conscious human being. Everything you know will be brought to bear to solve the question, "Do I buy or do I not buy?"

For example, geopolitics are important. Understanding of human relationships is important. Knowing the religious history of Iran versus the religious history of, say, Syria is important. Understanding that the Anglo-Saxons invaded . . . or that England was invaded by the Normans . . . and how that affected them—that's all important; you have to understand all of that. So there's nothing that you know that is not important. And there's nothing to me more powerful than feeling potent ties, like, "Wow. Everything that I am is relevant. I don't have to hide any part of me. I don't have to make a decision that uses less than all I am."

So for me, that would be the goal. To me, in finance, that's the ultimate job right there. It's to be out there in the alchemical world where my choices have real world ramifications. All of who I am can be brought to bearing a choice, and by the way, I get an objective signal. You either made money or you didn't. I get that feedback from the world . . . in terms of how well did I measure the truth? So my advice is always be an investor. I wouldn't want to be in the other professions. Now, that said, there are people who are really good at trading. And trading is a very similar thing. But their timescale is different. Maybe they don't understand things at the glacial scale. So my intuition tends to work on what I understand on what's happening today and what the world will look like ten to fifteen years from now. I'm not so good knowing what the world will look like ten minutes from now.

WALL STREET 50
Alex Green *Advice for The Street*

MAKE WALL STREET A BETTER PLACE

Alexander Green is an author and the Chief Investment Strategist of The Oxford Club and Chief Investment Strategist for Investment U. A Wall

Street veteran, he has over twenty-five years' experience as a research analyst, investment advisor, financial writer, and portfolio manager.

KIM: If you were to give advice to someone who wanted to work in finance, what would it be?

ALEX: Well, I wouldn't deter them. I would say, first of all, that there are plenty of ethical and hardworking people on Wall Street, and they can always use more, so be that kind of a person. By all means, go to Wall Street. Make your fortune, but make it helping other people. I worked as a researcher, a broker, and a money manager, and I never harmed anyone. I'm not saying everybody made money. If they open the account at the top of the market and started to get out at the bottom of the market, I probably didn't make them any money, but at least I dealt with them honestly and forthrightly, and I tried to make them aware of the upside potentials of every investment and the downside that's inherent in every investment. So there are plenty of people who'd be a great addition to Wall Street. I wouldn't discourage anyone. Go there and make it a better place.

WALL STREET 50
Joseph Grano   *Advice for The Street*
FIRST IMPRESSIONS AND INTERPERSONAL SKILLS

Joseph Grano is Chairman and CEO of Centurion Holdings LLC, a company that advises private and public companies. From 2001–2004, he was Chairman of UBS Financial Services Inc. (formerly UBS PaineWebber). Grano joined PaineWebber in 1988 and became President of PaineWebber Group in 1994. As its president, he oversaw a series of important restructurings including the acquisition of Kidder, Peabody, and J.C. Bradford. Grano was instrumental in helping to bring about the merger of PaineWebber with UBS in 2000, when Grano was named President and CEO of UBS PaineWebber and the following year named Chairman and CEO. Previously, he was with Merrill Lynch for sixteen years, holding senior management positions.

Before joining Merrill Lynch, Mr. Grano served in the U.S. Special Forces (Green Berets). He became one of the Army's youngest officers, achieving the rank of Captain.

KIM: What is your advice to young people who want to work on Wall Street?

JOSEPH: What I tell young people entering the workforce in any industry, first, and foremost, is that first impressions count, so for the first three months, you should be the first one in and last one out. Second, don't expect your supervisors and managers to be clairvoyant. Raise your damn hand and ask a question if you need direction or you're confused. That's better than you making a mistake. Too many young people think "I am going to show weakness." No, it's just the opposite. Let me tell you something: every good manager wants to grab a wounded bird. Find out who you want to be your mentor, who you have the right chemistry with, and go to that person. They will love it. That's why they are a manager, and unfortunately, you can get lost in the maze in a big organization. You do need sponsors, but it's incumbent upon you to either earn them or create them. You can't do that if you are in your own little cocoon.

Here's an example. I was invited to speak to an Asian society two years ago and those in the audience were all vice presidents—twenty-five to thirty-five of the smartest, the brightest, all went to the best schools, Stanford, Harvard—I speak about the economy, the world, and their careers. I said, "My guess is you grew up in a household where you went to school and you outworked everybody. Matter of fact, when you leave here, you will go home and you're going to turn that computer on. In your early career, you shot up the ladder and now you are here sitting with vice presidents. My instincts say you are totally frustrated because you hit a ceiling. I'll tell you why: you never developed your interpersonal skills. You out-thought, out-studied, everybody, but you never learned interpersonal skills. You cannot move up in management until you do." And I gave them a bunch of things they should be doing to correct that.

The next day, they made me the master of this society and, I kid you not, it went from a one-hour event to three hours. It's this they and so many others need to hear.

WALL STREET 50
Don Seymour   *Advice for The Street*

BE PROUD OF THE FINANCIAL SERVICES INDUSTRY

Don Seymour, the Founder of DMS Offshore Investment Services Ltd., is directly responsible for the creation of the regulatory framework of the Investment Services Division of the Cayman Islands Monetary Authority (CIMA). In 2007, he created "The Joanna Clarke Excellence in Education Award" to honor local educator Ms. Joanna Clarke—a teacher who made a critical difference in his life—to encourage and recognize the efforts of other people and organizations that contribute to education in the Cayman Islands.

KIM: What would you say to those who want to go into finance today?

DON: Oh, I'd definitely recommend it. I think that Wall Street and finance—is a force for good in the world. It is very necessary. I don't believe in this Main Street, Wall Street divide. There's really one street that leads throughout the United States. And that farmer in Idaho needs the financial markets as much as we need food. They really go together. The entire United States should be proud of its financial services industry—as proud as it is of its military and all the great things the United States can do. Because the U.S. leads the world in many aspects, but the U.S. is clearly a leader in financial services. And because of all the innovation that occurs in finance, the world is a much better place. You can't remove finance from the world; it's very necessary. That the United States excels in that should be a source of pride for Americans, not something to be despised and demonized.

CONSCIOUSNESS TEACHER
Rasanath Das   *Advice for The Street*

ASK YOURSELF, "WHY?"

Rasanath Das is a monk and former management consultant and investment banker. His TEDx talk describes his incredible journey—from being what he describes as an "external achievement machine" to one who is rich in spiritual introspection, integrity, and true connectivity.

KIM: What would be your advice to those who want to work in finance today?

RASANATH: Ask why. If not for others at least answer that question for yourself. You don't have to tell others, but you do have to know for yourself. I remember in my investment banker interview, when I was sitting there, and I mentioned this in my TEDx talk, the first interview question I received was handed to me on a piece of paper and it said, "Investment Banking is a business—where thieves and pimps run freely in the corridors and the few good men die the death of a dog." And in big bold letters beneath that it read: "There is also a negative side." Then my interviewer looked me straight in the eye and asked, "Which one of the three are you?"

When you are sitting in an interview, you tell them how much you love banking, but that is not necessarily true. There actually might be other reasons for it. It's important to be aware of the true reasons. There are answers you might say because you want to get a job. But there are answers you do have to give yourself. Why you are in this field? What is your motive? What is your purpose? The answer may be that there is something else you truly love and this will provide me with the means to pursue that. So be conscious. Be really conscious of all the connections in your life. There are very few things we truly love in our life. Life must be structured in such a way that everything else we do is somehow connected to what we truly love. So when we go into work, we will understand why it is being done. Our life is integrated—it is one piece. It is not many disjointed pieces. Ultimately, life is connected to one thing, and one wants to be sure that is ultimately where one's heart is, in service to support that one thing.

KIM: By the way, what was your answer to his question?

RASANATH: Well, I said that I am the thief. The person asked me, "Why do you think you are the thief?" It sounds cheesy, but I said because I steal hearts. I really impress people. That is what I said. If I were given those three choices today, I would say I am trying to be a good man.

A Final Note and Invitation

———

Never doubt that a small group of thoughtful, committed, citizens can change the world. Indeed, it is the only thing that ever has.
—MARGARET MEAD

Transforming Wall Street. You might feel that this title and mere phrase is an indication of my having my head in the sand or in the clouds and that I am being impractical. As I stated in the beginning of this book, there is no doubt that Wall Street has epic issues and challenges and, for that matter, probably always will as we live in a world that will never be perfect. Yet while greed and unconscious behavior may never go away completely, we can still choose to live in possibility and co-create solutions instead of just rail against it. We can begin by asking for a new set of standards and regulations— standards and regulations that honor humanity and our planet. Many behaviors and laws in this great country were changed because of the dreamers who saw what could be. I'm no Pollyanna, but I am definitely a dreamer.

Whether or not you work on Wall Street, it's clear that the way the game is being played now is not sustainable for any of us, including those who currently sit on the top. They too will eventually fall if the rest of society falls.

So the question is: How do we transform Wall Street? What can you, reader, do when you are only one person? It begins as all things do—with yourself. Whether or not you work there, the more awake and aware you are, the better your life will be, and believe it or not, the better it will be for the rest of us who share this planet with you. As Marianne Williamson says, "As we let our own light shine, we unconsciously give others permission to do the same. As we are liberated from our own fear, our presence automatically liberates others."

Awareness: The Perils and Opportunities of Reality by Anthony DeMello speaks of our needing to develop a "readiness to see something new." He also says, as do Adam Smith, Ayn Rand, and Marshall Rosenberg (creator of NonViolent Communication), that we are always going to be motivated by self-interest. DeMello also says that things don't need to be fixed but understood. If we begin to understand ourselves and then others, things will change. He also says the labels are bullshit. I'm a fallible human; you're a fallible human. There is no distinction or types. It's just an illusion that continues to keep alive our ability to otherize, which keeps us from understanding each other and thus working together. The more we become alive to our own and one another's needs and potential, the more we dissolve the illusion, or one could say, the more we dissolve the Matrix.

Being more in tune to others' needs and one's own, is one of the most powerful paradigms I've come across. When I first stumbled upon Marshall Rosenberg's Nonviolent Communication, it blew me away, and now over fifteen years later, it still does when I witness the results. NVC's two tenets are: 1) All humans are motivated by need, and 2) Mankind is empathic by nature. When you really understand these tenets, you can see that each of us is either getting our needs met or not getting our needs met and that the costs to meeting our needs can be either high or low. Learning how to listen and communicate while keeping this in mind supplies us with the ability to secure our own needs while keeping the costs to a minimum and honoring another's needs. How you view people, not to mention the way you view yourself, is transformed forever when you grasp this. This is why I am such an advocate of Rosenberg's work especially in the corporate world. When people in organizations realize the power of empathy, their understanding and experience of themselves, their clients, their coworkers, supervisors, peers, and boards completely transform. Miyashiro's book *The Empathy Factor Your Competitive Advantage for Personal, Team, and Business Success* (drawn from Marshall Rosenberg's NVC work) explains how *being alive to the needs of others* in the office can transform your experience with yourself, your family, your work-place, your community, and the world.

As Ben Zander says in his remarkable book, *The Art of Possibility*, which is based on Werner Erhard's philosophy, "In the face of diffi-culty, we can despair, get angry . . . or choose possibility."

I believe you and I can be that possibility. I believe these 50 Wall Street men and women featured in this book are living that possibility and we all can be encouraged and motivated by their lives to realize our own desire for success while honoring our integrity. And that doing so is not unusual or rare. I want you to know that you are not alone and that you are actually a part of the majority and, therefore, more powerful than you have realized.

I propose that capitalism isn't our problem but rather our lack of consciousness. Looking deeply at what our "Father of Capitalism," the moral philosopher Adam Smith, spoke of and advocated is what we need to adhere to. What we now refer to as *Conscious Capitalism*, or what Harvard Business School's Professor Michael Porter calls *Shared Value*, is actually more in alignment with what Smith had in mind. When we concern ourselves not only with our own self-interest, but with that of all the stakeholders involved, including society and our planet, we have more powerful returns and not only monetarily. Our very own Wall Street 50 Amy Domini and her Domini 400 Social Index proves this every time it outperforms the S&P's 500. As her website states, "Domini's approach to responsible investing begins with our *Global Investment Standards*. These standards are directed toward two fundamental objectives: *the promotion of universal human dignity and the enrichment of our natural environment.*"

We also learned that just because people are smart and educat-ed, doesn't mean they won't make mistakes. Milton Friedman and company misread the corporate law because they weren't lawyers but economists. And that error, the belief that it mandates shareholder primacy, has misled and misinformed many of our current leaders in education, politics, and business for almost forty years.

One of the reasons I believe forty years could go by without this ever being seriously questioned sooner is that our culture in the United States discourages our being the authorities of our own lives. We have been taught to surrender to the "experts." In Seth Godin's book, *Linchpin: Are You Indispensable?*, Godin describes this ugly truth's genesis. It goes back to the creation of our public educational system. It was not created so we might become the best we can be, but to teach us how to think like everyone else. In other words, become sheep and not shepherds. Godin goes into great detail explaining how, to keep the factories filled with workers during the Industrial Revolution, the public school system was created so students would adapt early to the experience of a "factory." Learning early how to function in a system that rewards obedience and discourages individuality grooms one to live and work like sheep. I would say it encourages a life lived unconsciously. Godin believes that the reason there is such an employment crisis in our nation is that our educational system has produced followers, not leaders. Organizations and industries are no longer in need of followers who "do it like everyone else." Today's firms and industries, even governments, are in dire need of innovators and linchpins. People who know how to think for themselves. People who ask hard to answer questions. People who are willing to speak hard truths. People who see things not as they are but as they could be. People who focus on what works instead of what doesn't. But it's hard to find these people when most have been rewarded for *not* being that way.

The mythologist Joseph Campbell said, "You become mature when you become the authority of your own life." It's time for each of us to become the authority of our own life and to do that requires that we meet ourselves with an honesty that we may not have engaged in before. Taking the time to be thoughtful about who and what we are and what we value takes courage. Living a life awake and aware may at times be challenging, but we must remember it is not a quest for perfection but a willingness to be with our own humanity—and that will make it worth all the effort, not to mention enable us to be with one another's.

I'm inviting you to consider living and working on Wall Street or Main Street as a fully authentic conscious individual who knows how to honor his or her own dignity while honoring the rest of humanity's. I'm inviting you to be the change you want to see on Wall Street and beyond. I'm inviting you to become the authority you are waiting for to transform it.

This is an invitation to live more consciously—professionally and personally. To refuse to participate in anything other than conscious capitalism. To "see something new" and be the Hero I know you were born to be. I am calling you to the adventure of a lifetime.

What is your reply?

Consciousness Steps

Let him who would move the world first move himself.
—SOCRATES

These following **Five Practices** are specific actions one can take to be more awake and aware, more conscious. To review, they are:

1. Be responsible (not "wrong") for what shows up in your life
2. Practice Self and Other Empathy
3. Practice Emotional Non-Resistance
4. Be the Hero of Your Own Life: Embracing Your Internal/External Journey
5. Practice Self-Awareness/Mindfulness

These steps are all ways to cultivate consciousness. Most take lifelong practice. The benefits you will receive from them will immediately offer you some relief, although if you truly embrace them over time with practice, you will find that your life will change exponentially.

Is it possible to live as a capitalist while living a consciously lived life? I believe these *Wall Street 50* and *Teachers of Consciousness* have unequivocally proven my theory that, yes, indeed you can. To embrace one does not mean an abandonment of the other. Early on in my coaching, I learned the power of saying "Yes, and," meaning that when we live in an either/or world, we shut out so much opportunity; in fact, we stop the action. Walls go up instantly when the word "No" arrives in any conversation either with ourselves or with someone else in a negotiation or even a meeting. Watch for it; you'll see. In fact, in improvisation classes, that is the first thing you are taught: Don't say, "No." Always say, "Yes, and" to keep the action moving.

Living a soulful or even mystic life does not mean one can't be practical. I am someone who embraces my soulfulness and spirituality, yet I am also someone who is pragmatic. I don't see the two as being incongruent; in fact, I find they support each other.

Nathaniel Branden says in his book, *The Art of Living Consciously: The Power of Awareness to Transform Everyday Life*, that "Living consciously entails being in the present without losing the wider context." That's what my **Five Practices** will enable you to do.

What are some other steps? Well, how about taking the self-assessment that's right at the end of this book. And when you get your score, send it over to me. Let me know how you did, and whether you're satisfied with where you are. If you're not satisfied, then I request you consider doing some work to increase it. How? One step is to work with a coach. I can't tell you how much my own consciousness grew when I began working with one. In coaching you are asked deep open-ended questions that are not necessarily easy to answer, but even in the not-knowing, you are changed. How you approach all aspects of your life begins to shift when you wrestle with big open-ended questions. By doing so, you stop living from a default setting and instead begin consciously choosing your life and what is in it.

> Be patient toward all that is unsolved in your heart and try to love the questions themselves, like locked rooms and like books that are now written in a very foreign tongue. Do not now seek the answers, which cannot be given to you because you would not be able to live them. And the point is, to live everything. Live the questions now. Perhaps you will then gradually, without noticing it, live along some distant day into the answer.
>
> —Rainer Maria Rilke

Rilke's quote speaks to how each of us is here to "live the questions," and I assure you, when you live your questions, you eventually do, "Live your way into the answer."

What else can you do? By all means read! Read all you possibly can. At the end of this book is a long list of just some of the books that have served me in becoming more awake. Reading has changed my life with every book I've read.

Engage in transformational work. At the end of this book, you will find a resource list with numerous courses like Landmark Education, and retreat centers, like Kripalu, or intensives, like The Mankind Project, that if you engage in, either a little or a lot, will assist you in waking up.

Seek out teachers and/or mentors—ones that have both wealth *and meaning* in their lives. If you're fortunate, you might get to work with someone one-on-one, but even if you don't, so many masters will teach you with their writings, blogs, quotes, and video-taped talks online.

Learn how to meditate and practice it as often as possible. There are multiple styles of meditation. Find the style that suits you. Find a small group to practice with because having contact with others who have the same intention always facilitates a more streamlined connection when you are first starting out. Meditation schools that I recommend are also listed in the resource list at the back and my firm actually has two executive coaches who specialize in instructing how to begin meditating on a regular basis.

Get out into nature weekly, if not more often. And without an electronic device. This means no phone, no camera, no nothing but perhaps an old fashioned compass. We all are working way more than ever before. We have our electronic devices almost attached to our bodies. It's not healthy. Being in nature allows you to connect to the rhythm of the earth. When we immerse ourselves inside of her, our heart rate and pulse relax and are reset. Our internal motor gets re-connected to that which is the earth's universal rhythm. Our heart and soul needs to plug into nature on occasion to remember where we come from and who we are. Nature simultaneously humbles and em-powers you. Being in it allows you to experience reverence. Whether you are Jewish, a Muslim, Episcopalian, or an atheist, one can't but enter into reverence when in a deep forest. David Abram in his book, *The Spell of the Sensuous: Perception and Language in a More-Than-Human World,* speaks about how our human cognition is dependent on the natural environment. He wonders how Western civilization became so disconnected from nature and how much this alienation costs us. In his other book, *Becoming Animal: An Earthly Cosmology*, he says:

> How monotonous our speaking becomes when we speak only to ourselves! And how *insulting* to the other beings—to foraging black bears and twisted old cypresses—that no longer sense us talking to them, but only about them, as though they were not present in our world. . . . Small wonder that rivers and forests no longer compel our focus or our fierce devotion. For we walk about such entities only behind their backs, as though they were not participant in our lives. Yet if we no longer call out to the moon slipping between the clouds, or whisper to the spider setting the silken struts of her web, well, then the numerous powers of this world will no longer address *us*—and if they still try, we will not likely hear them.

The future of capitalism, not to mention our country and our world, rests on your shoulders. It rests on my shoulders. Together, we can transform all that needs transforming by being transformed. Now you have met some men and women who are living and working with integrity and have succeeded at balancing both wealth *and meaning*. I am not saying they are perfect or they haven't or won't ever make mistakes; they are human, so of course, they are fallible. But they are striving toward this balance each day, and that is worth admiring and learning from.

The Wall Street 50 have given us some bold and out-of-the-box solutions for Wall Street and our world. Let's implement what we can in our little corner. Let's heed their advice for how we work in and on Wall Street and beyond. Let us together transform our own lives, and by doing so, transform what our world of business and capitalism looks like. Together, we can create a conscious path for a new future.

We have not even to risk the adventure alone, for the heroes of all time have gone before us. The Labyrinth is thoroughly known. We have only to follow the thread of the hero path. And where we had thought to find an abomination, we shall find a god. And where we had thought to slay another, we shall slay ourselves. And where we had thought to travel outward, we shall come to the center of our own existence. And where we had thought to be alone, we shall be with all the world.

—Joseph Campbell

Acknowledgments

———

First, I want to acknowledge and thank the men and women of Wall Street and finance who are living in and working with integrity. Thank you for being the kind of people you are. Without fanfare, praise, or acknowledgment you have, in spite of the temptations faced, stayed true to what was in your clients' best interest or done the right thing when no one was looking. You have taken the high road and done what you knew you had to do in order to be true to your own soul's moral code, even in the face of high costs to yourself and perhaps your family. A special shout out to the over ninety New York State Community Bankers who were my first introduction to the world of finance—whom I call the "George Baileys of Banking." I watched with admiration your efforts to support, encourage, and empower your communities. Each of you exemplified the qualities we want in our bankers. You also were kind and dignified in how you treated me and everyone else at the offices of Community Bankers Association of New York State. A special thank you to Mariel Donath, CBANY's President and CEO, its indomitable leader for over nine years whom I had the pleasure and honor of assisting for six years. Thank you for your mentorship, encouragement, and love. You took a chance on me—a young woman with no corporate or executive assisting experience. Your wisdom and patience brought all my strengths forth. Working for you changed my life and I am now the founder of *The Wall Street Coach* because you were willing to give me my first break—this book wouldn't exist if it weren't for you.

A big thank you to every one of The Wall Street 50 for allowing me to interview you. Thank you for your trust, your time, and sharing your journey. Thank you for not restricting me in any way. All of you are the true leaders of Wall Street. You are what is great about it and what is noble about capitalism. Thank you to all of the professors, teachers, spiritual leaders, and vanguards who see our bright future—thank you for giving me your time, wisdom, and the stories of your personal voyages that continue to assist me in my own quest for enlightenment as well as providing me and the readers of this book a clearer path to follow.

I'd also like to express my empathy to those in finance who have been judged wrongly or grouped inadvertently with those who are unethical or unconscious. Let this book reassure you that you are seen and you are not alone. In fact, you are legion in number. I hope this book will inspire you to become more empowered and to come together to make the necessary changes in this industry. You have made a difference and it's time to make more of one.

Thank you Bob Eichinger; you initiated this journey with the words you spoke to me in our first conversation on August 1st, 2011, that I needed to write my own book. Here it is, Bob.

A special mahalo to the Goddess Pele and her beautiful island of Hawai'i also known as the Healing Island or Big Island—you are now my second home. You healed and encouraged me while I worked on this book, and I know your Mana is infused in these pages and will bring healing and encouragement to those who read them. Mahalo to my Hawaiian 'ohana who invited, welcomed, and supported me. Thank you Jordan and Jamie Forth for opening the door to this beautiful island. To Matthew Hakala, for reminding me to breathe deeply. Thank you to my friend and brother-by-choice, the Rev. David Stout, Rector of St. James Episcopal Church in Waimea and the amazing Bobby Clement. Not only did Hawai'i get to happen because of both of you, but you also opened your home and community to me. Not to mention filled me up with love, delicious chocolate martinis, mai tais, and green flashes.

Thank you to the rest of my Big Island Hawaiian 'ohana and friends: Phyllis and Evarts Fox for treating me and loving me like a daughter; Margo Wray and Marquita Denison for your advising, wisdom, and support; Pat and Dave Allbee for your love, support, and for sharing your home; Susan Hunt and Marius Ellis for the opportunity to house and pet sit for you and for having the greatest writing desk . . .

I mean dining room table one could ask for. Mike and Erin Petrosian for being the best neighbors. Thank you Amber Rowland for wisdom and support. Thank you Mark McGuffie for your encouragement. Thank you Danny Akaka for clarity. Thank you Michael Zola and Shea Grimm for the introduction to Batman and your Hualalai connections, and Uncle Manny Vincent and my fellow 6 a.m. paddlers at Kawaihae Canoe Club who rooted me on. Thanks to everyone at the Waimea Coffee Company where I spent a lot of hours drinking chai latte, writing on their outside deck, and waxing on about the benefits of capitalism to anyone who would listen.

Thank you to my very special clients (you know who you are) who continued to work with me when my time away lasted longer that we all expected.

Thank you to my parents for the gift of life and to my sister for always having my back.

My dear Ella Francis, may this book's sheer existence encourage you to always live in possibility.

To Gail Bennett, Wendi Huestis, Frank Jaccarino, Christine Kiesling, Joseph Laranjeiro, Elizabeth Lewin, and James Thomas— each of you were there every step of the way and never wavered once in your support or belief in me. I thank you with all the love in my heart for your friendship.

Thank you Rabbi Michael Katz for everything.

My love and gratitude to the Gomez family, formerly of Brooklyn, for loving me so many years ago.

Thank you Raphael Cushnir for being my Yoda.

Thank you Dave Shoemaker for so much but most of all for supporting the book idea from the very beginning.

To Robert Dilenschneider, thank you for your support, encouragement, and the introduction to many of these men and women of integrity, and thank you, Alex von Bidder, for our introduction.

Thank you Mary Ruth Tomasiewicz for your love, support, and encouragement and for allowing me to use the beautiful offices of Phantom Audio in the iconic Flatiron district of New York City to conduct so many early interviews.

I completed over ninety interviews. Some of the interviews, in the end, were not able to be recapped due to the editing process, but I was affected by every one of them and would like to thank everyone for sharing his or her time, knowledge, experience, and perspective with me: Ziad Abdelnour, Stacey Asher, Shari Brown, Don Callahan, Mariel Donath, Brady Dougan, Connie Duckworth, Royce Froehlich, Ofir Hirsch, Raymond Joseph, Ann Kaplan, Dmitry Koltunov, Mike Krieger, Justin Mahy, Jim McNair, Alfonso Montiel, Marcy Murninghan, Simon Murray, Gil Olsen, Alan Patricoff, Christian Ramsey, Peter Ressler, Roland Rojas, Susan Strausberg, Katie, Alex, Jim and Julianna Stuart, and Mark Thompson.

Thank you to all my teachers, coaches, mentors, gurus, and shamans: especially Patricia Aburdene, Adyashanti, Joseph Aldo, Joseph Campbell, Coaches Training Institute staff, Alan Cohen, Chip Conley, Felix Conradi, Raphael Cushnir, Jessica Derksen, Laura Doyle, Elaine Egidio, Werner Erhard, Keith Ferrazzi, Tim Ferriss, Royce Froehlich, Mama Gena, Yasuhiko Genku Kimura, Seth Godin, Marshall Goldsmith, Joseph Jaworski, W. Brugh Joy, Samantha Keen, Anna Kelly, Dr. Peter Kostenbaum, Stanley Krippner, Charles Lawrence, Matteus Level, Dr. Peter Levin, Dr. Pat Love, John Martin, Jed McKenna, Steve Mitten, Marie Miyashiro, Maki Nanatawara, Chikako Hoshino Powers, Kate Roeske, Marshall Rosenberg, Dr. Samuel Sagan, Roger Smith, Eckhart Tolle, Cindy Wigglesworth, and William Zinsser.

Thank you to my friends who supported me and this process along the way—I couldn't have done it without you or your encouragement: Modupe Afilaka, Laurie Altschuler, Annette Baron, Michelle Baydo, Andrew Bennett, Yaf Boye-Flaegel, Rev. Mark Bozzuti-Jones, Jesse Campanaro, Eric Carangelo, Mo Chanmugham, Jorge Colon, Julie Cramer, Chelsea Dommert, Dishan Elise, Todd Fairbairn, Linda Finkle, Ken Foster, Steve Gaither, Jen Galatioto, Maria Gamb, Jasra Gottingar, Sara Grace, Aliya Hallim-Byne, Matthew "Zeke" Hughes, Rebecca Jackson, Samantha Keen, Lisa Krohn, Jim Kukral, Sergeant Frank Lancellotti, Elizabeth Langtry, Graham Lawlor, Nick Lazonby, Elina LeClaire, Mattius Levell, Eric Lyons, Jana Manning, Dr. Fred

Mayer, Cindy Morgan, Siobhane Murphy, Wayne Nato Basa, Colleen Newvine Tebeau, Susan and Victor Niederhoffer, Olivia Nuzzi, Marc Oromaner, Erica Peitler, Jim Persing, Rob Piacitelli, Brian Pittman, Dana Price, Danny Prussman, Lisa Rangel, Tahl Raz, David Reich, Annelies Richmond, Ellen Rogin, Jill Ross, Natalie Runyon, Gunny Scarfo, Karl Schmieder, Samir Selmanovic, Denise Shull, the Sidebotham and Wirkula Clan, Liz Smith, Aaron Smyle, Kelly Stern, Fran Stockley, Rodney Sullivan, Jamie Troia, Simon Tyler, Bill Tully, Rob Urban, Mary Van Geffen, Stephen Viederman, Alex von Bidder, Jason Apollo Voss, Lee Watkiss, Tyler Whitney, Theresa Wiles, Stephanie Woo, and Silvana Zepedia.

Thank you Chris Taylor and Leah Taylor Duncan, the journalists that covered my coaching on Wall Street.

To my amazing US attorney Daniel Basov of Kaplan Breyer Schwarz & Ottesen, LLP and to my attorney in the UK Stuart Pearson aka Batman, of Grower Freeman Solicitors.

To my editors: Tyler Tichelaar, you are a miracle worker. Larry Alexander, you have the eyes of an eagle. Thank you, too, Peg Henrickson, for all your early listening.

To Karen Giangreco, thank you for the extraordinary amount of time and effort and love you gave to my interior layout.

To my book advisors, Patrick Snow, thank you for everything, especially that cold call so many years ago and Natasa Lekic of NY Book Editors for your contacts and support.

To Frank Jaccarino, who read my first and last drafts using a fine tooth comb and gave me invaluable insight and feedback.

To Lauren Lee Anderson, Evarts Fox, Sara Grace, Joseph Laranjeiro, Christine Kiesling, Tahl Raz, and Jack D. Schwager for your input and suggestions to early drafts.

To my amazing website designer Alina Wilczynski who designed the stunning cover and our websites, and Andrew Bennett my IT consultant on everything.

Thanks to David Frankel for his belief in me and this project and his entire team at ZipDX® LLC for their amazing transcriptions of over ninety interviews.

To Mike Wilson and his extraordinary team at ditto.tv for their generous and brilliant work.

Thanks to Syed Faraz Mehmood and his team at Orazone Technologies.

Thank you to the most incredible assistant and intern I could have ever asked for, Camille Ducourant, who kept my spirits up when I doubted I could indeed pull this off.

Thank you to my assistants Adina Sherman, Gabrielle Miller, Jonathan Sherman, and Devorah Ellerton.

Thank you Maia Tarnas for all your work on my never-ending bibliography.

Thank you to my amazing interns: Jose Javier Balmaceda, Eric Bellin, Sean Lasher, Abraham C. Mendelson, Pear Ryadina Utami, and Nayma Silver.

And to my four-legged friend Buddy, thank you for keeping me company.

Consciousness Self-Assessment

———

Anthony DeMello said that the real question isn't: *Is there life after death, but is there life before death?* This assessment isn't to make you feel bad about yourself; it's simply an informal tool to see whether you need more encouragement to have more *"life before death."* Be gentle with yourself no matter the results.

Please score yourself with 1 through 5

1 = never   2 = rarely   3 = sometimes   4 = often   5 = all the time

1. You practice self-empathy.

   1   2   3   4   5

2. You are clear on what your values are.

   1   2   3   4   5

3. Your emotions/feelings are never in control of you.

   1   2   3   4   5

4. You know that "you don't know what you don't know."

   1   2   3   4   5

5. When life is challenging you never blame yourself or God/ the world/others.

   1   2   3   4   5

6. You practice non-attachment.

   1   2   3   4   5

7. You know that who you are has nothing to do with your net worth, title, education, profession, car, and/or the home you own/rent.

   1   2   3   4   5

8. You handle mistakes or failures remarkably well.

   1   2   3   4   5

9. You've been true to your heart or soul in spite of the cost.

   1   2   3   4   5

10. You realize your actions impact others.

   1   2   3   4   5

50 = Wow! Good job. Who are your teachers? :) Remember, there is more. Keep going.

40–50 = You're so close to staying awake more. You know what is needed. Do that.

30–40 = You are willing to be with "what's hard to be with." Well done. Go further.

20–30 = You're taking too many catnaps; with a little effort you will see change.

10–20 = You've hit the snooze button one too many times. Time to rouse yourself out of bed.

10 = You have slept in and it is late—time to wake up!

Please email me your score: kim@thewallstreetcoach.com

I truly want to support you on your journey of becoming more awake and aware. We are all on this journey together and each and every day we will find ourselves faced with a choice. We can either stay awake or stay asleep. It's a daily practice. Seek out the support you need and find encouragement from those who travel this road and remember to provide it to those you see struggling.

Each day, enlightenment sits right in front of us, and all we need to do is be present to it. Consciousness is ours for the taking. Together, let us each embrace it.

The biggest barrier to awakening is the belief that it is something rare.

—ADYASHANTI

My Story

──────

Ever since I was about fourteen, I thought, "There has to be a way one can make a profit and still help the world." I remember turning that thought over and over in my imagination, thinking about the ways one could do just that.

I think I thought that way from an early age because of the financial extremes I experienced growing up. I have had an unusual life. I have experienced homelessness and I've flown privately. I've known what it's like to scrape by, put groceries on credit cards, and borrow money from friends as well as make a quarter of a million dollars in a very short time, enjoy a first class vacation in St. John in the U.S. Virgin Islands, and travel globally. I know what it's like to go hungry and what it's like to live in luxury. Having lived on both sides of the tracks, I know luxury is definitely more enjoyable, but what one gets from living without a home and experiencing poverty is you aren't afraid of very much. After what I've seen and lived through, very little scares me. But there is something else. You begin to see below the surface. You begin to see qualities of a person's character and not judge people based on their bank accounts, titles, degrees, or lifestyles.

Growing up in two different households, one with my mother and one with my father, I remember my mom struggling financially. I qualified for free lunch in school and can remember going to the gas station and putting five dollars in the tank. I've gone to the market and bought only one roll of toilet paper. I remember our car not having heat in the winter and the brakes going out while my mother drove down a hill. Meanwhile my experience on the weekends at my father's home was quite different. It included visits to a fancy country club, Broadway plays, and Tiffany's. I went to school in St. James on Long Island which was a financially diverse neighborhood. While shuffling between these two different households, I began to pay attention to the way people were to me. I knew that some of the fancier clothing I had from my dad (like velvet Calvin Klein jeans) elicited some commentary from my "friends" and were best not worn the days I needed to use my free lunch card. I also began to feel a subtle sense of discomfort when I spoke about some of the Broadway shows my dad had taken me to with those friends who weren't financially in good shape. Yet when I was with friends at my Dad's home who were more well off, they didn't seem to judge me in the same sort of way.

As I grew up, I wanted to find a way to balance these things. How to make a profit, how to have what I wanted in life, and still be a good person and do good in the world. I just didn't know how it could be done. Then one day years later, I found out about Muhammad Yunus. His Grameen Bank makes micro loans to women in India—micro amounts like $30.00 to $50.00. When I found this out, I thought, "Yunus did it! He figured out how to do both: make a profit and make the world better."

My life would take many twists and turns after that, but I never forgot my goal to make a profit and make the world a better place. My career went from being the operations manager of a large bookstore to being the executive assistant for the President and CEO of Community Bankers Association of New York State, and then as an executive and personal assistant to the CEO of a hedge fund that paid me a tremendous salary. It was after all this, though, that I finally found what Joseph Campbell calls "bliss" when I became an executive coach.

It began when I attended the Landmark forum—a three-and-a-half-day intense seminar that asked me to consider that I might actually be living my life from a place of limitation and old paradigms. By the time it was over, I felt empowered and wondered, "What must it be like to empower people? To give people back their lives? To be able to put people back in the driver's seat of their experience? That would be amazing." But, "How?" was the question. Eventually, the answer came in my becoming an executive coach.

The path to become a coach was fascinating, and in time, I had my coaching certification and business off the ground. As a coach, I was asked to join Idea Tribe, a leadership, coaching, and workshop team. At that time, Chip Conley was advocating Idea Tribe in his hotel chain, Joie De Vivre, on the West Coast. I didn't know much about Chip at the time, but shortly, Chip's book, *Peak: How Great Companies Get Their Mojo from Maslow*, came out. I was the only Idea Tribe coach located on the East Coast at the time of his book release, so I went to his release party to show support. I bought his book that evening and read it in almost one sitting. I wept when I read it. Here was a man talking about how to be really successful in business by treating people well, and in fact, helping them to experience meaning in their jobs and their lives. Here it was again—proof that my childhood theory of marrying profit to improving the world was possible. I was so moved by Chip's book and his willingness to be vulnerable and open about his own journey that I wrote him a lengthy, heartfelt email telling him how important his book was to me, how inspired I was to see someone at his level of success really getting this, and how honored I was to be a part of his hotel chain in the form of Idea Tribe. Not long after, we began to correspond and Chip turned me on to the Conscious Capitalist Institute.

My beliefs were proving to be achievable, but the "how" still eluded me. My coaching business had hit a plateau in the summer of 2008 and was barely growing. It was becoming difficult to support myself financially. Then my friend Elizabeth said to me, "What if you did Free Coaching?" I looked at her like she was crazy, but I figured I had nothing to lose. My friend James also had told me, "If you really love what you do, you'll do it for free." It was important for me to share my gift with the world, and maybe I would meet some prospects. I thought about where to go, and after a couple of bumpy starts, I settled on doing it down on Wall Street. I knew there was tension down there and I knew how stressful it was in finance when things were going well, never mind when they weren't going well, so I thought people on Wall Street could use it.

In preparation for what I presumed would be some sideways looks, I wore my most formal suit to counteract my homemade sign. And on October 7, 2008, down I went to bring my coaching to those whom

I hoped might use it. Within a couple of hours of sitting there on my cement bench on the corner of Broad and Wall Street, there was some static in the air. I could feel the tension. I asked a passerby what was going on and he said, "The market is in free fall." Then people started to approach me—the sort of executives I didn't expect would. I could see from their ashen faces that they were in shock. I had stumbled into what would be for the next few months, if not the entire year, one of the more trying times to work on Wall Street, and thanks to the wisdom of another colleague, Stefan Doering, I continued to go down there almost weekly for the rest of that year. In heat and cold, I sat on that bench and coached the walking wounded at lunch hour on my cement bench. I met incredible people during that year-long activity, and I was inspired by their passion, perseverance, and dedication.

Within a couple of weeks, the media was swarming all over the place; reporters would approach me with a disdainful look, and ask, "What the hell are you doing?" I'd respond, "I'm coaching people." And before I knew it, eight reporters wanted to interview me. And with each story I began to be called something I had not once called myself: The Wall Street Coach. And with that my new company was born.

And that brings me to this project. Over the next couple of years, I and everyone else began to hear a lot of really negative stories and bad news about those in the world of finance and Wall Street, ranging from Bernie Madoff to the big banks receiving extraordinary assistance as we found out they had made their own problems. It became very frustrating. And I was angry like most people—angry over the greed; angry over how the little guy pays yet again. Every day another report in the paper about the greed, lack of integrity, and an absence of consciousness.

In March of 2011, I attended the Conscious Capitalists Institute's Conference thanks to Chip Conley and Susan Niederhoffer. I listened to John Mackey speak about how capitalism has and can continue to put an end to poverty in so many ways. It was an extraordinary talk that reminded me once again how passionate I was about making a profit and making a difference. I was moved to tears during Mackey's talk and the conversations around me. It was like these people all "got it." And I felt hopeful and thrilled to be able to see that, yes indeed, this could be done. I met Doug Rausch from Trader Joe's. Kip Tindell from The Container Store was there. These were very successful people who were definitely making a difference in the world, yet living as true capitalists. It was a watershed event for me.

I also met Samir Selmanovic, a self-described "born again capitalist." At some point, Samir realized he had begun to define capitalists as the "other." And because he had always advocated that people participate in any group they found themselves "otherizing," he took his own medicine, dived into the world of capitalism, and discovered to his surprise that there were a lot of amazing, generous, integrity-filled capitalists out there. Samir was always surprised by my love of Ayn Rand. I tried to explain to him that in many ways, she had set me free since I had grown up in a household where we were taught the word "we" and not "I." Rand's literature was healing, profound, and liberating for me when I first read her in my early twenties. I felt her philosophy was about taking responsibility for one's life and owning one's own power—never to sell out on your beliefs or sacrifice your soul to appease another. I found her characters to be men and women who were coming from a place of integrity. Sure they were fictional characters, but man, did they have the courage of their convictions.

Because I spent so much time outside the stock exchange during my year of free coaching, I visited Occupy Wall Street and spoke to a number of protestors early on in the demonstrations. Although I am a supporter of civil disobedience, something about the Occupy Movement rubbed me the wrong way, yet I couldn't initially put my finger on it. The same with the media coverage. I couldn't understand why we were not hearing anything from the men and women of integrity who worked on the Street, why wasn't anyone asking them for suggestions on how to improve or transform it? I kept asking myself, "Why is there so much focus on what is wrong instead of a focus on solutions?"

What really prompted me to consider finding what I now call *The Wall Street 50* was seeing people who were self-made have their moral characters questioned during these early protests. Those who were successful were suddenly finding themselves defending their right to make a profit. People were almost apologizing for their success. Capitalism was being collapsed with corruption. I began to hear young people speak about Capitalism as if it were evil and an advocacy of self-absorption. And yet what looked and smelled a lot like Socialism was being touted as the solution to our problems, when it was that very philosophy that had gotten us into this situation in the first place. It wasn't capitalism that was the enemy but "crony capitalism."

I found the mood in the air during that time very un-American. Wasn't capitalism one of the things that had made this country so great? Hadn't all of our great-grandparents come here because this was the land of opportunity? So I thought, "What if we could hear from those on Wall Street who were living and working with integrity so we could find out how they were able to resist the temptations they faced. I wondered what behaviors they had in common. I thought if we could learn from them, we could then encourage more of it. To live a life consciously and morally takes courage. I began to wonder, how did those with great success balance both when a lot of money was on the line? I thought it was time to start to hear solutions and start demanding of the system a new way of doing business. Who better to learn from and co-create effective solutions with than those who had already balanced the two sides of the scale—wealth *and meaning*. Who better than the leaders who worked on the Street who could be viewed as role models? It seemed to me that we were in dire need of men and women we could look up to and emulate. Men and women that were examples of conscious capitalism. We were in need of solutions to improve Wall Street. How could we begin and where did we need to start? These were the questions I began to hear in my head and I felt compelled to find the answers—I thought if I found the conscious capitalists of Wall Street they would point the way. And so my journey to write this book began.

Resources

TO ENGAGE IN PRACTICE ONE: SELF-RESPONSIBILITY

Landmark Education: http://www.landmarkworldwide.com

The Mankind Project: http://mankindproject.org

The SQ21/Spiritual Intelligence Assessment:
https://www.deepchange.com/assessments

Movie: *Transformation: The Life & Legacy of Werner Erhard*:
http://www.transformationfilm.com

Engage in a 360: http://www.thewallstreetcoach.com

Books

The Art of Possibility by Rosamund Stone Zander and Benjamin Zander

Atlas Shrugged by Ayn Rand

Conscious Money by Patricia Aburdene

Choose Yourself! by James Altucher

The Fountainhead by Ayn Rand

How Then Shall We Live by Wayne Muller

The Three Laws of Performance by Steve Zaffon and Dave Logan

TO ENGAGE IN PRACTICE TWO:
SELF/OTHER EMPATHY

These two sites have massive amounts of free resources to understand NonViolent Communication better:
    www.NonViolentCommunication.com and www.CNVC.org

The NonViolent Communication Training Course with Marshall Rosenberg is a 9 CD disc set teaching all the tenets of his work.

Volunteer a little or a lot with any non-profit; I recommend:
    www.RoomtoRead.org/Chapters and www.CouldYou.org

Books

Becoming Animal by David Abram

The Empathy Factor by Marie R. Miyashiro

I and Thou by Martin Buber

NonViolent Communication by Marshall Rosenberg

Speak Peace in a World of Conflict by Marshall Rosenberg

TO ENGAGE IN PRACTICE THREE:
EMOTIONAL NON-RESISTANCE

Raphael Cushnir has free and low cost information on this practice on his website: www.cushnir.com

Books

Linchpin: Are You Indispensable? by Seth Godin

The One Thing Holding You Back by Raphael Cushnir

Surfing Your Inner Sea: Essential Lessons for Lasting Serenity by Raphael Cushnir

Waking the Tiger by Peter A. Levine

When the Heart Waits by Sue Monk Kidd

TO ENGAGE IN PRACTICE FOUR:
THE INTERNAL AND EXTERNAL JOURNEY

Watch or buy the 6-hour video series *The Power of Myth*: Bill Moyer's Interview of Joseph Campbell.

Rent or own the movie *Finding Joe*: www.FindingJoeTheMovie.com

Landmark Education: http://www.landmarkworldwide.com

Mama Gena's School of the Womanly Arts:
http://www.mamagenas.com

The Mankind Project: http://mankindproject.org

Burning Man: http://www.burningman.com

Books

Crossing the Unknown Sea: Work as a Pilgrimage of Identity by David Whyte

The Heart Aroused: Poetry & the Preservation of the Soul in Corporate America by David Whyte

The Hero with a Thousand Faces by Joseph Campbell

I Had It All the Time by Alan Cohen

Pathways to Bliss by Joseph Campbell

Personal Mythology by David Feinstein and Stanley Krippner

Women Who Run with the Wolves by Clarissa Pinkola Estés

Work as a Heroic Journey: Using the Workplace to Evolve Your Character and Consciousness by Marion Moss Hubbard

TO ENGAGE IN PRACTICE FIVE:
SELF-AWARENESS/MINDFULNESS

The Art of Living Foundation: http://www.artofliving.org/us-en

Clairvision Meditation: http://www.clairvision.org

Gabrielle Roth's 5Rhythms: http://www.5rhythms.com

U.S. Based Retreat Centers

Kripalu Center for Yoga & Health: http://www.kripalu.org

Hollyhock: https://www.hollyhock.ca/cms

The Esalen Institute: http://www.esalen.org

Omega: http://www.eomega.org

Books

Awareness by Anthony DeMello

The Art of Living Consciously by Nathaniel Branden

Falling Into Grace by Adyashanti

How Will You Measure Your Life by Clayton M. Christensen

The Inner Voice of Trading by Michael Martin

The Intuitive Investor by Jason Apollo Voss

A New Earth: Awakening to Your Life's Purpose by Eckhart Tolle

The Perils and Opportunities of Reality by Anthony DeMello

Setting Your Heart on Fire by Raphael Cushnir

Synchronicity: The Inner Path of Leadership by Joe Jaworski

APPENDIX D:
Further Reading

Abdelnour, Ziad. *Economic Warfare: Secrets of Wealth Creation in the Age of Welfare Politics.* Hoboken: John Wiley & Sons, Inc., 2012.

Abram, David. *Becoming Animal: An Earthly Cosmology.* New York: Vintage Books, 2011.

Abram, David. *The Spell of the Sensuous: Perception and Language in a More-Than-Human World.* New York: Vintage Books, 1997.

Aburdene, Patricia. *Conscious Money: Living, Creating, and Investing with Your Values for a Sustainable New Prosperity.* New York: Atria Books/Beyond Words, 2012.

Aburdene, Patricia. *Megatrends 2010: The Rise of Conscious Capitalism.* Charlottesville: Hampton Roads Publishing Company, Inc., 2005.

Adyashanti. *Falling into Grace: Insights on the End of Suffering.* Louisville: Sounds True, 2013.

Allison, John. *The Financial Crisis and the Free Market Cure: Why Pure Capitalism Is the World Economy's Only Hope.* McGraw-Hill, 2012.

Altucher, James. *Choose Yourself!* Lioncrest Publishing, 2013.

Anielski, Mark. *The Economics of Happiness.* Gabriola Island: New Society Publisher, 2007.

Babur, Martin. *I and Thou.* New York: Touchstone, 1971.

Baumeister, Roy F., and John Tierney. *Willpower: Rediscovering the Greatest Human Strength.* London, Gr. Brit.: Allen Lane, 2012.

Beebe, John. *Integrity in Depth*. College Station: Texas A&M University Press, 2005.

Block, Peter. *Flawless Consulting: A Guide to Getting Your Expertise Used*. San Francisco: Pfeiffer, 2011.

Block, Peter. *The Answer to How is Yes: Acting on What Matters*. San Francisco: Berrett-Koehler Publishers, 2003.

Bogle, John C. *Enough: True Measures of Money, Business, and Life*. Hoboken: John Wiley & Sons, Inc., 2010.

Bogle, John C. *The Battle for the Soul of Capitalism*. New Haven: Yale University Press, 2005.

Bornstein, David. *The Price of a Dream: The Story of the Grameen Bank*. Chicago: University of Chicago Press, 1997.

Branden, Nathaniel. *The Art of Living Consciously: The Power of Awareness to Transform Everyday Life*. New York: Simon & Schuster, 1999.

Brown, Ellen. *The Web of Debt*. 5th ed. Baton Rouge: Third Millennium Press, 2012.

Brown, Joshua M. *Backstage Wall Street: An Insider's Guide to Knowing Who to Trust, Who to Run From, and How to Maximize Your Investments*. New York: The McGraw-Hill Companies, 2012.

Bryon, William J. *The Power of Principles: Ethics for the New Corporate Culture*. Maryknoll: Orbis Books, 2006.

Cameron, Julia. *The Artist's Way*. 10th anniversary ed. New York: Jeremy P. Tarcher/Putnam, 2002.

Campbell, Joseph. *The Hero with a Thousand Faces*. New York: Pantheon Books, 1949.

Campbell, Joseph. *The Power of Myth*. New York: Anchor Books, 1991.

Castaneda, Carlos. *The Teachings of Don Juan: A Yaqui Way of Knowledge*. New York, Ballantine, 1973.

Christensen, Clayton M., James Allworth, and Karen Dillon. *How Will You Measure Your Life?* New York: HarperCollins Publishers, 2012.

Cohen, Alan H. *I Had It All the Time: When Self-Improvement Gives Way to Ecstasy*. Haiku, Alan Cohen Publications, 1995.

Cohen, Alan H. *The Dragon Doesn't Live Here Anymore*. New York: Ballantine Books, 1993.

Cohen, Roy. *The Wall Street Professional's Survival Guide: Success Secrets of a Career Coach*. Upper Saddle River: FT Press, 2010.

Conley, Chip. *Emotional Equations: Simple Steps for Creating Happiness + Success in Business + Life*. New York: Patria Paperback, 2012.

Conley, Chip. *Peak: How Great Companies Get Their Mojo from Maslow*. San Francisco: Jossey-Bass, 2007.

Counts, Alex. *Give Us Credit*. New York: Times Books/Random House, 1996.

Csikszentmihalyi, Mihaly. *Flow: The Psychology of Optimal Experience*. New York: Harper and Row, 1990.

Cushnir, Raphael. *Setting Your Heart on Fire: Seven Invitations to Liberate Your Life*. New York: Broadway Books, 2004.

Cushnir, Raphael. *Surfing Your Inner Sea: Essential Lessons for Lasting Serenity*. San Francisco: Chronicle Books LLC, 2009.

Cushnir, Raphael. *The One Thing Holding You Back: Unleashing the Power of Emotional Connection*. New York: HarperOne, 2008.

Damasio, Antonio. *Self Comes to Mind: Constructing the Conscious Brain*. New York: Vintage Books, 2012.

Dass, Ram. *Be Here Now*. San Cristobal, NM: Lama Foundation, 1971.

Davis, Susan. *The Trojan Horse of Love*. 2010.

DeMartini, John F. *How to Make One Hell of a Profit and Still Get to Heaven*. Carlsbad: Hay House, Inc., 2004.

De Mello, Anthony. *Awareness: The Perils and Opportunities of Reality*. New York: Image Books, 1990.

Domini, Amy L., and Peter D. Kinder. *Ethical Investing*. Boston: Addison Wesley Publishing Company, 1986.

Domini, Amy L., Steven Lydenberg, and Peter Kinder. *Investing for Good: Making Money While Being Socially Responsible*. New York: HarperCollins, 1994.

Domini, Amy. *Socially Responsible Investing: Making a Difference and Making Money*. Chicago: Dearborn Trade, 2001.

Doyle, Laura. *Things Will Get as Good as You Can Stand: (. . . When you learn that it is better to receive than to give) The Superwoman's Practical Guide to Getting as Much as She Gives*. New York: Simon & Schuster, 2004.

Eisenstein, Charles. *Sacred Economics: Money, Gift, and Society in the Age of Transition*. Berkeley: Evolver Editions, 2011.

Eisler, Riane. *Sacred Pleasure: Sex, Myth, and the Politics of the Body— New Paths to Power and Love*. New York: HarperOne, 1996.

Estés, Clarissa Pinkola. *Women Who Run with the Wolves*. New York: Ballantine Books, 1992.

Feinstein, David and Stanley Krippner. *Personal Mythology: Using Ritual, Dreams, and Imagination to Discover Your Inner Story*. Fulton: Energy Psychology Press, 2009.

Ferrazzi, Keith, and Tahl Raz. *Never Eat Alone: And Other Secrets to Success, One Relationship at a Time.* New York: Crown Business, 2005.

Gaines, Edwene. *The Four Spiritual Laws of Prosperity: A Simple Guide to Unlimited Abundance.* Rodale Books, 2005.

Godin, Seth. *Linchpin: Are You Indispensable?* New York: Portfolio Trade, 2011.

Goswami, Amit. *The Self-Aware Universe.* New York: Jeremy P. Tarcher/Putnam, 1995.

Gould, Roger L. *Transformations: Growth and Change in Adult Life.* New York: Simon & Schuster, 1979.

Grano, Joseph J., and Mark Levine. *You Can't Predict a Hero: From War to Wall Street, Leading in Times of Crisis.* San Francisco: Jossey-Bass, 2009.

Green, Alexander. *Beyond Wealth: The Road Map to a Rich Life.* Hoboken: John Wiley & Sons, Inc., 2011.

Greene, Robert. *Mastery.* New York: Penguin Books, 2013.

Harris, Carla. *Expect to Win: Proven Strategies for Success from a Wall Street Vet.* New York: Penguin Group (USA) Incorporated, 2009.

Hawken, Paul. *The Ecology of Commerce: A Declaration of Sustainability.* New York: HarperBusiness, 1993.

Henderson, Hazel, and Simran Sethi. *Ethical Markets: Growing the Green Economy.* White River Junction: Chelsea Green Publishing Company, 2007.

Hendren, Michael E. *Spiritual Capitalism.* Michael Hendren, 2007.

Herman, R. Paul. *The HIP Investor: Make Bigger Profits by Building a Better World.* Hoboken: John Wiley & Sons, Inc., 2010.

Hill, Napoleon. *Outwitting the Devil: The Secret to Freedom and Success*. New York: Sterling Publishing, 2012.

Hill, Napoleon. *Think and Grow Rich*. Radford: Wilder Publications, LLC., 2008.

Holmes, Ernest. *The Science of Mind*. New York: Tarcher, 2010.

Houle, David. *Entering the Shift Age: The End of the Information Age and the New Era of Transformation*. Naperville: Sourcebooks, Inc., 2012.

Hubbard, Marion Moss. *Work as a Heroic Journey: Using the Workplace to Evolve Your Character and Consciousness*. San Diego: Orion Publishing Company, 2005.

Jaworski, Joseph. *Synchronicity: the Inner Path of Leadership*. San Francisco: Berrett-Koehler Publishers, 1996.

Kaufman, Henry. *On Money and Markets: A Wall Street Memoir*. New York: McGraw-Hill Companies, 2000.

Kaufman, Henry. *The Road to Financial Reformation: Warnings, Consequences, Reforms*. Hoboken: John Wiley & Sons, Inc., 2009.

Kay, John. *Obliquity: Why Our Goals Are Best Achieved Indirectly*. New York: The Penguin Press, 2011.

Kelley, Tom and Jonathan Littman. *The Ten Faces of Innovation: IDEO's Strategies for Defeating the Devil's Advocate and Driving Creativity Throughout Your Organization*. New York: Currency/ Doubleday, 2005.

Kelly, Marjorie. *The Divine Right of Capital: Dethroning the Corporate Aristocracy*. San Francisco: Berrett-Koehler Publishers, Inc., 2003.

Kidd, Sue Monk. *The Dance of the Dissident Daughter: A Women's Journey from Christian Tradition to the Sacred Feminine*. New York: HarperOne, 2006.

Kidd, Sue Monk. *When the Heart Waits: Spiritual Direction for Life's Sacred Questions.* New York: HarperOne, 2006.

Kimsey-House, Henry, et al. *Co-Active Coaching: Changing Business, Transforming Lives.* 3rd ed. Boston: Nicholas Brealey America, 2011.

Kiyosaki, Robert T. *Rich Dad Poor Dad: What The Rich Teach Their Kids About Money That the Poor and Middle Class Do Not!* New York: Warner Books, Inc., 2001.

Kuper, Andrew. *Democracy Beyond Borders: Justice and Representation in Global Institutions.* Oxford University Press, 2006.

Kuper, Andrew. *Global Responsibilities: Who Must Deliver on Human Rights?* New York: Routledge, 2005.

Lechter, Sharon L., and Greg S. Reid. *Three Feet from Gold: Turn Your Obstacles into Opportunities (Think and Grow Rich).* New York: Sterling Publishing, 2011.

Levine, Peter A. *Waking the Tiger: Healing Trauma.* Berkeley: North Atlantic Books, 1997.

Lewis, Michael. *The Big Short: Inside the Doomsday Machine.* New York: W.W. Norton & Company, Inc., 2011.

Lewis, Michael. *Flash Boys: A Wall Street Revolt.* New York: W.W. Norton & Company, Inc., 2014.

Lewis, Michael. *Liar's Poker.* New York: W.W. Norton & Company, Inc., 2010.

Mackey, John and Rajendra Sisodia. *Conscious Capitalism: Liberating the Heroic Spirit of Business.* Boston: Harvard Business School Publishing Corporation, 2013.

Martin, Michael. *The Inner Voice of Trading: Eliminate the Noise, and Profit from the Strategies That Are Right for You.* Upper Saddle River: FT Press, 2012.

McLean, Bethany and Joe Nocera. *All the Devils Are Here: The Hidden History of the Financial Crisis.* New York: Portfolio Hardcover, 2010.

Mellan, Olivia. *Money Harmony: Resolving Money Conflicts in Your Life and Relationships.* New York: Walker & Company, 1995.

Millman, Dan. *The Way of the Peaceful Warrior: A Book that Changes Lives,* H.J. Kramer, Inc., 1984.

Miyashiro, Marie R. *The Empathy Factor: Your Competitive Advantage for Personal, Team, and Business Success.* Encinitas: PuddleDancer Press, 2011.

Monks, Robert. *Citizens DisUnited: Passive Investors, Drone CEOs, and the Corporate Capture of the American Dream.* Miniver Press, 2013.

Monks, Robert A.G. *The New Global Investors: How Shareowners can Unlock Sustainable Prosperity Worldwide.* Oxford: Capstone Publishing Limited, 2001.

Monks, Robert and Nell Minow. *Watching the Watchers: Corporate Governance for the 21st Century.* Hoboken: John Wiley & Sons, Inc., 1996.

Muller, Wayne. *A Life of Being, Having, and Doing Enough.* New York: Harmony Books, 2010.

Muller, Wayne. *How Then, Shall We Live? Four Simple Questions That Reveal the Beauty and Meaning of Our Lives.* New York: Bantam Book, 1996.

Needleman, Jacob. *Money and the Meaning of Life.* New York: Doubleday, 1994.

Neiderhoffer, Victor. *The Education of a Speculator.* Hoboken: John Wiley & Sons, Inc., 1997.

Nemeth, Marie. *Mastering Life's Energies: Simple Steps to a Luminous Life at Work and Play.* Novato: New World Library, 2007.

Nemeth, Maria. *The Energy of Money: A Spiritual Guide to Financial and Personal Fulfillment.* New York: Wellspring/Ballantine, 2000.

Neumann, Erich. *The Origins and History of Consciousness (Bollingen Series, 42).* Princeton: Princeton University Press, 1970.

O'Hara, Nancy. *Find a Quiet Corner: A Simple Guide to Self-Peace.* New York: Warner Books, Inc., 1995.

Peck, M. Scott. *The Road Less Traveled: A New Psychology of Love, Traditional Values and Spiritual Growth.* New York: Simon & Schuster, 1988.

Porter, Michael E. and Mark R. Kramer, "Creating Shared Value: How to Reinvent Capitalism—And Unleash a Wave of Innovation and Growth." *Harvard Business Review* (Jan-Feb 2011): 2–17.

Porter, Michael E. *On Competition.* Boston: Harvard Business School Publishing, 1998.

Rajan, Raghuram G., and Luigi Zingales. *Saving Capitalism from the Capitalists: Unleashing the Power of Financial Markets to Create Wealth and Spread Opportunity.* New York: Crown Business, 2003.

Rand, Ayn. *Anthem.* London: Cassell, 1938.

Rand, Ayn. *Atlas Shrugged.* New York: Random House, 1957.

Rand, Ayn. *Capitalism: The Unknown Ideal.* New York: New American Library, 1966.

Rand, Ayn. *Philosophy: Who Needs It.* Indianapolis: Bobbs-Merrill Company, 1982.

Rand, Ayn. *The Fountainhead*. Indianapolis: Bobbs-Merrill Company, 1943.

Rand, Ayn. *The Virtue of Selfishness: A New Concept of Egoism*. New York: New American Library, 1964.

Rand, Ayn. *We the Living*. London: Macmillan Publishers Ltd., 1936.

Redfield, James. *The Celestine Prophecy: An Adventure*. New York: Warner Books, Inc., 1997.

Ressler, Peter and Monika Mitchell. *Conversations with Wall Street: The Inside Story of the Financial Armageddon and How to Prevent the Next One*. Campbell: FastPencil Premiere, 2011.

Ressler, Peter and Monika Mitchell Ressler. *Spiritual Capitalism: What the FDNY Taught Wall Street About Money*. New York: Chilmark Books, 2005.

Richard, Christine S. *Confidence Game: How Hedge Fund Manager Bill Ackman Called Wall Street's Bluff*. Hoboken: John Wiley & Sons, Inc., 2010.

Ritholtz, Barry and Aaron Task. *Bailout Nation: How Greed and Easy Money Corrupted Wall Street and Shook the World Economy*. Hoboken: John Wiley & Sons, Inc., 2009.

Rogers, Jim. *A Gift to My Children: A Father's Lessons for Life and Investing*. New York: Random House, 2009.

Rogers, Jim. *Investment Biker: Around the World with Jim Rogers*. New York: Random House Trade Paperback, 2003.

Rogers, Jim. *Street Smarts: Adventures on the Road and in the Markets*. New York: Crown Business, 2013.

Rosenberg, Marshall B. *Nonviolent Communication: A Language of Life*. Encinitas: PuddleDancer Press, 2003.

Rosenberg, Marshall B. *Speak Peace in a World of Conflict: What You Say Next Will Change Your World*. Encinitas: PuddleDancer Press, 2005.

Sardello, Robert. *Facing the World with Soul: The Reimagination of Modern Life*. 2nd ed. Great Barrington: Lindisfarne Press, 2004.

Schwager, Jack D. *Market Sense and Nonsense: How the Markets Really Work (and How They Don't)*. Hoboken: John Wiley & Sons, Inc., 2012.

Schwager, Jack D. *Market Wizards, Updated: Interviews With Top Traders*. Hoboken: John Wiley & Sons, Inc., 2012.

Schwager, Jack D. *The New Market Wizards: Conversations with America's Top Traders*. New York: HarperBusiness, 1992.

Siegel, Daniel J. *The Developing Mind: How Relationships and the Brain Interact to Shape Who We Are*. New York: The Guilford Press, 2001.

Siegel, Daniel J. *The Mindful Brain: Reflection and Attunement in the Cultivation of Well-Being*. New York: W.W. Norton & Company, 2007.

Shore, Bill. *The Light of Conscience: How a Simple Act Can Change Your Life*. New York: Random House Trade Paperbacks, 2005.

Shull, Denise. *Market Mind Games: A Radical Psychology of Investing, Trading and Risk*. The McGraw-Hill Companies, Inc, 2011.

Singer, June. *Boundaries of the Soul: The Practice of Jung's Psychology*. New York: Anchor Books, 1994.

Sisodia, Rajendra S., David B. Wolfe, and Jagdish N. Sheth. *Firms of Endearment: How World-Class Companies Profit from Passion and Purpose*. Upper Saddle River: Wharton School Publishing, 2007.

Skousen, W. Cleon. *The Naked Capitalist*. Cutchogue: Buccaneer Books, 1998.

Smith, Adam. *An Inquiry into the Nature and Causes of the Wealth of Nations*. 1776.

Smith, Adam. *The Theory of Moral Sentiments*. 1759.

Stout, Lynn. *Cultivating Conscience: How Good Laws Make Good People*. Princeton: Princeton University Press, 2011.

Stout, Lynn. *The Shareholder Value Myth: How Putting Shareholders First Harms Investors, Corporations, and the Public*. San Francisco: Berrett-Koehler Publishers, Inc., 2012.

Thomashauer, Regena. *Mama Gena's School of Womanly Arts: Using the Power of Pleasure to Have Your Way with the world (How to Use the Power of Pleasure)*. New York: Simon & Schuster, 2003.

Tolle, Eckhart. *A New Earth: Awakening to Your Life's Purpose*. New York: Penguin Group, 2005.

Tolle, Eckhart. *The Power of Now: A Guide to Spiritual Enlightenment*. Novato: New World Library, 1999.

Tuckett, David, and Richard J. Taffler. *Fund Management: An Emotional Finance Perspective*. Charlottesville: The Research Foundation of CFA Institute, 2012.

Twist, Lynne. *The Soul of Money: Reclaiming the Wealth of Our Inner Resources*. New York: W.W. Norton & Company, Inc., 2003.

Ury, William L. *The Third Side: Why We Fight and How We Can Stop*. New York: Penguin Books Ltd., 2000.

Voss, Jason Apollo. *The Intuitive Investor: A Radical Guide for Manifesting Wealth*. New York: SelectBooks, 2010.

Walsch, Neale Donald. *Conversations with God: An Uncommon Dialogue, Book 1*. New York: G. P. Putnam's Sons, 1996.

Wattles, Wallace D. *The Science of Getting Rich: Your Master Key to Success*. Blacksburg: Thrift Books, 2009.

Whitehead, John C. *A Life in Leadership: From D-Day to Ground Zero: An Autobiography*. New York: Basic Books, 2005.

Whyte, David. *Crossing the Unknown Sea: Work as a Pilgrimage of Identity*. New York: The Berkley Publishing Group, 2001.

Whyte, David. *The Heart Aroused: Poetry and the Preservation of the Soul in Corporate America*. New York: Doubleday, 1994.

Whyte, David. *The Three Marriages: Reimagining Work, Self and Relationship*. New York: Riverhead Books, 2009.

Wilber, Ken. *The Atman Project: A Transpersonal View of Human Development*. 2nd ed. Wheaton: Quest Books, 1996.

Wilder, Barbara. *Money is Love: Reconnecting to the Sacred Origins of Money*. Longmont: Wild Ox Press, 1999.

Woodruff, Paul. *Reverence: Renewing a Forgotten Virtue*. New York: Oxford University Press, 2001.

Zaffron, Steve and Dave Logan. *The Three Laws of Performance: Rewriting the Future of Your Organization and Your Life*. San Francisco: Jossey-Bass, 2009.

Zander, Rosamund Stone and Benjamin Zander. *The Art of Possibility: Transforming Professional and Personal Life*. New York: Penguin Books Ltd., 2002.

The Wall Street Coach

Wall Street can be stressful on a good day, never mind a bad one. So when the market began to struggle in 2007–2008, I knew that I could make an impact there. On October 7, 2008, I sat down outside the NYSE in a nice suit with a homemade sign to do what I do best: coach.

It just so happened that, on that day, the market dropped 500 points and the crash of '08 officially began. That day, and for weeks afterward, folks who would never have approached me under normal circumstances sat down to talk to me. TheStreet.com dubbed me "The Wall Street Coach," and so *The Wall Street Coach* was born.

Kim Ann Curtin on her Wall Street bench, October 2008

About the Author

KIM ANN CURTIN is an author, professional keynote speaker, Executive Coach, and Founder of *The Wall Street Coach*.

She helps C-Suite Executives accelerate their personal and professional success through consciousness, to help them become as successful on the inside as they are on the outside.

Since the financial market crashed in October 2008, Kim has been working to build a more optimistic and sustainable vision for the finance industry. As *The Wall Street Coach*, Kim is a trusted advisor and consultant to executives, teams, conferences, and Fortune 500 companies, both in the US and across the globe.

Visit Kim at:

www.TheWallStreetCoach.com
Kim@thewallstreetcoach.com | 646-420-2099

> *Kim will donate a portion of her profits from this book to Room to Read, to increase global literacy and girls' education.*